PRENTICE HALL
LITERATURE

Common Core Companion

Grade Eight

Pearson
Upper Saddle River, New Jersey
Boston, Massachusetts
Chandler, Arizona
Glenview, Illinois

Copyright © Pearson Education, Inc., or its affiliates. All Rights Reserved. Printed in the United States of America. This publication is protected by copyright, and permission should be obtained from the publisher prior to any prohibited reproduction, storage in a retrieval system, or transmission in any form or by any means, electronic, mechanical, photocopying, recording, or likewise. For information regarding permissions, write to Pearson Curriculum Group Rights & Permissions, One Lake Street, Upper Saddle River,

Pearson, Prentice Hall, and Pearson Prentice Hall are trademarks, in the U.S. and/or other countries, of Pearson Education, Inc., or its affiliates.

ISBN-13: 978-0-133-19065-6
ISBN-10:   0-133-19065-X

1 2 3 4 5 6 7 8 9 10 V031 15 14 13 12 11

Table of Contents

The instruction and activities in this book are organized around the Common Core State Standards for English and Language Arts.

Reading Standards for Literature

Reading Standards for Informational Texts

Writing Standards

Writing 1: Write arguments to support claims with clear reasons and relevant evidence.

a) Introduce claim(s), acknowledge and distinguish the claim(s) from alternate or opposing claims, and organize the reasons and evidence logically.

b) Support claim(s) with logical reasoning and relevant evidence, using accurate, credible sources and demonstrating an understanding of the topic or text.

c) Use words, phrases, and clauses to create cohesion and clarify the relationships among claim(s), counterclaims, reasons, and evidence.

d) Establish and maintain a formal style.

e) Provide a concluding statement or section that follows from and supports the argument presented.

Writing 2: Write informative/explanatory texts to examine a topic and convey ideas, concepts, and information through the selection, organization, and analysis of relevant content.

a) Introduce a topic clearly, previewing what is to follow; organize ideas, concepts, and information into broader categories; include formatting (e.g., headings), graphics (e.g., charts, tables), and multimedia when useful to aiding comprehension.

b) Develop the topic with relevant, well-chosen facts, definitions, concrete details, quotations, or other information and examples.

c) Use appropriate and varied transitions to create cohesion and clarify the relationships among ideas and concepts.

d) Use precise language and domain-specific vocabulary to inform about or explain the topic.

e) Establish and maintain a formal style.

f) Provide a concluding statement or section that follows from and supports the information or explanation presented.

Writing 3: Write narratives to develop real or imagined experiences or events using effective technique, relevant descriptive details, and well-structured event sequences.

a) Engage and orient the reader by establishing a context and point of view and introducing a narrator and/or characters; organize an event sequence that unfolds naturally and logically.

b) Use narrative techniques, such as dialogue, pacing, description, and reflection, to develop experiences, events, and/or characters.

c) Use a variety of transition words, phrases, and clauses to convey sequence, signal shifts from one time frame or setting to another, and show the relationships among experiences and events.

d) Use precise words and phrases, relevant descriptive details, and sensory language to capture the action and convey experiences and events.

e) Provide a conclusion that follows from and reflects on the narrated experiences or events.

Writing 4: Produce clear and coherent writing in which the development, organization, and style are appropriate to task, purpose, and audience. (Grade-specific expectations for writing types are defined in standards 1–3 above.)

Writing 5: With some guidance and support from peers and adults, develop and strengthen writing as needed by planning, revising, editing, rewriting, or trying a new approach, focusing on how well purpose and audience have been addressed. (Editing for conventions should demonstrate command of Language standards 1–3 up to and including grade 8.)

Writing 6: Use technology, including the Internet, to produce and publish writing and present the relationships between information and ideas efficiently as well as to interact and collaborate with others.

Writing 7: Conduct short research projects to answer a question (including a self-generated question), drawing on several sources and generating additional related, focused questions that allow for multiple avenues of exploration.

Writing 8: Gather relevant information from multiple print and digital sources, using search terms effectively; assess the credibility and accuracy of each source; and quote or paraphrase the data and conclusions of others while avoiding plagiarism and following a standard format for citation.

Writing 9: Draw evidence from literary or informational texts to support analysis, reflection, and research.

a) Apply grade 8 Reading standards to literature (e.g., "Analyze how a modern work of fiction draws on themes, patterns of events, or character types from myths, traditional stories, or religious works such as the Bible, including describing how the material is rendered new").

b) Apply grade 8 Reading standards to literary nonfiction (e.g., "Delineate and evaluate the argument and specific claims in a text, assessing whether the reasoning is sound and the evidence is relevant and sufficient; recognize when irrelevant evidence is introduced").

Writing 10: Write routinely over extended time frames (time for research, reflection, and revision) and shorter time frames (a single sitting or a day or two) for a range of discipline-specific tasks, purposes, and audiences.

Speaking and Listening Standards

Speaking and Listening 1: Engage effectively in a range of collaborative discussions (one-on-one, in groups, and teacher- led) with diverse partners on grade 8 topics, texts, and issues, building on others' ideas and expressing their own clearly.

a) Come to discussions prepared, having read or researched material under study; explicitly draw on that preparation by referring to evidence on the topic, text, or issue to probe and reflect on ideas under discussion.

b) Follow rules for collegial discussions and decision-making, track progress toward specific goals and deadlines, and define individual roles as needed.

c) Pose questions that connect the ideas of several speakers and respond to others' questions and comments with relevant evidence, observations, and ideas.

d) Acknowledge new information expressed by others, and, when warranted, qualify or justify their own views in light of the evidence presented.

Speaking and Listening 2: Analyze the purpose of information presented in diverse media and formats (e.g., visually, quantitatively, orally) and evaluate the motives (e.g., social, commercial, political) behind its presentation.

Language Standards

Language 1: Demonstrate command of the conventions of standard English grammar and usage when writing or speaking.

a) Explain the function of verbals (gerunds, participles, infinitives) in general and their function in particular sentences.

b) Form and use verbs in the active and passive voice.

c) Form and use verbs in the indicative, imperative, interrogative, conditional, and subjunctive mood.

d) Recognize and correct inappropriate shifts in verb voice and mood.

Language 2: Demonstrate command of the conventions of standard English capitalization, punctuation, and spelling when writing.

a) Use punctuation (comma, ellipsis, dash) to indicate a pause or break.

b) Use an ellipsis to indicate an omission.

c) Spell correctly.

Language 3: Use knowledge of language and its conventions when writing, speaking, reading, or listening.

a) Use verbs in the active and passive voice and in the conditional and subjunctive mood to achieve particular effects (e.g., emphasizing the actor or the action; expressing uncertainty or describing a state contrary to fact).

Language 4: Determine or clarify the meaning of unknown and multiple-meaning words or phrases based on grade 8 reading and content, choosing flexibly from a range of strategies.

a) Use context (e.g., the overall meaning of a sentence or paragraph; a word's position or function in a sentence) as a clue to the meaning of a word or phrase.

b) Use common, grade-appropriate Greek or Latin affixes and roots as clues to the meaning of a word (e.g., precede, recede, secede).

c) Consult general and specialized reference materials (e.g., dictionaries, glossaries, thesauruses), both print and digital, to find the pronunciation of a word or determine or clarify its precise meaning or its part of speech.

d) Verify the preliminary determination of the meaning of a word or phrase (e.g., by checking the inferred meaning in context or in a dictionary).

Language 5: Demonstrate understanding of figurative language, word relationships, and nuances in word meanings.

  a) Interpret figures of speech (e.g. verbal irony, puns) in context.

  b) Use the relationship between particular words to better understand each of the words.

  c) Distinguish among the connotations (associations) of words with similar denotations (definitions) (e.g., *bullheaded, willful, firm, persistent, resolute*).

Language 6: Acquire and use accurately grade-appropriate general academic and domain-specific words and phrases; gather vocabulary knowledge when considering a word or phrase important to comprehension or expression.

Performance Tasks

About the *Common Core Companion*

The Common Core Companion student workbook provides instruction and practice in the Common Core State Standards. The standards are designed to help all students become college and career ready by the end of grade 12. Here is a closer look at this workbook:

Reading Standards

Reading Standards for Literature and Informational Texts are supported with instruction, examples, and multiple copies of worksheets that you can use over the course of the year. These key standards are revisited in the Performance Tasks section of your workbook.

Writing Standards

Full writing workshops are provided for Writing standards 1, 2, 3, and 7. Writing standards 4, 5, 6, 8, 9, and 10 are supported with direct instruction and worksheets that provide targeted practice. In addition, writing standards are revisited in Speaking and Listening activities and in Performance Tasks.

Speaking and Listening Standards

Detailed instruction and practice are provided for each Speaking and Listening standard. Additional opportunities to master these standards are provided in the Performance Tasks.

Language Standards

Explicit instruction and detailed examples support each Language standard. In addition, practice worksheets and graphic organizers provide additional opportunities for students to master these standards.

Performance Tasks

Using the examples in the Common Core framework as a guide, we provide opportunities for you to test your ability to master each reading standard, along with tips for success and rubrics to help you evaluate your work.

Reading Standards for
Literature

Literature 1

> **1. Cite the textual evidence that most strongly supports an analysis of what the text says explicitly as well as inferences drawn from the text.**

Explanation

When you analyze a text, think about different parts of it and how they relate to each other. Your analysis leads you to ideas about what the text means. However, you must support your analysis with evidence from the text. Even when you analyze **explicit** details, or direct statements, in a text, you must support what you are saying. You may also **make inferences**, or reach conclusions, about what a text hints at but does not say directly. It is important to support an inference with evidence from the text that will convince others your inference is correct.

Examples

- Explicit details provide basic information for readers and are directly stated. "Josie ran down the crowded street after her barking dog," and "Twister darted into the Smiths' backyard and hid in the bushes" are explicit details.

- Inferences are logical guesses readers make based on details in the text, as well as on their own knowledge and experiences. For example, in the story above, the author might also provide this passage:

   "Oh, no," Josie thought. "Not the Smiths' yard again!" Following the path to the backyard, she walked quietly next to the house and sneaked into the bushes. Then she heard the door open.

- The textual evidence of Josie's reaction to Twister running into the neighbor's backyard, the sneaking through the bushes, and the opening of the door support these inferences: The dog has run into the Smiths' yard before, that Josie knows the Smiths don't like it, and that she is trying to get Twister away before they notice. Unfortunately, they're home.

Academic Vocabulary

inference a logical guess based on details in the text and on personal experience

textual evidence words or phrases in a text that support an analysis of the text

Apply the Standard

Use the worksheets that follow to help you apply the standard as you read. Several copies of each worksheet have been provided for you to use with different literature selections.

- Citing Textual Evidence: Supporting an Analysis of Explicit Statements

- Citing Textual Evidence: Supporting an Inference

Name _____ Date _____ Selection _____

Citing Textual Evidence: Supporting an Analysis of Explicit Statements

Analyze a literary work to identify four important things it says explicitly. Enter those statements in the left column of the chart, below. Then, in the right column, cite textual evidence to support and explain your choices.

Explicit Statement from the Text	Textual Evidence: Why the Statement Is Important
1.	a. b. c.
2.	a. b. c.

A

Name _____ Date _____ Selection _____

Citing Textual Evidence: Supporting an Analysis of Explicit Statements

Analyze a literary work to identify four important things it says explicitly. Enter those statements in the left column of the chart, below. Then, in the right column, cite textual evidence to support and explain your choices.

Explicit Statement from the Text	Textual Evidence: Why the Statement Is Important
1.	a. b. c.
2.	a. b. c.

B

Name _____ Date _____ Selection _____

Citing Textual Evidence: Supporting an Analysis of Explicit Statements

Analyze a literary work to identify four important things it says explicitly. Enter those statements in the left column of the chart, below. Then, in the right column, cite textual evidence to support and explain your choices.

Explicit Statement from the Text	Textual Evidence: Why the Statement Is Important
1.	a. b. c.
2.	a. b. c.

C

Name _____ Date _____ Selection _____

Citing Textual Evidence: Supporting an Analysis of Explicit Statements

Analyze a literary work to identify four important things it says explicitly. Enter those statements in the left column of the chart, below. Then, in the right column, cite textual evidence to support and explain your choices.

Explicit Statement from the Text	Textual Evidence: Why the Statement Is Important
1.	a.
	b.
	c.
2.	a.
	b.
	c.

D

For use with Literature 1

Name _____ Date _____ Selection _____

Citing Textual Evidence: Supporting an Analysis of Explicit Statements

Analyze a literary work to identify four important things it says explicitly. Enter those statements in the left column of the chart, below. Then, in the right column, cite textual evidence to support and explain your choices.

Explicit Statement from the Text	Textual Evidence: Why the Statement Is Important
1.	a.
	b.
	c.
2.	a.
	b.
	c.

E

Name _____ Date _____ Selection _____

Citing Textual Evidence: Supporting an Analysis of Explicit Statements

Analyze a literary work to identify four important things it says explicitly. Enter those statements in the left column of the chart, below. Then, in the right column, cite textual evidence to support and explain your choices.

Explicit Statement from the Text	Textual Evidence: Why the Statement Is Important
1.	a. b. c.
2.	a. b. c.

F

Name _____ Date _____ Selection _____

Citing Textual Evidence: Supporting an Inference

Use the left column of this chart to make three inferences from the text. Then, in the right column, support each inference with textual evidence.

Inference from the Text	Textual Evidence Supporting the Inferences
1.	
2.	
3.	
4.	

A

Name _____ Date _____ Selection _____

Citing Textual Evidence: Supporting an Inference

Use the left column of this chart to make three inferences from the text. Then, in the right column, support each inference with textual evidence.

Inference from the Text	Textual Evidence Supporting the Inferences
1.	
2.	
3.	
4.	

B

Name _____ Date _____ Selection _____

Citing Textual Evidence: Supporting an Inference

Use the left column of this chart to make three inferences from the text. Then, in the right column, support each inference with textual evidence.

Inference from the Text	Textual Evidence Supporting the Inferences
1.	
2.	
3.	
4.	

C

Name _____ Date _____ Selection _____

Citing Textual Evidence: Supporting an Inference

Use the left column of this chart to make three inferences from the text. Then, in the right column, support each inference with textual evidence.

Inference from the Text	Textual Evidence Supporting the Inferences
1.	
2.	
3.	
4.	

D

Name _____ Date _____ Selection _____

Citing Textual Evidence: Supporting an Inference

Use the left column of this chart to make three inferences from the text. Then, in the right column, support each inference with textual evidence.

Inference from the Text	Textual Evidence Supporting the Inferences
1.	
2.	
3.	
4.	

E

Name _____ Date _____ Selection _____

Citing Textual Evidence: Supporting an Inference

Use the left column of this chart to make three inferences from the text. Then, in the right column, support each inference with textual evidence.

Inference from the Text	Textual Evidence Supporting the Inferences
1.	
2.	
3.	
4.	

F

Literature 2

> 2. **Determine a theme or central idea of a text and analyze its development over the course of the text, including its relationship to the characters, setting, and plot; provide an objective summary of the text.**

Explanation

Good triumphs over evil. Be careful what you wish for. You can probably think of many examples of books or movies that convey messages about life. An idea about life that an author explains in a literary work is called its **theme**. It is often expressed as a general statement about life or people. An author does not necessarily state the theme of a work directly. Often, the reader has to figure it out by studying the story details that develop and refine the theme. You can begin to analyze how an author develops a theme by making an objective **summary**, a brief restatement of the important details in a work.

Examples

- **Summary** To write an **objective summary**, you briefly restate the important details in a work—without including your own opinions. Here is a summary of a story about an elderly man and his housekeeper.

  John Grandy is an elderly widower. His son lives hundreds of miles away. His only company is his housekeeper, Alice, who comes three days a week to clean and cook. One day he notices that an expensive necklace he gave his wife is missing from her jewelry box. He assumes that Alice, always short of money, took it. Despite his anger, he decides not to confront her because he has no proof. Over the years, Grandy and Alice develop a friendship, and the necklace is forgotten. Then one day, looking through an old suitcase, he finds the necklace caught in the lining. Recalling his unfair suspicions of Alice, he happily gives it to her for her birthday.

- **Theme** To determine a story's **theme**, or central idea, analyze details in the text for clues about the message the writer is trying to convey. *Don't jump* to *conclusions* is one theme of the story above. Grandy's suspicions, Alice's need for money, the friendship between the characters, and the discovery of the lost necklace are all clues important to determining the theme.

Academic Vocabulary

theme a story's central idea or message about life

summary a brief restatement of the important details in a work

Apply the Standard

Use the worksheets that follow to help you apply the standard as you read. Several copies of each worksheet have been provided for you to use with different literature selections.

- Summarizing: Important Details

- Analyzing: Central Idea or Theme

Name _____ Date _____ Selection _____

Summarizing Key Supporting Details

Use the organizer to list the characters, setting, and key events from a text you have read. Then use that information to write an objective summary of the text. Remember to leave out personal opinions and judgments.

Title:

Main Characters
Setting
Key Events

1.

2.

3.

4.

5.

Summary ....

....

....

....

....

....

....

A

Name _____ Date _____ Selection _____

Summarizing Key Supporting Details

Use the organizer to list the characters, setting, and key events from a text you have read. Then use that information to write an objective summary of the text. Remember to leave out personal opinions and judgments.

Title:

Main Characters
Setting
Key Events
1.
2.
3.
4.
5.

Summary ....

....

....

....

....

....

....

B

Name _____ Date _____ Selection _____

Summarizing Key Supporting Details

Use the organizer to list the characters, setting, and key events from a text you have read. Then use that information to write an objective summary of the text. Remember to leave out personal opinions and judgments.

Title:

Main Characters
Setting

Key Events

1.

2.

3.

4.

5.

Summary ....

....

....

....

....

....

....

C

Name _____ Date _____ Selection _____

Summarizing Key Supporting Details

Use the organizer to list the characters, setting, and key events from a text you have read. Then use that information to write an objective summary of the text. Remember to leave out personal opinions and judgments.

Title:

Main Characters
Setting
Key Events
1.
2.
3.
4.
5.

Summary ....

....

....

....

....

....

D

For use with Literature 2

Name _____ Date _____ Selection _____

Summarizing Key Supporting Details

Use the organizer to list the characters, setting, and key events from a text you have read. Then use that information to write an objective summary of the text. Remember to leave out personal opinions and judgments.

Title:

Main Characters

Setting

Key Events
1.
2.
3.
4.
5.

Summary ....

....

....

....

....

....

....

E

Name _____ Date _____ Selection _____

Summarizing Key Supporting Details

Use the organizer to list the characters, setting, and key events from a text you have read. Then use that information to write an objective summary of the text. Remember to leave out personal opinions and judgments.

Title:

Main Characters
Setting
Key Events 1. 2. 3. 4. 5.

Summary ....

....

....

....

....

....

....

....

F

Name _____ Date _____ Selection _____

Analyzing a Central Idea or Theme

Use this diagram to list character, setting, and plot details that give clues about the theme of a text you have read.

Details about Characters:

+

Details about the Setting:

+

Details about the Plot:

=

Theme:

A

Name _____ Date _____ Selection _____

Analyzing a Central Idea or Theme

Use this diagram to list character, setting, and plot details that give clues about the theme of a text you have read.

Details about Characters:

+

Details about the Setting:

+

Details about the Plot:

=

Theme:

B

Name _____ Date _____ Selection _____

Analyzing a Central Idea or Theme

Use this diagram to list character, setting, and plot details that give clues about the theme of a text you have read.

Details about Characters:

+

Details about the Setting:

+

Details about the Plot:

=

Theme:

C

Name _____ Date _____ Selection _____

Analyzing a Central Idea or Theme

Use this diagram to list character, setting, and plot details that give clues about the theme of a text you have read.

Details about Characters:

+

Details about the Setting:

+

Details about the Plot:

=

Theme:

D

Name _____ Date _____ Selection _____

Analyzing a Central Idea or Theme

Use this diagram to list character, setting, and plot details that give clues about the theme of a text you have read.

Details about Characters:

+

Details about the Setting:

+

Details about the Plot:

=

Theme:

E

Name _____ Date _____ Selection _____

Analyzing a Central Idea or Theme

Use this diagram to list character, setting, and plot details that give clues about the theme of a text you have read.

Details about Characters:

+

Details about the Setting:

+

Details about the Plot:

=

Theme:

F

Literature 3

> **3.** Analyze how particular lines of dialogue or incidents in a story or drama propel the action, reveal aspects of a character, or provoke a decision.

Explanation

You learn about your friends based on what they say, how they act, and what others say about them. You learn about characters in a story or drama in the same way. **Dialogue** is a conversation between or among characters. Dialogue, or what characters say to one another, helps the reader understand the characters' traits, attitudes, and values. It reveals their motivations, or the reasons why they take a particular action. It also reveals how characters feel about each other. Are they friends or bitter enemies? Have they known each other long? Often the answers are in the dialogue.

Dialogue can also move the plot along by telling what happened. The **plot** of a literary work is the series of events that move the action forward. Plot events reveal aspects of a character by creating **conflicts,** or struggles within or between characters. Characters show what they are like when they struggle with others or with their own feelings. The plot incidents may cause characters to change and take further actions in the story. By analyzing these elements, you can better understand how the author uses these devices to reveal aspects of the character or to move the plot forward.

Examples

- **Dialogue** can propel the action of a story, as when a character says, "Move aside, or I'll *make* you move!" Clearly, something will happen as a result of this statement. It's a threat. Additionally, this line of dialogue reveals a menacing aspect of the character that may not have been previously obvious. It will also provoke a decision from the person this character is addressing.

- **Plot** incidents often cause further action. When a character loses his or her footing on a mountainside, something else is bound to happen. The events of a plot can also reveal aspects of a character. For example, after that same character slides into a ravine, he or she may demonstrate skill and determination by successfully using a rope to climb out.

Academic Vocabulary

dialogue a conversation between or among characters

plot a sequence of related events that move the story forward

Apply the Standard

Use the worksheets that follow to help you apply the standard as you read. Several copies of each worksheet have been provided for you to use with different literature selections.

- Analyzing Story Elements: Dialogue

- Analyzing Story Elements: Plot

Name _____ Date _____ Selection _____

Analyzing Story Elements: Dialogue

Use the organizer to analyze how dialogue affects other elements of a story or drama that you have read. Enter excerpts of dialog that affect the action of the story in the left column. Then, in the right column, explain what affect the dialogue had on the plot or character.

Dialogue	How the Dialogue Affects Action

Dialogue	How the Dialogue Reveals Character Traits

Dialogue	How the Dialogue Provokes a Decision

A

Name _____ Date _____ Selection _____

Analyzing Story Elements: Dialogue

Use the organizer to analyze how dialogue affects other elements of a story or drama that you have read. Enter excerpts of dialog that affect the action of the story in the left column. Then, in the right column, explain what affect the dialogue had on the plot or character.

Dialogue	How the Dialogue Affects Action

Dialogue	How the Dialogue Reveals Character Traits

Dialogue	How the Dialogue Provokes a Decision

B

For use with Literature 3

Name _____ Date _____ Selection _____

Analyzing Story Elements: Dialogue

Use the organizer to analyze how dialogue affects other elements of a story or drama that you have read. Enter excerpts of dialog that affect the action of the story in the left column. Then, in the right column, explain what affect the dialogue had on the plot or character.

Dialogue	How the Dialogue Affects Action

Dialogue	How the Dialogue Reveals Character Traits

Dialogue	How the Dialogue Provokes a Decision

C

For use with Literature 3

Name _____ Date _____ Selection _____

Analyzing Story Elements: Dialogue

Use the organizer to analyze how dialogue affects other elements of a story or drama that you have read. Enter excerpts of dialog that affect the action of the story in the left column. Then, in the right column, explain what affect the dialogue had on the plot or character.

Dialogue	How the Dialogue Affects Action

Dialogue	How the Dialogue Reveals Character Traits

Dialogue	How the Dialogue Provokes a Decision

D

Name _____ Date _____ Selection _____

Analyzing Story Elements: Dialogue

Use the organizer to analyze how dialogue affects other elements of a story or drama that you have read. Enter excerpts of dialog that affect the action of the story in the left column. Then, in the right column, explain what affect the dialogue had on the plot or character.

Dialogue	How the Dialogue Affects Action

Dialogue	How the Dialogue Reveals Character Traits

Dialogue	How the Dialogue Provokes a Decision

E

Name _____ Date _____ Selection _____

Analyzing Story Elements: Dialogue

Use the organizer to analyze how dialogue affects other elements of a story or drama that you have read. Enter excerpts of dialog that affect the action of the story in the left column. Then, in the right column, explain what affect the dialogue had on the plot or character.

Dialogue	How the Dialogue Affects Action

Dialogue	How the Dialogue Reveals Character Traits

Dialogue	How the Dialogue Provokes a Decision

F

Name _____ Date _____ Selection _____

Analyzing Story Elements: Plot

Use the organizer to analyze how plot incidents affect other elements of a story or drama that you have read. In the left column, list plot events that affect the action of a story or drama. Then, in the right column, explain what affect the plot events have on character or action.

Plot Event	How the Event Affects Action
Event 1	
Event 2	

Plot Event	How the Event Reveals Character Traits
Event 1	
Event 2	

Plot Event	How the Event Provokes a Decision
Event 1	
Event 2	

A

Name _____ Date _____ Selection _____

Analyzing Story Elements: Plot

Use the organizer to analyze how plot incidents affect other elements of a story or drama that you have read. In the left column, list plot events that affect the action of a story or drama. Then, in the right column, explain what affect the plot events have on character or action.

Plot Event	How the Event Affects Action
Event 1	
Event 2	

Plot Event	How the Event Reveals Character Traits
Event 1	
Event 2	

Plot Event	How the Event Provokes a Decision
Event 1	
Event 2	

B

Name _____ Date _____ Selection _____

Analyzing Story Elements: Plot

Use the organizer to analyze how plot incidents affect other elements of a story or drama that you have read. In the left column, list plot events that affect the action of a story or drama. Then, in the right column, explain what affect the plot events have on character or action.

Plot Event	How the Event Affects Action
Event 1	
Event 2	

Plot Event	How the Event Reveals Character Traits
Event 1	
Event 2	

Plot Event	How the Event Provokes a Decision
Event 1	
Event 2	

C

For use with Literature 3

Name _____ Date _____ Selection _____

Analyzing Story Elements: Plot

Use the organizer to analyze how plot incidents affect other elements of a story or drama that you have read. In the left column, list plot events that affect the action of a story or drama. Then, in the right column, explain what affect the plot events have on character or action.

Plot Event	How the Event Affects Action
Event 1	
Event 2	

Plot Event	How the Event Reveals Character Traits
Event 1	
Event 2	

Plot Event	How the Event Provokes a Decision
Event 1	
Event 2	

D

Name _____ Date _____ Selection _____

Analyzing Story Elements: Plot

Use the organizer to analyze how plot incidents affect other elements of a story or drama that you have read. In the left column, list plot events that affect the action of a story or drama. Then, in the right column, explain what affect the plot events have on character or action.

Plot Event	How the Event Affects Action
Event 1	
Event 2	

Plot Event	How the Event Reveals Character Traits
Event 1	
Event 2	

Plot Event	How the Event Provokes a Decision
Event 1	
Event 2	

E

Name _____ Date _____ Selection _____

Analyzing Story Elements: Plot

Use the organizer to analyze how plot incidents affect other elements of a story or drama that you have read. In the left column, list plot events that affect the action of a story or drama. Then, in the right column, explain what affect the plot events have on character or action.

Plot Event	How the Event Affects Action
Event 1	
Event 2	

Plot Event	How the Event Reveals Character Traits
Event 1	
Event 2	

Plot Event	How the Event Provokes a Decision
Event 1	
Event 2	

F

Literature 4

> **4.** Determine the meaning of words and phrases as they are used in a text, including figurative and connotative meanings; analyze the impact of specific word choices on meaning and tone, including analogies or allusions to other texts.

Explanation

Good writers choose words that will enrich the meaning of their work and create the desired **tone,** or attitude toward the subject. They pay attention to these qualities of language:

- **Figurative language** refers to words that go beyond their dictionary meanings. Writers use figures of speech like the following to make their writing fresh and engaging:

  simile — a comparison of two unlike things using the word *like* or *as*

  metaphor — an implied comparison in which something is described as though it were something else

- **Connotative meanings** are the ideas, emotions, and associations that a word calls to mind.

  Sometimes authors use **analogies** or **allusions** to help explain a concept.

Examples

- **Figurative language** "The room was a nightmare of disheveled clothes and unfinished homework" is a metaphor for a messy bedroom.

- **Connotative meaning** *Cheap* and *thrifty* both describe a person's shopping behavior.

- **Analogy** Comparing the odds of getting your bedroom cleaned on time to the odds of winning a lottery shows the improbability of the situation.

- **Allusion** "Debt was Jane's Achilles heel" stresses her most vulnerable trait.

Academic Vocabulary

figurative language language that is not meant to be taken literally

connotative meaning feelings and emotions associated with a word or phrase

tone a writer's attitude toward his or her subject

analogy a comparison between two different things that are similar in a number of ways

allusion a reference to a well-known person, place, event, literary work, or work of art.

Apply the Standard

Use the worksheets that follow to help you apply the standard as you read. Several copies of each worksheet have been provided for you to use with different literature selections.

- Understanding Connotations and Figurative Language

- Analyzing Word Choices

Name _____ Date _____ Assignment _____

Understanding Connotations and Figurative Language

Use the organizer to help you determine the figurative or connotative meaning of words and phrases you encounter in your reading. In the first column, record a word or phrase. Write its figurative meaning in the next column. Then note if a word's connotation is positive, negative, or neutral.

Word or Phrase	Figurative Meaning	Connotative Meaning
1.		❏ positive ❏ negative ❏ neutral
2.		❏ positive ❏ negative ❏ neutral
3.		❏ positive ❏ negative ❏ neutral
4.		❏ positive ❏ negative ❏ neutral
5.		❏ positive ❏ negative ❏ neutral

A

Name _____ Date _____ Assignment _____

Understanding Connotations and Figurative Language

Use the organizer to help you determine the figurative or connotative meaning of words and phrases you encounter in your reading. In the first column, record a word or phrase. Write its figurative meaning in the next column. Then note if a word's connotation is positive, negative, or neutral.

Word or Phrase	Figurative Meaning	Connotative Meaning
1.		❏ positive ❏ negative ❏ neutral
2.		❏ positive ❏ negative ❏ neutral
3.		❏ positive ❏ negative ❏ neutral
4.		❏ positive ❏ negative ❏ neutral
5.		❏ positive ❏ negative ❏ neutral

B

For use with Literature 4

Name _____ Date _____ Assignment _____

Understanding Connotations and Figurative Language

Use the organizer to help you determine the figurative or connotative meaning of words and phrases you encounter in your reading. In the first column, record a word or phrase. Write its figurative meaning in the next column. Then note if a word's connotation is positive, negative, or neutral.

Word or Phrase	Figurative Meaning	Connotative Meaning
1.		❏ positive ❏ negative ❏ neutral
2.		❏ positive ❏ negative ❏ neutral
3.		❏ positive ❏ negative ❏ neutral
4.		❏ positive ❏ negative ❏ neutral
5.		❏ positive ❏ negative ❏ neutral

C

For use with Literature 4

Name _____ Date _____ Assignment _____

Understanding Connotations and Figurative Language

Use the organizer to help you determine the figurative or connotative meaning of words and phrases you encounter in your reading. In the first column, record a word or phrase. Write its figurative meaning in the next column. Then note if a word's connotation is positive, negative, or neutral.

Word or Phrase	Figurative Meaning	Connotative Meaning
1.		❏ positive ❏ negative ❏ neutral
2.		❏ positive ❏ negative ❏ neutral
3.		❏ positive ❏ negative ❏ neutral
4.		❏ positive ❏ negative ❏ neutral
5.		❏ positive ❏ negative ❏ neutral

D

For use with Literature 4

Name _____ Date _____ Assignment _____

Understanding Connotations and Figurative Language

Use the organizer to help you determine the figurative or connotative meaning of words and phrases you encounter in your reading. In the first column, record a word or phrase. Write its figurative meaning in the next column. Then note if a word's connotation is positive, negative, or neutral.

Word or Phrase	Figurative Meaning	Connotative Meaning
1.		❏ positive ❏ negative ❏ neutral
2.		❏ positive ❏ negative ❏ neutral
3.		❏ positive ❏ negative ❏ neutral
4.		❏ positive ❏ negative ❏ neutral
5.		❏ positive ❏ negative ❏ neutral

E

Name _____ Date _____ Assignment _____

Understanding Connotations and Figurative Language

Use the organizer to help you determine the figurative or connotative meaning of words and phrases you encounter in your reading. In the first column, record a word or phrase. Write its figurative meaning in the next column. Then note if a word's connotation is positive, negative, or neutral.

Word or Phrase	Figurative Meaning	Connotative Meaning
1.		❏ positive ❏ negative ❏ neutral
2.		❏ positive ❏ negative ❏ neutral
3.		❏ positive ❏ negative ❏ neutral
4.		❏ positive ❏ negative ❏ neutral
5.		❏ positive ❏ negative ❏ neutral

F

For use with Literature 4

Name _____ Date _____ Assignment _____

Analyzing Word Choices

Use the organizer to help you analyze the effect of specific word choices on tone and meaning. In the first column, write examples of analogies and allusions you find in your reading. In the second column, explain the effect they have on a poem, story, or drama's tone and meaning.

Word Choices	Effect on Tone and Meaning
Examples of Analogies:	
Examples of Allusions:	

A

Name _____ Date _____ Assignment _____

Analyzing Word Choices

Use the organizer to help you analyze the effect of specific word choices on tone and meaning. In the first column, write examples of analogies and allusions you find in your reading. In the second column, explain the effect they have on a poem, story, or drama's tone and meaning.

Word Choices	Effect on Tone and Meaning
Examples of Analogies:	
Examples of Allusions:	

B

Name _____ Date _____ Assignment _____

Analyzing Word Choices

Use the organizer to help you analyze the effect of specific word choices on tone and meaning. In the first column, write examples of analogies and allusions you find in your reading. In the second column, explain the effect they have on a poem, story, or drama's tone and meaning.

Word Choices	Effect on Tone and Meaning
Examples of Analogies:	
Examples of Allusions:	

C

Name _____ Date _____ Assignment _____

Analyzing Word Choices

Use the organizer to help you analyze the effect of specific word choices on tone and meaning. In the first column, write examples of analogies and allusions you find in your reading. In the second column, explain the effect they have on a poem, story, or drama's tone and meaning.

Word Choices	Effect on Tone and Meaning
Examples of Analogies:	
Examples of Allusions:	

D

Name _____ Date _____ Assignment _____

Analyzing Word Choices

Use the organizer to help you analyze the effect of specific word choices on tone and meaning. In the first column, write examples of analogies and allusions you find in your reading. In the second column, explain the effect they have on a poem, story, or drama's tone and meaning.

Word Choices	Effect on Tone and Meaning
Examples of Analogies:	
Examples of Allusions:	

E

Name _____ Date _____ Assignment _____

Analyzing Word Choices

Use the organizer to help you analyze the effect of specific word choices on tone and meaning. In the first column, write examples of analogies and allusions you find in your reading. In the second column, explain the effect they have on a poem, story, or drama's tone and meaning.

Word Choices	Effect on Tone and Meaning
Examples of Analogies:	
Examples of Allusions:	

F

Literature 5

> 5. Compare and contrast the structure of two or more texts and analyze how the differing structure of each text contributes to its meaning and style.

Explanation

When you read a story, you may experience feelings of joy, fear, or inspiration. Each of these effects results from choices authors make about the structure of their work. **Narrative structure** is the pattern that a story's plot follows. Most narratives are told in **chronological order,** meaning that events are related in the order in which they occur. Narrative devices such as flashback and foreshadowing may sometimes break this sequence of events.

A **flashback** interrupts the chronological order of the action to present events that happened in the past. Flashbacks provide background information or explain a character's motivation. Words and phrases such as *yesterday* or *when I was a child* might signal a flashback. Words such as *today* or *now* mark a return to the present.

Foreshadowing gives hints about something that will occur in the future. It creates suspense by making the reader want to know how a story will end. Foreshadowing can come from details in the setting, from a character's statements, or from events.

Examples

- **Flashback** A flashback reveals the source of Jake's interest in building.

  Brenda Wilson was cleaning a closet when she came across one of her son's old wooden blocks. Her mind drifted back decades to Jake, age 2, stacking his blocks. The jangling of the phone jolted her back to the present. It was grown-up Jake telling her that his construction company had just won an award.

- **Foreshadowing** The suspense created about what will happen to Anna is created by foreshadowing.

  It was growing dark, but Anna wanted to reach her aunt's house before dinner. As she trudged along, a heavy snow began to fall, and she turned onto the wrong road.

Academic Vocabulary

chronological order events are related in the order in which they occur

foreshadowing hints or clues about events that will happen later

flashback an interruption in the action of a narrative to reveal events that occurred in the past

Apply the Standard

Use the worksheet that follows to help you apply the standard as you read. Several copies have been provided for you to use with different literature selections.

- Comparing and Contrasting Text Structures

Name _____ Date _____ Assignment _____

Comparing and Contrasting Text Structures

Use the organizer to compare and contrast the narrative structure of two texts you have read. Identify examples of foreshadowing and flashback in each story. Then, answer the questions at the bottom of the page.

Title of Story 1:	Title of Story 2:
Examples of Flashbacks: **Impact on Meaning:**	**Examples of Flashbacks:** **Impact on Meaning:**
Examples of Foreshadowing: **Impact on Meaning:**	**Examples of Foreshadowing:** **Impact on Meaning:**

How do the texts differ in structure? ....

....

....

What effect do these differences have on each text's meaning and style? ....

....

....

A

Name _____ Date _____ Assignment _____

Comparing and Contrasting Text Structures

Use the organizer to compare and contrast the narrative structure of two texts you have read. Identify examples of foreshadowing and flashback in each story. Then, answer the questions at the bottom of the page.

Title of Story 1:	Title of Story 2:
Examples of Flashbacks: **Impact on Meaning:**	**Examples of Flashbacks:** **Impact on Meaning:**
Examples of Foreshadowing: **Impact on Meaning:**	**Examples of Foreshadowing:** **Impact on Meaning:**

How do the texts differ in structure? ....

....

....

What effect do these differences have on each text's meaning and style? ....

....

....

B

Name _____ Date _____ Assignment _____

Comparing and Contrasting Text Structures

Use the organizer to compare and contrast the narrative structure of two texts you have read. Identify examples of foreshadowing and flashback in each story. Then, answer the questions at the bottom of the page.

Title of Story 1:	Title of Story 2:
Examples of Flashbacks: **Impact on Meaning:**	**Examples of Flashbacks:** **Impact on Meaning:**
Examples of Foreshadowing: **Impact on Meaning:**	**Examples of Foreshadowing:** **Impact on Meaning:**

How do the texts differ in structure? ....
....
....

What effect do these differences have on each text's meaning and style? ....
....
....

C

Name _____ Date _____ Assignment _____

Comparing and Contrasting Text Structures

Use the organizer to compare and contrast the narrative structure of two texts you have read. Identify examples of foreshadowing and flashback in each story. Then, answer the questions at the bottom of the page.

Title of Story 1:	Title of Story 2:
Examples of Flashbacks: **Impact on Meaning:**	**Examples of Flashbacks:** **Impact on Meaning:**
Examples of Foreshadowing: **Impact on Meaning:**	**Examples of Foreshadowing:** **Impact on Meaning:**

How do the texts differ in structure? ....

....

What effect do these differences have on each text's meaning and style? ....

....

....

D

Name _____ Date _____ Assignment _____

Comparing and Contrasting Text Structures

Use the organizer to compare and contrast the narrative structure of two texts you have read. Identify examples of foreshadowing and flashback in each story. Then, answer the questions at the bottom of the page.

Title of Story 1:	Title of Story 2:
Examples of Flashbacks: **Impact on Meaning:**	**Examples of Flashbacks:** **Impact on Meaning:**
Examples of Foreshadowing: **Impact on Meaning:**	**Examples of Foreshadowing:** **Impact on Meaning:**

How do the texts differ in structure? ....

....

....

What effect do these differences have on each text's meaning and style? ....

....

....

E

Name _____ Date _____ Assignment _____

Comparing and Contrasting Text Structures

Use the organizer to compare and contrast the narrative structure of two texts you have read. Identify examples of foreshadowing and flashback in each story. Then, answer the questions at the bottom of the page.

Title of Story 1:	Title of Story 2:
Examples of Flashbacks: **Impact on Meaning:**	**Examples of Flashbacks:** **Impact on Meaning:**
Examples of Foreshadowing **Impact on Meaning:**	**Examples of Foreshadowing** **Impact on Meaning:**

How do the texts differ in structure? ....

....

....

What effect do these differences have on each text's meaning and style? ....

....

....

F

Literature 6

> **6.** Analyze how differences in the points of view of the characters and the audience or reader (e.g., created through the use of dramatic irony) create such effects as suspense or humor.

Explanation

Authors develop the **points of view** of the narrator and characters in their stories through the details they give about these characters. By telling what a character says, does, and thinks, as well as what others say about this person, the author reveals important information about the character's traits and motivations.

Many writers will reveal information to the audience or the reader that the characters do not know. This discrepancy is often used to entertain, or to create **humor** or to create tension or **suspense.** While most humorists are trying to entertain, humor can also be used to convey a serious theme.

Irony is a discrepancy or contradiction between appearance and reality, between expectation and outcome, or between meaning and intention. You can contrast the viewpoints of different characters by paying attention to the varying kinds of information provided about each of them.

The readers or audience sometimes know more about what is occurring in a story or play than the characters do. This situation is referred to as **dramatic irony.** The effects of such dramatic irony might include humor, suspense, or pathos.

Examples

- **Humor** In a comedy, a shop girl pretends to be a successful businesswoman in an effort to impress the rich, snobbish family of the young man she loves.

- **Suspense** In a science-fiction story, a motorist gives a ride to a hitchhiker whom the reader knows to be a murderous creature from another planet.

- **Dramatic irony** The reader or audience knows something about the plot that the character does not.

Academic Vocabulary

irony the contradiction between appearance and reality

dramatic irony a contradiction between what a character thinks and what the reader or audience knows to be true

suspense the growing curiosity, tension, or anxiety the reader feels about the outcome of events in a literary work

Apply the Standard

Use the worksheet that follows to help you apply the standard as you read. Several copies have been provided for you to use with different literature selections.

- Analyzing Point of View

Name _____ Date _____ Assignment _____

Analyzing Point of View

Use the organizer to analyze how dramatic irony can create such effects as humor or suspense.

Character	What the Character Knows	What the Reader Knows	Effect Created by the Dramatic Irony (humor, suspense, or other)
Character 1			
Character 2			
Character 3			

A

Name _____ Date _____ Assignment _____

Analyzing Point of View

Use the organizer to analyze how dramatic irony can create such effects as humor or suspense.

Character	What the Character Knows	What the Reader Knows	Effect Created by the Dramatic Irony (humor, suspense, or other)
Character 1			
Character 2			
Character 3			

B

Name _____ Date _____ Assignment _____

Analyzing Point of View

Use the organizer to analyze how dramatic irony can create such effects as humor or suspense.

Character	What the Character Knows	What the Reader Knows	Effect Created by the Dramatic Irony (humor, suspense, or other)
Character 1			
Character 2			
Character 3			

C

Name _____ Date _____ Assignment _____

Analyzing Point of View

Use the organizer to analyze how dramatic irony can create such effects as humor or suspense.

Character	What the Character Knows	What the Reader Knows	Effect Created by the Dramatic Irony (humor, suspense, or other)
Character 1			
Character 2			
Character 3			

D

Name _____ Date _____ Assignment _____

Analyzing Point of View

Use the organizer to analyze how dramatic irony can create such effects as humor or suspense.

Character	What the Character Knows	What the Reader Knows	Effect Created by the Dramatic Irony (humor, suspense, or other)
Character 1			
Character 2			
Character 3			

E

Name _____ Date _____ Assignment _____

Analyzing Point of View

Use the organizer to analyze how dramatic irony can create such effects as humor or suspense.

Character	What the Character Knows	What the Reader Knows	Effect Created by the Dramatic Irony (humor, suspense, or other)
Character 1			
Character 2			
Character 3			

F

Literature 7

> 7. **Analyze the extent to which a filmed or live production of a story or drama stays faithful to or departs from the text or script, evaluating the choices made by the director or actors.**

Explanation

Fictions and dramas frequently inspire people to produce filmed or live performances. The process of turning a written text into a film or live production often requires changes to the original work. For example, a story may be too long, too short, or too complicated to be translated easily into a film or play. In other instances, directors have different ideas of how to develop the story. They might eliminate subplots or minor characters; they might emphasize certain aspects of characters, or change the setting of the story. They may even alter the ending to gain more audience appeal.

All of these changes can lead people to say: "I liked the book better than the movie" or "I liked the movie better than the book." When you see a play or a movie version of a story or drama you have read, evaluate the choices the director and actors made. Did they stay faithful to the original text? Did their changes improve or harm your enjoyment of the story?

Examples

- When producing a film or live performance from a script, directors and actors must stick to the script and stage directions. For example, in *The Diary of Anne Frank,* the director cannot change the words, the number of characters, or the location of the story. He or she can, however, emphasize certain qualities of Anne Frank and other characters by how they say their lines and how they behave.

- Translating a novel or short story to a filmed or live performance usually requires significant changes from the written version. For example, the movie *Charley* contains dialogue, characters, and subplots not present in the story *Flowers for Algernon*. Sometimes the changes and additions seem to flow naturally from the book version. At other times, the changes make a story so different it no longer seems familiar.

Apply the Standard

Use the worksheet that follows to help you apply the standard as you read literature selections. Several copies of the worksheet have been provided for you.

- Evaluating Different Formats

Name _____ Date _____ Selection _____

Evaluating Different Formats

Use the organizer to help you evaluate the director's and actors' choices when transforming a story or script into a filmed or live performance.

I am comparing the short story, novel, or drama with ....

❏ filmed production called ....

❏ a live production called ....

Ways in which film or live performance stayed faithful to script or story	Ways in which film or live performance departed from the script or story
1.	1.
2.	2.
3.	3.
4.	4.
5.	5.

Which did you prefer, the text version or the filmed or live performance? Why?

....

....

....

A

Name _____ Date _____ Selection _____

Evaluating Different Formats

Use the organizer to help you evaluate the director's and actors' choices when transforming a story or script into a filmed or live performance.

I am comparing the short story, novel, or drama with ....

❑ filmed production called ....

❑ a live production called ....

Ways in which film or live performance stayed faithful to script or story	Ways in which film or live performance departed from the script or story
1.	1.
2.	2.
3.	3.
4.	4.
5.	5.

Which did you prefer, the text version or the filmed or live performance? Why?

....

....

....

B

Name _____ Date _____ Selection _____

Evaluating Different Formats

Use the organizer to help you evaluate the director's and actors' choices when transforming a story or script into a filmed or live performance.

I am comparing the short story, novel, or drama with ....

❏ filmed production called ....

❏ a live production called ....

Ways in which film or live performance stayed faithful to script or story	Ways in which film or live performance departed from the script or story
1.	1.
2.	2.
3.	3.
4.	4.
5.	5.

Which did you prefer, the text version or the filmed or live performance? Why?

....

....

....

C

Name _____ Date _____ Selection _____

Evaluating Different Formats

Use the organizer to help you evaluate the director's and actors' choices when transforming a story or script into a filmed or live performance.

I am comparing the short story, novel, or drama with ....

❏ filmed production called ....

❏ a live production called ....

Ways in which film or live performance stayed faithful to script or story	Ways in which film or live performance departed from the script or story
1.	1.
2.	2.
3.	3.
4.	4.
5.	5.

Which did you prefer, the text version or the filmed or live performance? Why?

....

....

....

D

Name _____ Date _____ Selection _____

Evaluating Different Formats

Use the organizer to help you evaluate the director's and actors' choices when transforming a story or script into a filmed or live performance.

I am comparing the short story, novel, or drama with ....

❏ filmed production called ....

❏ a live production called ....

Ways in which film or live performance stayed faithful to script or story	Ways in which film or live performance departed from the script or story
1.	1.
2.	2.
3.	3.
4.	4.
5.	5.

Which did you prefer, the text version or the filmed or live performance? Why?

....

....

....

E

Name _____ Date _____ Selection _____

Evaluating Different Formats

Use the organizer to help you evaluate the director's and actors' choices when transforming a story or script into a filmed or live performance.

I am comparing the short story, novel, or drama with ....

❏ filmed production called ....

❏ a live production called ....

Ways in which film or live performance stayed faithful to script or story	Ways in which film or live performance departed from the script or story
1.	1.
2.	2.
3.	3.
4.	4.
5.	5.

Which did you prefer, the text version or the filmed or live performance? Why?

....

....

....

F

For use with Literature 7

Literature 9

> 9. **Analyze how a modern work of fiction draws on themes, patterns of events, or character types from myths, traditional stories, or religious works such as the Bible, including describing how the material is rendered new.**

Explanation

Before stories were written down, they were told orally by storytellers. Every culture has an oral tradition that includes **myths**, legends, and folk tales that are passed down through the generations. These stories help us understand our past, describe our present, and communicate our beliefs. Authors of modern works of fiction learn a lot from storytellers. They draw upon familiar themes, events, and character types to create new stories that are rooted in tradition.

Traditional stories have unique characteristics. They generally express **universal themes**. These are themes that appear in stories from different cultures and throughout many time periods. Traditional stories center on heroes who are larger than life, and they often contain elements of the supernatural. Another characteristic of is their use of idioms to reflect the rhythms of spoken language.

Examples

- "Water Names" is a modern story built around a traditional story. The grandmother in "Water Names" grew up along the Yangtze River in China but now lives with her family in Wisconsin. Her granddaughters have never seen the water country where she was born, so she tells them a traditional story. The story contains an element of the supernatural, as a restless girl falls in love with the reflection of a handsome young man looking back at her from under the water. The river puts a spell on her, and she sits by the water waiting for him every day. One day she is swept away by a torrential rain and disappears. When the grandmother finishes telling the traditional story, the modern story resumes and her granddaughters ask for an explanation. She says, "Perhaps she lost her mind to desiring." Her answer expresses a universal theme of unfulfilled longing.

Academic Vocabulary

universal theme a theme that is found throughout the literature of all time periods

myth a traditional story that tries to explain the causes of natural phenomena such as the changing of the seasons

Apply the Standard

Use the worksheet that follows to help you apply the standard as you read literature selections. Several copies of the worksheet have been provided for you.

- Analyzing Literary Influences

Name _____ Date _____ Selection _____

Analyzing Literary Influences

Use the organizer below to analyze the common elements in a modern story and a traditional story.

	Modern Story	**Traditional Story**
Theme		
Events		
Character Types		

A

Name _____ Date _____ Selection _____

Analyzing Literary Influences

Use the organizer below to analyze the common elements in a modern story and a traditional story.

	Modern Story	**Traditional Story**
Theme		
Events		
Character Types		

B

Name _____ Date _____ Selection _____

Analyzing Literary Influences

Use the organizer below to analyze the common elements in a modern story and a traditional story.

	Modern Story	Traditional Story
Theme		
Events		
Character Types		

C

Name _____ Date _____ Selection _____

Analyzing Literary Influences

Use the organizer below to analyze the common elements in a modern story and a traditional story.

	Modern Story	Traditional Story
Theme		
Events		
Character Types		

D

Name _____ Date _____ Selection _____

Analyzing Literary Influences

Use the organizer below to analyze the common elements in a modern story and a traditional story.

	Modern Story	**Traditional Story**
Theme		
Events		
Character Types		

E

Name _____ Date _____ Selection _____

Analyzing Literary Influences

Use the organizer below to analyze the common elements in a modern story and a traditional story.

	Modern Story	Traditional Story
Theme		
Events		
Character Types		

F

Literature 10

> 10. By the end of the year, read and comprehend literature, including stories, dramas, and poems, at the high end of grades 6–8 text complexity band independently and proficiently.

Explanation

Complexity is the difficulty level of a work of any kind. Works of literature can vary widely in their complexity, or how difficult they are to understand. Some stories, dramas, and poems are less complex than others—they use familiar subjects, directly stated ideas and themes, and simple vocabulary with short sentences. Other work of literature, however, are more complex because they introduce unfamiliar concepts, are based on implied ideas and themes, and include advanced vocabulary, figurative language, and long sentences.

You will read literary works in different genres, such as stories, dramas, and poems. You will also be expected to **comprehend**, or understand the meaning and importance of, more complex texts than you have read before. To comprehend complex texts, use reading strategies such as the ones described below.

Examples

- To **monitor** your comprehension, stop occasionally as you read and ask yourself questions about what you have just read. For example, in O. Henry's story "A Retrieved Reformation," stop to ask yourself what Jimmy Valentine intends to do when he gets out of prison. Then **reread** or read ahead to find out exactly what he does. Later in the story, stop and ask yourself why he changes his name. Then back up and reread the section in which he changes his name.

- In the same story, use **context clues** to understand the unfamiliar vocabulary, such as the word "retribution." Clues such as "quick getaways" and "a successful dodger of retribution" hint that Jimmy does not always receive punishment for his crimes.

- **Paraphrase** sections that are difficult to understand. For example, you should paraphrase the paragraph that begins when the detective, Ben Price, says "That's Dandy Jim Valentine's autograph. He's resumed business." By restating the meaning of this entire paragraph in your own words, you will understand what the detective really means when he says "autograph." He is really saying that he recognizes that a new crime has been committed by Jimmy Valentine, an ex-con.

Academic Vocabulary

complexity the degree to which a story, poem, drama, or other work is difficult to understand

comprehend understand the meaning and importance of something

Apply the Standard

Use the worksheet that follows to help you apply the standard as you read. Several copies of the worksheet have been provided for you to use with different literature selections.

- Comprehending Complex Texts

Name _____ Date _____ Selection _____

Comprehending Complex Texts

Explain what makes the story, poem, drama, or other selection you are reading complex. Then explain how the strategy in the chart helps you comprehend the selection.

What makes this selection complex?

....

....

Strategy	How the Strategy Helped Me Comprehend the Selection
monitoring comprehension	
using context	
paraphrasing	
reread	

A

Name _____ Date _____ Selection _____

Comprehending Complex Texts

Explain what makes the story, poem, drama, or other selection you are reading complex. Then explain how the strategy in the chart helps you comprehend the selection.

What makes this selection complex?

....

....

Strategy	How the Strategy Helped Me Comprehend the Selection
monitoring comprehension	
using context	
paraphrasing	
reread	

B

Name _____ Date _____ Selection _____

Comprehending Complex Texts

Explain what makes the story, poem, drama, or other selection you are reading complex. Then explain how the strategy in the chart helps you comprehend the selection.

What makes this selection complex?

....

....

Strategy	How the Strategy Helped Me Comprehend the Selection
monitoring comprehension	
using context	
paraphrasing	
reread	

C

For use with Literature 10

Name _____ Date _____ Selection _____

Comprehending Complex Texts

Explain what makes the story, poem, drama, or other selection you are reading complex. Then explain how the strategy in the chart helps you comprehend the selection.

What makes this selection complex?

....

....

Strategy	How the Strategy Helped Me Comprehend the Selection
monitoring comprehension	
using context	
paraphrasing	
reread	

D

Name _____ Date _____ Selection _____

Comprehending Complex Texts

Explain what makes the story, poem, drama, or other selection you are reading complex. Then explain how the strategy in the chart helps you comprehend the selection.

What makes this selection complex?

....

....

Strategy	How the Strategy Helped Me Comprehend the Selection
monitoring comprehension	
using context	
paraphrasing	
reread	

E

Name _____ Date _____ Selection _____

Comprehending Complex Texts

Explain what makes the story, poem, drama, or other selection you are reading complex. Then explain how the strategy in the chart helps you comprehend the selection.

What makes this selection complex?

....

....

Strategy	How the Strategy Helped Me Comprehend the Selection
monitoring comprehension	
using context	
paraphrasing	
reread	

F

Reading Standards for Informational Text

Informational Text 1

> 1. **Cite the textual evidence that most strongly supports an analysis of what the text says explicitly as well as inferences drawn from the text.**

Explanation

Informational texts give explicit information (facts, examples, definitions, and explanations) about a topic. This explicit information provides details about a subject or topic. Good readers use these **explicit details** and other information to draw inferences about a topic. An **inference** is a logical guess based on clues in the text, or **textual evidence**, and the reader's knowledge and experience. When discussing a text, always support your inferences or analyses with the strongest text evidence you have.

Successful readers take note of and analyze important explicit details in a text. They also make inferences to comprehend more fully the meaning of a story.

Examples

- **Explicit details** provide basic information for readers and are directly stated. For example, "The most poisonous snake in the United States is the coral snake" and "It buries itself in the ground or in leaves and generally comes out at night" are explicit details.

- **Inferences** are logical guesses readers make based on details in the text and their own personal experience and knowledge. For example, the author might also say the following about snakes: "Copperhead snakes are poisonous and account for the largest number of snake bites in the U.S. If somebody steps on or near one, a copperhead may give a warning bite or a 'dry bite,' a bite with no venom. Copperhead bites are rarely, if ever, fatal." Although the text doesn't explicitly say it, you can infer that copperheads probably are not very aggressive snakes and have a weak poison.

- **Textual evidence** refers to examples from the text used to support a response or analysis. When providing textual evidence, you answer the question "How do you know?" Always cite the strongest evidence you can find to support your analysis.

Academic Vocabulary

explicit details information that is directly stated in the text

inference logical guess based on details in the text as well as personal experience

textual evidence words or phrases that support an analysis

Apply the Standard

Use the worksheets that follow to help you apply the standard as you read. Several copies of each worksheet have been provided for you to use with different informational texts.

- Citing Textual Evidence: Supporting an Analysis of Explicit Statements

- Citing Textual Evidence: Making Inferences

Name _____ Date _____ Selection _____

Identifying Strong Textual Evidence

Use this chart to record your analysis of a text. Then provide text evidence to support your analysis.
Circle the 3 strongest pieces of text evidence for each analysis.

Analysis of Text	Evidence from the Text
1.	a. b. c.
2.	a. b. c.

A

For use with Informational Text 1

Name _____ Date _____ Selection _____

Identifying Strong Textual Evidence

Use this chart to record your analysis of a text. Then provide text evidence to support your analysis. Circle the 3 strongest pieces of text evidence for each analysis.

Analysis of Text	Evidence from the Text
1.	a. b. c.
2.	a. b. c.

B

For use with Informational Text 1

Name _____ Date _____ Selection _____

Identifying Strong Textual Evidence

Use this chart to record your analysis of a text. Then provide text evidence to support your analysis.
Circle the 3 strongest pieces of text evidence for each analysis.

Analysis of Text	Evidence from the Text
1.	a. b. c.
2.	a. b. c.

C

For use with Informational Text 1

Name _____ Date _____ Selection _____

Identifying Strong Textual Evidence

Use this chart to record your analysis of a text. Then provide text evidence to support your analysis. Circle the 3 strongest pieces of text evidence for each analysis.

Analysis of Text	Evidence from the Text
1.	a. b. c.
2.	a. b. c.

D

Name _____ Date _____ Selection _____

Identifying Strong Textual Evidence

Use this chart to record your analysis of a text. Then provide text evidence to support your analysis. Circle the 3 strongest pieces of text evidence for each analysis.

Analysis of Text	Evidence from the Text
1.	**a.** **b.** **c.**
2.	**a.** **b.** **c.**

E

Name _____ Date _____ Selection _____

Identifying Strong Textual Evidence

Use this chart to record your analysis of a text. Then provide text evidence to support your analysis. Circle the 3 strongest pieces of text evidence for each analysis.

Analysis of Text	Evidence from the Text
1.	a. b. c.
2.	a. b. c.

F

Name _____ Date _____ Selection _____

Making Inferences

Use this chart to make inferences from the text. Combine details you have gathered from the story or passage with your own knowledge or experience to make inferences.

Details from the Text	Inference from the Text
1.	
2.	
3.	

A

For use with Informational Text 1

Name _____ Date _____ Selection _____

Making Inferences

Use this chart to make inferences from the text. Combine details you have gathered from the story or passage with your own knowledge or experience to make inferences.

Details from the Text	Inference from the Text
1.	
2.	
3.	

B

Name _____ Date _____ Selection _____

Making Inferences

Use this chart to make inferences from the text. Combine details you have gathered from the story or passage with your own knowledge or experience to make inferences.

Details from the Text	Inference from the Text
1.	
2.	
3.	

C

Name _____ Date _____ Selection _____

Making Inferences

Use this chart to make inferences from the text. Combine details you have gathered from the story or passage with your own knowledge or experience to make inferences.

Details from the Text	Inference from the Text
1.	
2.	
3.	

D

Name _____   Date _____   Selection _____

Making Inferences

Use this chart to make inferences from the text. Combine details you have gathered from the story or passage with your own knowledge or experience to make inferences.

Details from the Text	Inference from the Text
1.	
2.	
3.	

E

Name _____ Date _____ Selection _____

Making Inferences

Use this chart to make inferences from the text. Combine details you have gathered from the story or passage with your own knowledge or experience to make inferences.

Details from the Text	Inference from the Text
1.	
2.	
3.	

F

Informational Text 2

> **2. Determine a central idea of a text and analyze its development over the course of the text, including its relationship to supporting ideas; provide an objective summary of the text.**

Explanation

The **central idea** is the main point of a piece of writing. It is what the author is trying to say to readers. Sometimes the central idea is stated directly, but usually the reader has to figure it out by studying the supporting details in the text. **Supporting details** are examples, facts, reasons, and descriptions that give more information about the central idea. As you read, notice how the writer groups the details, and look for sentences that pull details together.

A good way to clarify central ideas is to summarize the text. A **summary** is a brief restatement of the text in your own words. It includes only the most important details, and it presents the information objectively. When writing a summary, first determine the central idea the author is trying to convey; then restate in your own words the supporting details.

Examples

- **Summarize** Read this summary of an article about the Underground Railroad.

   Although an estimated 100,000 enslaved people successfully escaped to the North along the Underground Railroad, thousands more never made it to freedom. Some were taken by slave catchers; others died from the hardships of the journey. Those who were recaptured were punished harshly with beatings and imprisonment. But even if enslaved individuals did not gain their freedom, their attempts were not in vain. Information about which paths to take and where the safe places to hide were was passed on to others.

- **Central Idea** Although it is not stated directly, the supporting details in the text point to a clear central idea: *The journey to freedom on the Underground Railroad was dangerous but worthwhile*. Details about the risk of death and punishment highlight the danger.

Academic Vocabulary

central idea the main idea or central message of a text

summary a statement of the central idea and important details in a work

supporting details facts, details, reasons, and descriptions that support the central idea

Apply the Standard

Use the worksheets that follow to help you apply the standard as you read. Several copies of each worksheet have been provided for you to use with different informational texts.

- Summarizing Key Supporting Details

- Analyzing Central Ideas

Name _____ Date _____ Selection _____

Summarizing Key Supporting Details

Use the organizer to summarize a text. First present the central idea; then record the most important details. Use your own words, and write in full sentences.

Central Idea ....

....

....

....

1. Detail

....

....

....

....

2. Detail

....

....

....

....

3. Detail

....

....

....

....

4. Detail

....

....

....

....

A

Name _____ Date _____ Selection _____

Summarizing Key Supporting Details

Use the organizer to summarize a text. First present the central idea; then record the most important details. Use your own words, and write in full sentences.

Central Idea ....
....
....
....
....

1. Detail
....
....
....
....
....

2. Detail
....
....
....
....
....

3. Detail
....
....
....
....
....

4. Detail
....
....
....
....
....

B

For use with Informational Text 2

Name _____ Date _____ Selection _____

Summarizing Key Supporting Details

Use the organizer to summarize a text. First present the central idea; then record the most important details. Use your own words, and write in full sentences.

Central Idea ....
....
....
....
....

1. Detail
....
....
....
....
....

2. Detail
....
....
....
....
....

3. Detail
....
....
....
....
....

4. Detail
....
....
....
....
....

C

For use with Informational Text 2

Name _____ Date _____ Selection _____

Summarizing Key Supporting Details

Use the organizer to summarize a text. First present the central idea; then record the most important details. Use your own words, and write in full sentences.

Central Idea ....

....

....

....

....

1. Detail

....

....

....

....

....

2. Detail

....

....

....

....

....

3. Detail

....

....

....

....

....

4. Detail

....

....

....

....

....

D

For use with Informational Text 2

Name _____ Date _____ Selection _____

Summarizing Key Supporting Details

Use the organizer to summarize a text. First present the central idea; then record the most important details. Use your own words, and write in full sentences.

Central Idea ....
....
....
....
....

1. Detail
....
....
....
....
....

2. Detail
....
....
....
....
....

3. Detail
....
....
....
....
....

4. Detail
....
....
....
....
....

E

Name _____ Date _____ Selection _____

Summarizing Key Supporting Details

Use the organizer to summarize a text. First present the central idea; then record the most important details. Use your own words, and write in full sentences.

Central Idea ....
....
....
....
....

1. Detail

....
....
....
....
....

2. Detail

....
....
....
....
....

3. Detail

....
....
....
....
....

4. Detail

....
....
....
....
....

F

Name _____   Date _____   Selection _____

Analyzing Central Ideas

Use the graphic organizer to state the central idea of the text and to list 5 important supporting details.

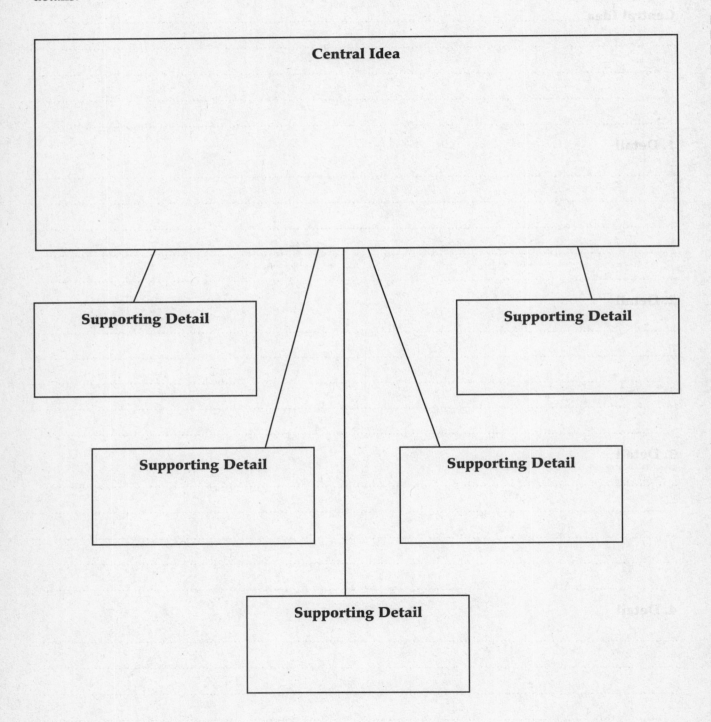

A

For use with Informational Text 2

Name _____ Date _____ Selection _____

Analyzing Central Ideas

Use the graphic organizer to state the central idea of the text and to list 5 important supporting details.

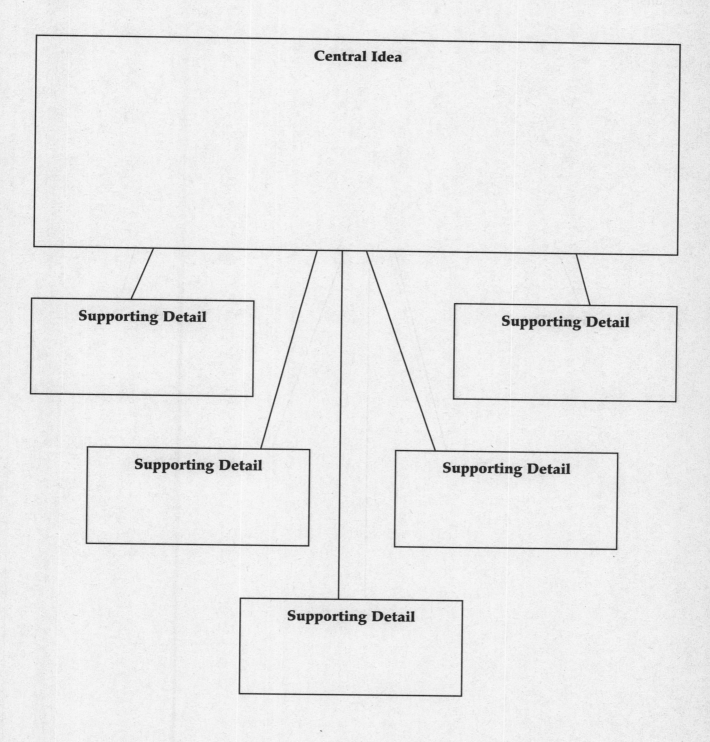

Central Idea

Supporting Detail

Supporting Detail

Supporting Detail

Supporting Detail

Supporting Detail

B

Name _____ Date _____ Selection _____

Analyzing Central Ideas

Use the graphic organizer to state the central idea of the text and to list 5 important supporting details.

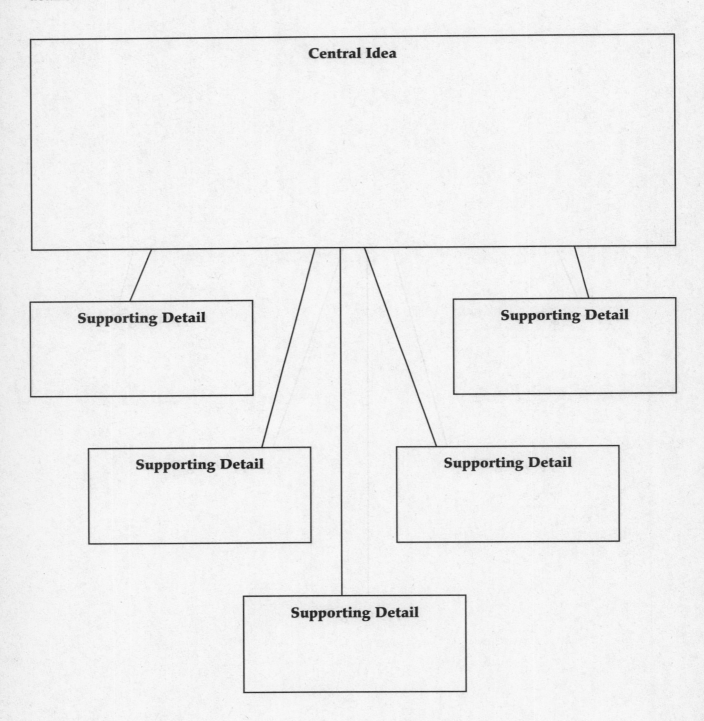

C

For use with Informational Text 2

Name _____ Date _____ Selection _____

Analyzing Central Ideas

Use the graphic organizer to state the central idea of the text and to list 5 important supporting details.

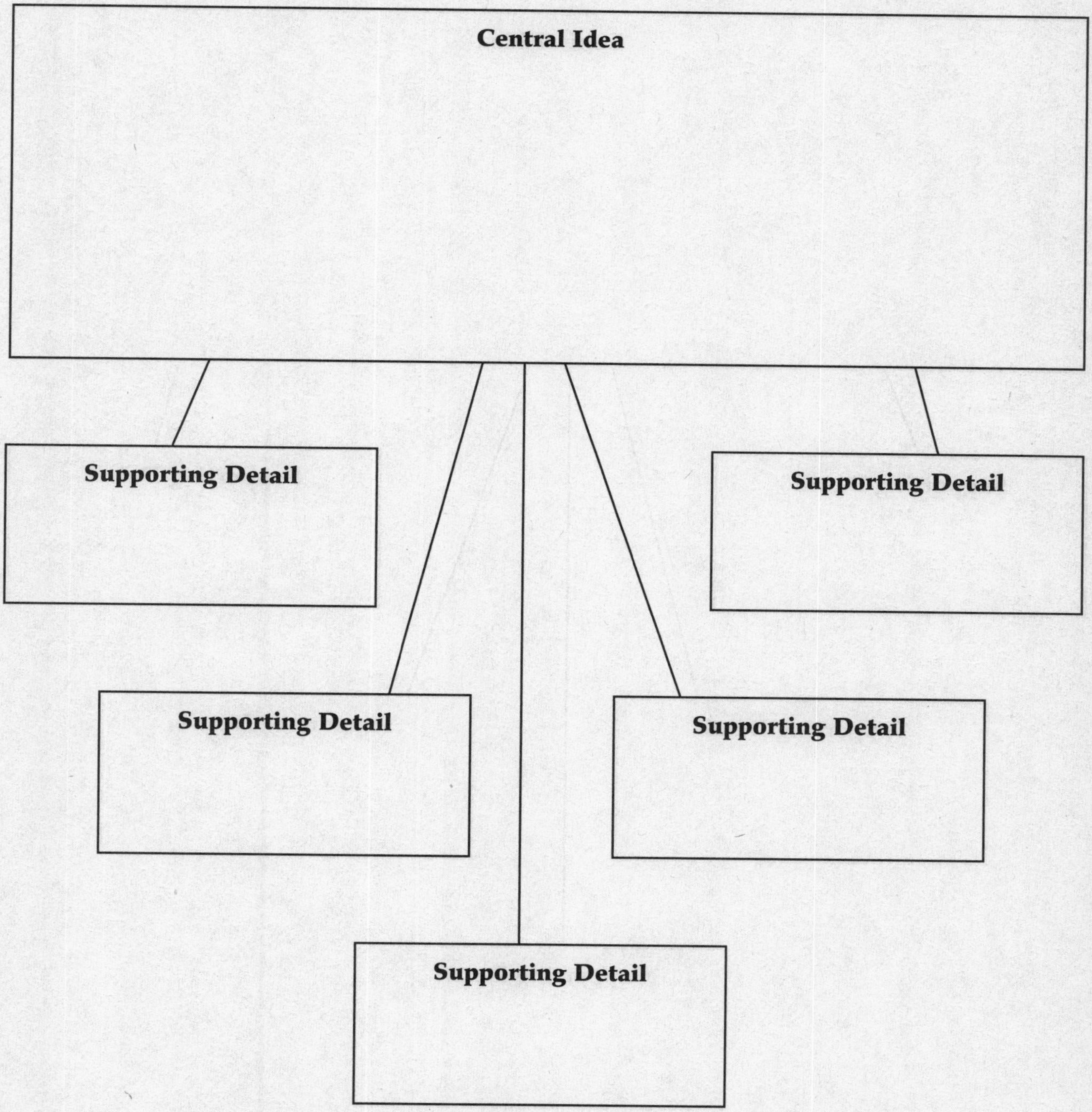

Central Idea

Supporting Detail

Supporting Detail

Supporting Detail

Supporting Detail

Supporting Detail

D

Name _____ Date _____ Selection _____

Analyzing Central Ideas

Use the graphic organizer to state the central idea of the text and to list 5 important supporting details.

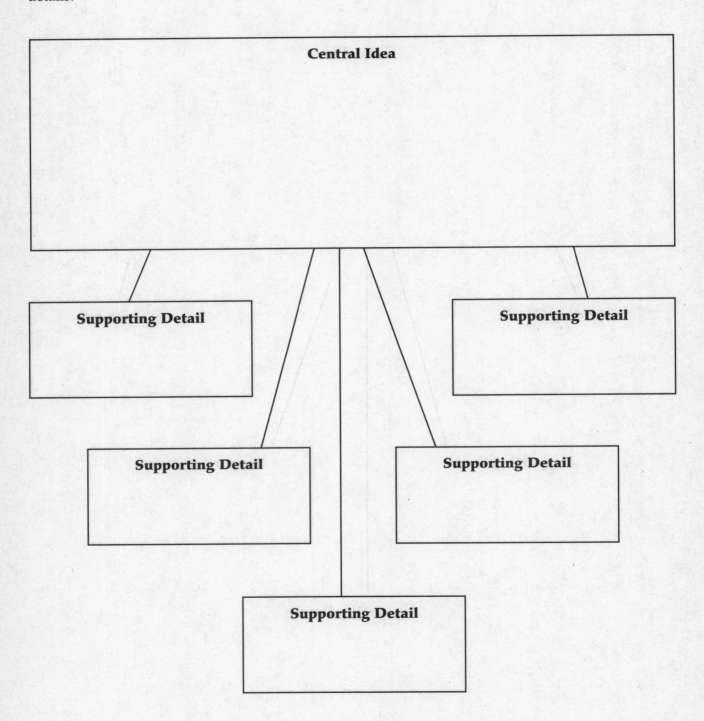

E

Name _____ Date _____ Selection _____

Analyzing Central Ideas

Use the graphic organizer to state the central idea of the text and to list 5 important supporting details.

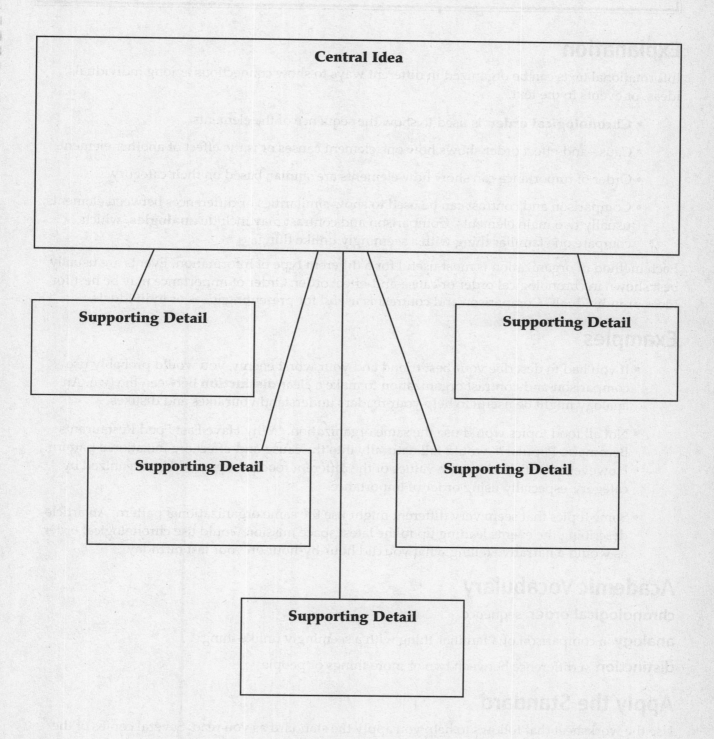

Central Idea

Supporting Detail

Supporting Detail

Supporting Detail

Supporting Detail

Supporting Detail

F

Informational Text 3

3. **Analyze how a text makes connections among and distinctions between individuals, ideas, or events (e.g., through comparisons, analogies, or categories).**

Explanation

Informational texts can be organized in different ways to show connections among individuals, ideas, or events in the text.

- **Chronological order** is used to show the sequence of the elements.

- Cause-and-effect order shows how one element causes or is the effect of another element.

- Order of importance can show how elements are similar, based on their category.

- Comparison and contrast can be used to show similarities or differences between elements, usually two main elements. Comparison and contrast may include **analogies,** which compare one familiar thing with a seemingly unlike thing.

Each method of organization is most useful for a different type of information. Events are usually best shown in chronological order or cause-and-effect order. Order of importance may be best for ideas or individuals. Comparison and contrast is useful for presenting ideas or individuals.

Examples

- If you had to describe your best friend and your worst enemy, you would probably use comparison-and-contrast organization to make a clear **distinction** between the two. An analogy might be useful to help your readers understand your likes and dislikes.

- Not all food topics would use the same organization. "Why Have Fast Food Restaurants Become so Popular?" would fall naturally into the cause-and-effect organizational pattern. However, an article about the values of the different food groups could be organized by category, especially using order of importance.

- Some topics that seem very different might use the same organizational pattern. An article describing the events leading up to the latest space mission would use chronological order, as would a narrative telling what you did hour-by-hour on your last birthday.

Academic Vocabulary

chronological order sequence

analogy a comparison of a familiar thing with a seemingly unlike thing

distinction a difference between two or more things or people

Apply the Standard

Use the worksheet that follows to help you apply the standard as you read. Several copies of the worksheet have been provided for you to use with different informational texts.

- Analyzing Connections

Name _____ Date _____ Assignment _____

Analyzing Connections

Use the organizer to analyze how the text compares and contrasts individuals, ideas, or events.

Comparison and Contrast Connections

Topics: (individuals, ideas, or events)	Comparisons: (how the topics are alike) 1. 2. 3.	Contrasts: (how the topics are different) 1. 2. 3.
Topics:	Comparisons: 1. 2. 3.	Contrasts: 1. 2. 3.
Topics:	Comparisons: 1. 2. 3.	Contrasts: 1. 2. 3.
Topics:	Comparisons: 1. 2. 3.	Contrasts: 1. 2. 3.

A

For use with Informational Text 3

Name _____ Date _____ Assignment _____

Analyzing Connections

Use the organizer to analyze how the text compares and contrasts individuals, ideas, or events.

Comparison and Contrast Connections

Topics: (individuals, ideas, or events)	Comparisons: (how the topics are alike)	Contrasts: (how the topics are different)
	1. 2. 3.	1. 2. 3.
Topics:	Comparisons: 1. 2. 3.	Contrasts: 1. 2. 3.
Topics:	Comparisons: 1. 2. 3.	Contrasts: 1. 2. 3.
Topics:	Comparisons: 1. 2. 3.	Contrasts: 1. 2. 3.

B

Name _____ Date _____ Assignment _____

Analyzing Connections

Use the organizer to analyze how the text compares and contrasts individuals, ideas, or events.

Comparison and Contrast Connections

Topics: (individuals, ideas, or events)	Comparisons: (how the topics are alike) 1. 2. 3.	Contrasts: (how the topics are different) 1. 2. 3.
Topics:	Comparisons: 1. 2. 3.	Contrasts: 1. 2. 3.
Topics:	Comparisons: 1. 2. 3.	Contrasts: 1. 2. 3.
Topics:	Comparisons: 1. 2. 3.	Contrasts: 1. 2. 3.

C

Name _____ Date _____ Assignment _____

Analyzing Connections

Use the organizer to analyze how the text compares and contrasts individuals, ideas, or events.

Comparison and Contrast Connections

Topics: (individuals, ideas, or events)	Comparisons: (how the topics are alike) 1. 2. 3.	Contrasts: (how the topics are different) 1. 2. 3.
Topics:	Comparisons: 1. 2. 3.	Contrasts: 1. 2. 3.
Topics:	Comparisons: 1. 2. 3.	Contrasts: 1. 2. 3.
Topics:	Comparisons: 1. 2. 3.	Contrasts: 1. 2. 3.

D

Name _____ Date _____ Assignment _____

Analyzing Connections

Use the organizer to analyze how the text compares and contrasts individuals, ideas, or events.

Comparison and Contrast Connections

Topics: (individuals, ideas, or events)	Comparisons: (how the topics are alike) 1. 2. 3.	Contrasts: (how the topics are different) 1. 2. 3.
Topics:	Comparisons: 1. 2. 3.	Contrasts: 1. 2. 3.
Topics:	Comparisons: 1. 2. 3.	Contrasts: 1. 2. 3.
Topics:	Comparisons: 1. 2. 3.	Contrasts: 1. 2. 3.

E

Name _____ Date _____ Assignment _____

Analyzing Connections

Use the organizer to analyze how the text compares and contrasts individuals, ideas, or events.

Comparison and Contrast Connections

Topics: (individuals, ideas, or events)	Comparisons: (how the topics are alike) 1. 2. 3.	Contrasts: (how the topics are different) 1. 2. 3.
Topics:	Comparisons: 1. 2. 3.	Contrasts: 1. 2. 3.
Topics:	Comparisons: 1. 2. 3.	Contrasts: 1. 2. 3.
Topics:	Comparisons: 1. 2. 3.	Contrasts: 1. 2. 3.

F

Informational Text 4

> **4.** Determine the meaning of words and phrases as they are used in a text, including figurative, connotative, and technical meanings; analyze the impact of specific word choices on meaning and tone, including analogies or allusions to other texts.

Explanation

In informational texts, you may come across words that you have never encountered before or that are used in unusual ways. For example, some authors use **figurative language** to explain ideas in a fresh way. In addition, you may encounter a familiar word whose **technical meaning** is unfamiliar. Words also have **connotative meanings,** or feelings and emotions that are associated with them.

Authors choose their words carefully because they know that their choices affect the meaning and **tone** of their writing. Sometimes authors use **analogies** or **allusions** to help explain a concept.

Examples

- Authors use **figurative language** to develop vivid images. In the sentence "The soldiers could feel their blood turn to ice," the soldiers' blood did not really become ice.

- The words *formal* and *stiff* can describe someone's manner, but the words also have different **connotative meanings.**

- The sentence "She was a real Scrooge" is an **allusion** to the character Scrooge in Dickens's *A Christmas Carol.* The allusion implies that the woman is very miserly with money.

- An **analogy** makes a comparison between two or more things that are similar in some ways but otherwise unlike. A writer might create an analogy comparing the turbulence in the air when flying to waves in the water when sailing.

Academic Vocabulary

figurative language words or phrases that are not meant to be taken literally

connotative meaning feelings and emotions associated with a word or phrase

allusion a reference to a well-known person, place, event, literary work, or work of art.

analogy comparison between two different things that are similar in a number of ways

tone the authors attitude towards a subject

technical meanings word meanings specifically related to a subject

Apply the Standard

Use the worksheets that follow to help you apply the standard as you read. Several copies of each worksheet have been provided for you to use with different informational texts.

- Understanding Connotations, Figurative Language, and Technical Terms

- Analyzing Word Choice

Name _____ Date _____ Assignment _____

Understanding Connotations, Figurative Language, and Technical Terms

Use the organizer below to help you determine the figurative, connotative, or technical meaning of words and phrases you encounter in reading informational texts. Use the first column to record 3-4 words and phrases that stand out or are memorable. Write their meanings in the second column. Use a dictionary, if necessary, to identify the meanings of technical terms.

Word or Phrase	Figurative, Connotative, or Technical Meaning
1.	
2.	
3.	
4.	

Name _____ Date _____ Assignment _____

Understanding Connotations, Figurative Language, and Technical Terms

Use the organizer below to help you determine the figurative, connotative, or technical meaning of words and phrases you encounter in reading informational texts. Use the first column to record 3-4 words and phrases that stand out or are memorable. Write their meanings in the second column. Use a dictionary, if necessary, to identify the meanings of technical terms.

Word or Phrase	Figurative, Connotative, or Technical Meaning
1.	
2.	
3.	
4.	

B

Name _____ Date _____ Assignment _____

Understanding Connotations, Figurative Language, and Technical Terms

Use the organizer below to help you determine the figurative, connotative, or technical meaning of words and phrases you encounter in reading informational texts. Use the first column to record 3-4 words and phrases that stand out or are memorable. Write their meanings in the second column. Use a dictionary, if necessary, to identify the meanings of technical terms.

Word or Phrase	Figurative, Connotative, or Technical Meaning
1.	
2.	
3.	
4.	

C

Name _____ Date _____ Assignment _____

Understanding Connotations, Figurative Language, and Technical Terms

Use the organizer below to help you determine the figurative, connotative, or technical meaning of words and phrases you encounter in reading informational texts. Use the first column to record 3-4 words and phrases that stand out or are memorable. Write their meanings in the second column. Use a dictionary, if necessary, to identify the meanings of technical terms.

Word or Phrase	Figurative, Connotative, or Technical Meaning
1.	
2.	
3.	
4.	

D

Name _____ Date _____ Assignment _____

Understanding Connotations, Figurative Language, and Technical Terms

Use the organizer below to help you determine the figurative, connotative, or technical meaning of words and phrases you encounter in reading informational texts. Use the first column to record 3-4 words and phrases that stand out or are memorable. Write their meanings in the second column. Use a dictionary, if necessary, to identify the meanings of technical terms.

Word or Phrase	Figurative, Connotative, or Technical Meaning
1.	
2.	
3.	
4.	

E

Name _____ Date _____ Assignment _____

Understanding Connotations, Figurative Language, and Technical Terms

Use the organizer below to help you determine the figurative, connotative, or technical meaning of words and phrases you encounter in reading informational texts. Use the first column to record 3-4 words and phrases that stand out or are memorable. Write their meanings in the second column. Use a dictionary, if necessary, to identify the meanings of technical terms.

Word or Phrase	Figurative, Connotative, or Technical Meaning
1.	
2.	
3.	
4.	

F

Name _____ Date _____ Assignment _____

Analyzing Word Choice

Use the organizer to help you analyze the effect of specific word choices on tone and meaning. In the first column, write examples of 2 or 3 analogies and allusions you find in your reading. In the second column, explain the effect they have on the author's tone and the meaning of the text.

Word Choices	Effect on Tone and Meaning
Examples of Analogies:	
Examples of Allusions:	

A

Name _____ Date _____ Assignment _____

Analyzing Word Choice

Use the organizer to help you analyze the effect of specific word choices on tone and meaning. In the first column, write examples of 2 or 3 analogies and allusions you find in your reading. In the second column, explain the effect they have on the author's tone and the meaning of the text.

Word Choices	Effect on Tone and Meaning
Examples of Analogies:	
Examples of Allusions:	

B

Name _____ Date _____ Assignment _____

Analyzing Word Choice

Use the organizer to help you analyze the effect of specific word choices on tone and meaning. In the first column, write examples of 2 or 3 analogies and allusions you find in your reading. In the second column, explain the effect they have on the author's tone and the meaning of the text.

Word Choices	Effect on Tone and Meaning
Examples of Analogies:	
Examples of Allusions:	

C

Name _____ Date _____ Assignment _____

Analyzing Word Choice

Use the organizer to help you analyze the effect of specific word choices on tone and meaning. In the first column, write examples of 2 or 3 analogies and allusions you find in your reading. In the second column, explain the effect they have on the author's tone and the meaning of the text.

Word Choices	Effect on Tone and Meaning
Examples of Analogies:	
Examples of Allusions:	

D

Name _____ Date _____ Assignment _____

Analyzing Word Choice

Use the organizer to help you analyze the effect of specific word choices on tone and meaning. In the first column, write examples of 2 or 3 analogies and allusions you find in your reading. In the second column, explain the effect they have on the author's tone and the meaning of the text.

Word Choices	Effect on Tone and Meaning
Examples of Analogies:	
Examples of Allusions:	

E

Name _____ Date _____ Assignment _____

Analyzing Word Choice

Use the organizer to help you analyze the effect of specific word choices on tone and meaning. In the first column, write examples of 2 or 3 analogies and allusions you find in your reading. In the second column, explain the effect they have on the author's tone and the meaning of the text.

Word Choices	Effect on Tone and Meaning
Examples of Analogies:	
Examples of Allusions:	

F

Informational Text 5

> 5. **Analyze in detail the structure of a specific paragraph in a text, including the role of particular sentences in developing and refining a key concept.**

Explanation

A paragraph is made up of sentences that work together to develop an idea. The main idea of a paragraph is the key concept that a writer wants to convey. Sometimes it is stated directly in a **topic sentence** that appears at the beginning or end of the paragraph. Sometimes it is not stated at all; the reader has to figure it out by studying the supporting details in the paragraph. **Supporting details** are examples, facts, reasons, or descriptions that develop the main idea.

Whether its topic sentence is stated or implied, a good paragraph must have unity and coherence. That means all the sentences must work together to support a single idea, and they must be organized logically, with transition words to connect them.

Examples

Each paragraph below uses different kinds of supporting details to develop the italicized topic sentence.

- **Sensory description** Running barefoot across the scorching sand to the shoreline, I dip my toes gratefully into the cool blue ocean. When I dive in, I feel its coolness against my hot skin. After a brief swim, I return to my blanket and dry off under the warm rays of the sun. *There is nothing more refreshing on a summer day than a trip to the beach.*

- **Reasons** *Mr. Panos is a dedicated teacher.* He makes math come alive in class by using real-life examples that students can relate to. When I was having trouble with algebra, he took the time to tutor me after school so that I wouldn't fail the midterm exam. He never gives up on us.

- **Facts and statistics** Of the estimated 2 million homeless people in America, about one-third are children. *Homeless children face many challenges.* They have more health problems than other children, and they often have trouble academically because they do not have a place to study or do their homework. They are also more likely than other students to drop out of high school.

Academic Vocabulary

supporting details examples, facts, reasons, or descriptions that develop the main idea

topic sentence a sentence that states the main idea of a paragraph

Apply the Standard

Use the worksheet that follows to help you apply the standard as you read. Several copies have been provided for you to use with different informational texts.

- Analyzing Paragraph Structure

Name _____ Date _____ Assignment _____

Analyzing Paragraph Structure

Choose a paragraph from an informational text you have read recently. In the organizer, identify the paragraph's topic sentence and then list the supporting details. You may add or delete circles as needed.

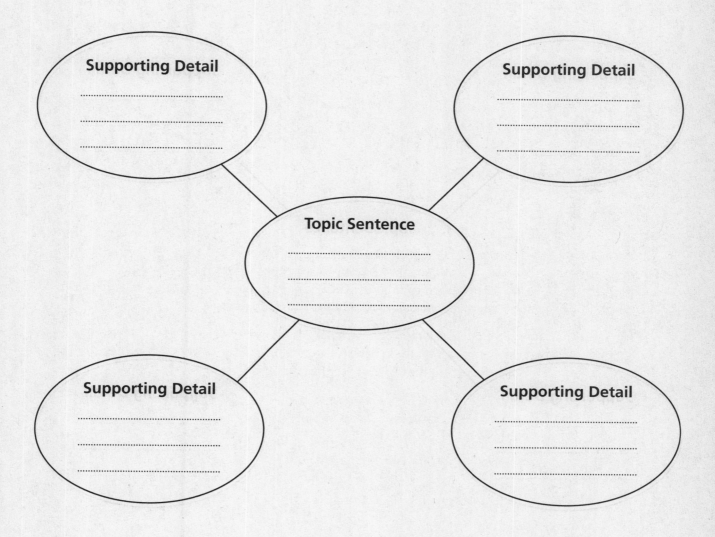

A

Name _____ Date _____ Assignment _____

Analyzing Paragraph Structure

Choose a paragraph from an informational text you have read recently. In the organizer, identify the paragraph's topic sentence and then list the supporting details. You may add or delete circles as needed.

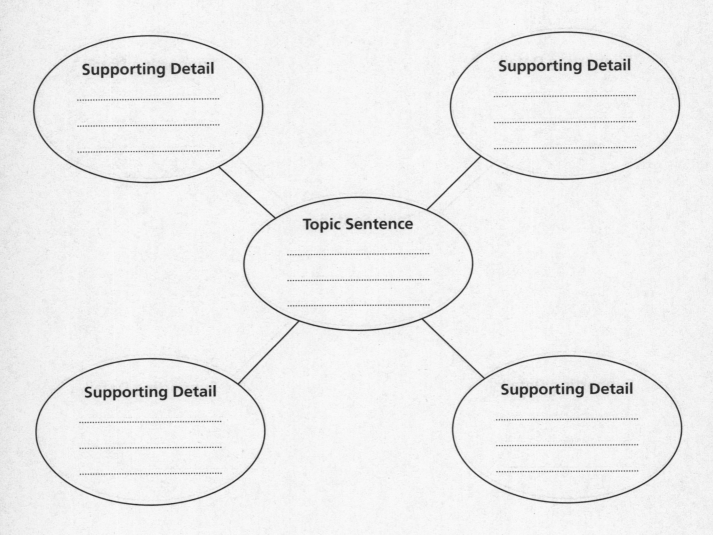

B

For use with Informational Text 5

Name _____ Date _____ Assignment _____

Analyzing Paragraph Structure

Choose a paragraph from an informational text you have read recently. In the organizer, identify the paragraph's topic sentence and then list the supporting details. You may add or delete circles as needed.

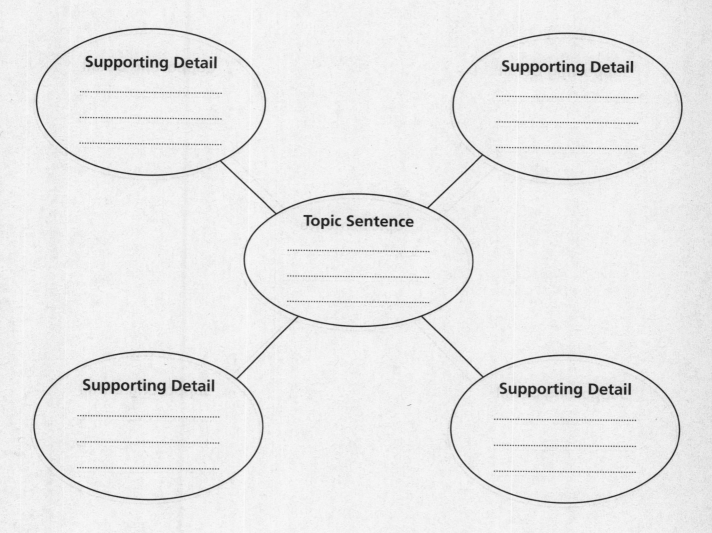

C

Name _____ Date _____ Assignment _____

Analyzing Paragraph Structure

Choose a paragraph from an informational text you have read recently. In the organizer, identify the paragraph's topic sentence and then list the supporting details. You may add or delete circles as needed.

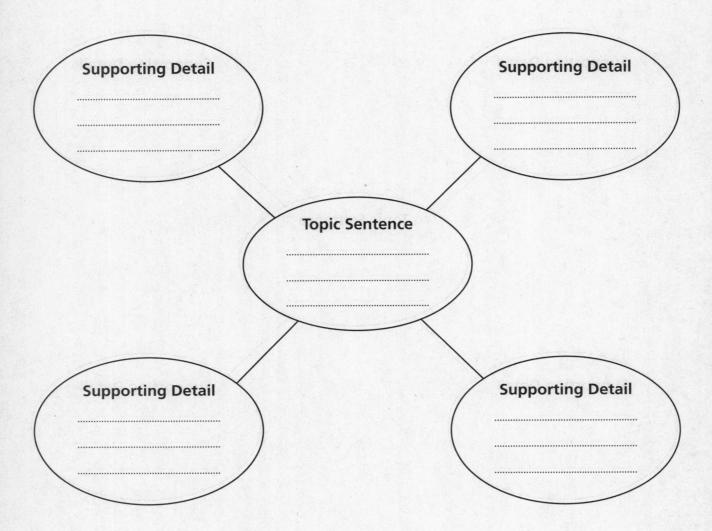

D

For use with Informational Text 5

Name _____ Date _____ Assignment _____

Analyzing Paragraph Structure

Choose a paragraph from an informational text you have read recently. In the organizer, identify the paragraph's topic sentence and then list the supporting details. You may add or delete circles as needed.

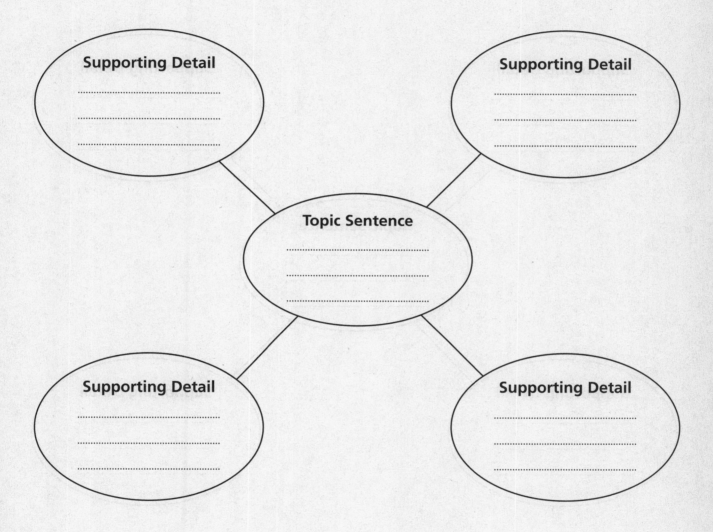

Supporting Detail

Supporting Detail

Topic Sentence

Supporting Detail

Supporting Detail

E

For use with Informational Text 5

Name _____ Date _____ Assignment _____

Analyzing Paragraph Structure

Choose a paragraph from an informational text you have read recently. In the organizer, identify the paragraph's topic sentence and then list the supporting details. You may add or delete circles as needed.

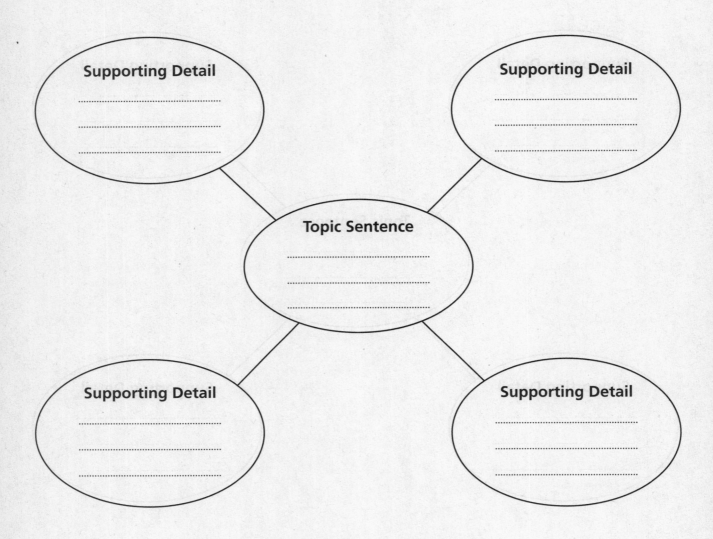

F

Informational Text 6

6. Determine an author's point of view or purpose in a text and analyze how the author acknowledges and responds to conflicting evidence or viewpoints.

Explanation

An author's **purpose** is his or her reason for writing a piece, such as *to inform, to persuade,* or *to entertain.* The details in the author's work help you learn the author's purpose. Facts, reasons, and statistics usually indicate that the purpose is to inform or persuade. Stories may have horrifying or amusing details that are included to entertain. Authors have both a general purpose and a specific purpose for writing. A general purpose might be to persuade, while a specific purpose might be "to convince readers to protect the endangered whales." The author's **point of view,** or opinion, is reflected in his or her specific purpose for writing.

When authors acknowledge conflicting evidence and viewpoints, they provide their readers with all the facts, not just the ones that support their own ideas. Readers are more likely to believe an author who tackles opposing viewpoints and evidence by providing **counterarguments** to them. Doing so persuades readers that the author's own viewpoint is the correct one.

Example

- A writer for the school paper has a clear purpose—to persuade readers to vote in favor of students wearing school uniforms. He supports his purpose by including details about the value of not having to buy a lot of expensive clothing and the positive effects of "fitting in" due to a lack of competition to wear the best clothes. He presents conflicting viewpoints by acknowledging that some people feel that uniforms take away students' individuality and creative outlets. He responds to the opposing viewpoint by presenting a counterargument that students should channel their creativity into art projects, not expensive clothing.

Academic Vocabulary

author's purpose the main reason an author writes a work

author's point of view an author's viewpoint, or opinion, on a topic

counterargument an argument made to respond to another argument

Apply the Standard

Use the worksheets that follow to help you apply the standard as you read. Several copies of each worksheet have been provided for you to use with different informational texts.

- Determining Point of View and Purpose

- Analyzing an Author's Response to Conflicting Evidence

Name _____ Date _____ Assignment _____

Determining Point of View and Purpose

Complete the organizer to determine the author's point of view and purpose in an informational text. First, write the title and topic of the selection. Then, in the left column, identify the author's point of view and purpose for writing. In the right column, provide details from the text that helped you determine the point of view and purpose.

Title of the Text:

Topic of the Text:

Author's Point of View:	Details from the Text:
Author's Purpose(s): ☐ to inform ☐ to persuade ☐ to entertain ☐ to reflect	

A

Name _____ Date _____ Assignment _____

Determining Point of View and Purpose

Complete the organizer to determine the author's point of view and purpose in an informational text. First, write the title and topic of the selection. Then, in the left column, identify the author's point of view and purpose for writing. In the right column, provide details from the text that helped you determine the point of view and purpose.

Title of the Text:

Topic of the Text:

Author's Point of View:	Details from the Text:
Author's Purpose(s): ❑ to inform ❑ to persuade ❑ to entertain ❑ to reflect	

B

Name _____ Date _____ Assignment _____

Determining Point of View and Purpose

Complete the organizer to determine the author's point of view and purpose in an informational text. First, write the title and topic of the selection. Then, in the left column, identify the author's point of view and purpose for writing. In the right column, provide details from the text that helped you determine the point of view and purpose.

Title of the Text:

Topic of the Text:

Author's Point of View:	Details from the Text:
Author's Purpose(s): ☐ to inform ☐ to persuade ☐ to entertain ☐ to reflect	

C

For use with Informational Text 6

Name _____ Date _____ Assignment _____

Determining Point of View and Purpose

Complete the organizer to determine the author's point of view and purpose in an informational text. First, write the title and topic of the selection. Then, in the left column, identify the author's point of view and purpose for writing. In the right column, provide details from the text that helped you determine the point of view and purpose.

Title of the Text:

Topic of the Text:

Author's Point of View:	Details from the Text:

| Author's Purpose(s):
 ❏ to inform
 ❏ to persuade
 ❏ to entertain
 ❏ to reflect | |

D

Name _____ Date _____ Assignment _____

Determining Point of View and Purpose

Complete the organizer to determine the author's point of view and purpose in an informational text. First, write the title and topic of the selection. Then, in the left column, identify the author's point of view and purpose for writing. In the right column, provide details from the text that helped you determine the point of view and purpose.

Title of the Text:

Topic of the Text:

Author's Point of View:	Details from the Text:
Author's Purpose(s): ☐ to inform ☐ to persuade ☐ to entertain ☐ to reflect	

E

Name _____ Date _____ Assignment _____

Determining Point of View and Purpose

Complete the organizer to determine the author's point of view and purpose in an informational text. First, write the title and topic of the selection. Then, in the left column, identify the author's point of view and purpose for writing. In the right column, provide details from the text that helped you determine the point of view and purpose.

Title of the Text:

Topic of the Text:

Author's Point of View:	Details from the Text:
Author's Purpose(s): ❑ to inform ❑ to persuade ❑ to entertain ❑ to reflect	

F

Name _____ Date _____ Assignment _____

Analyzing an Author's Response to Conflicting Evidence

Use the organizer to analyze an author's response to conflicting evidence and viewpoints.

```
┌─────────────────────────────────────────────┐
│ Title:                                      │
│ Author:                                     │
│                                             │
└─────────────────────────────────────────────┘
                     │
                     ▼
┌─────────────────────────────────────────────┐
│ Author's Position:                          │
│                                             │
│                                             │
│                                             │
│                                             │
└─────────────────────────────────────────────┘
                     │
                     ▼
┌─────────────────────────────────────────────┐
│ Conflicting evidence and viewpoints:        │
│                                             │
│                                             │
│                                             │
│                                             │
│                                             │
│                                             │
│                                             │
│                                             │
└─────────────────────────────────────────────┘
                     │
                     ▼
┌─────────────────────────────────────────────┐
│ Author's counterarguments:                  │
│                                             │
│                                             │
│                                             │
│                                             │
│                                             │
│                                             │
│                                             │
└─────────────────────────────────────────────┘
```

A

Name _____ Date _____ Assignment _____

Analyzing an Author's Response to Conflicting Evidence

Use the organizer to analyze an author's response to conflicting evidence and viewpoints.

Title:
Author:

↓

Author's Position:

↓

Conflicting evidence and viewpoints:

↓

Author's counterarguments:

B

Name _____ Date _____ Assignment _____

Analyzing an Author's Response to Conflicting Evidence

Use the organizer to analyze an author's response to conflicting evidence and viewpoints.

Title:
Author:

↓

Author's Position:

↓

Conflicting evidence and viewpoints:

↓

Author's counterarguments:

C

Name _____ Date _____ Assignment _____

Analyzing an Author's Response to Conflicting Evidence

Use the organizer to analyze an author's response to conflicting evidence and viewpoints.

Title:
Author:

↓

Author's Position:

↓

Conflicting evidence and viewpoints:

↓

Author's counterarguments:

D

Name _____ Date _____ Assignment _____

Analyzing an Author's Response to Conflicting Evidence

Use the organizer to analyze an author's response to conflicting evidence and viewpoints.

Title:
Author:

↓

Author's Position:

↓

Conflicting evidence and viewpoints:

↓

Author's counterarguments:

E

Name _____ Date _____ Assignment _____

Analyzing an Author's Response to Conflicting Evidence

Use the organizer to analyze an author's response to conflicting evidence and viewpoints.

Title:
Author:

$\downarrow$

Author's Position:

$\downarrow$

Conflicting evidence and viewpoints:

$\downarrow$

Author's counterarguments:

F

Informational Text 7

> 7. **Evaluate the advantages and disadvantages of using different mediums (e.g. print or digital text, video, multimedia) to present a particular topic or idea.**

Explanation

Every medium has advantages and disadvantages for presenting a particular topic or idea. To be a critical consumer of various media, you must be able to evaluate how well each medium communicates ideas.

Examples

- **Print or digital text** is particularly useful for presenting dense information and detail. Writers might choose text to present an argument or detailed research. For example, a writer could include detailed claims and evidence in a written text to persuade readers to recycle. When evaluating written text, ask yourself: Is this information clear and complete? Is there anything I do not understand that could be better communicated visually?

- **Video** is an effective medium for showing action, illustrating ideas, and demonstrating steps. For example, video can capture someone dancing or giving a speech. When evaluating video, ask yourself: How do the visuals add anything to my understanding, or how might the information have been provided in text and been just as effective?

- **Multimedia** is an ideal way to combine different elements into a single presentation. For example, if a person wanted to present the history of a city, multimedia would allow the person to combine live interviews, early maps of the city, video clips, and graphs showing the city's growth. When evaluating multimedia presentations, ask yourself: Have various elements been combined in a way that is useful and informative? Are the multimedia elements distracting or off topic?

Academic Vocabulary

digital text electronic text

multimedia a format for presenting information that combines media (text, graphics, sound, video)

Apply the Standard

Use the worksheet that follows to help you apply the standard as you read informational texts. Several copies of the worksheet have been provided for you.

- Evaluating Media

Name _____ Date _____ Assignment _____

Evaluating Media

As you review a variety of sources to learn about a topic or idea, use the organizer below to evaluate the advantages and disadvantages of different mediums. Then answer the questions at the bottom of the page.

Topic: ....

Medium	Advantages	Disadvantages
Print or Digital Text		
Video		
Multimedia		

What information did each medium provide? ....

....

....

Which medium was most effective in presenting ideas? Explain your answer. ....

....

....

A

Name _____ Date _____ Assignment _____

Evaluating Media

As you review a variety of sources to learn about a topic or idea, use the organizer below to evaluate the advantages and disadvantages of different mediums. Then answer the questions at the bottom of the page.

Topic: ....

Medium	Advantages	Disadvantages
Print or Digital Text		
Video		
Multimedia		

What information did each medium provide? ....

....

....

Which medium was most effective in presenting ideas? Explain your answer. ....

....

....

B

Name _____ Date _____ Assignment _____

Evaluating Media

As you review a variety of sources to learn about a topic or idea, use the organizer below to evaluate the advantages and disadvantages of different mediums. Then answer the questions at the bottom of the page.

Topic: ....

Medium	Advantages	Disadvantages
Print or Digital Text		
Video		
Multimedia		

What information did each medium provide? ....

....

....

Which medium was most effective in presenting ideas? Explain your answer. ....

....

....

C

Name _____ Date _____ Assignment _____

Evaluating Media

As you review a variety of sources to learn about a topic or idea, use the organizer below to evaluate the advantages and disadvantages of different mediums. Then answer the questions at the bottom of the page.

Topic: ....

Medium	Advantages	Disadvantages
Print or Digital Text		
Video		
Multimedia		

What information did each medium provide? ....

....

....

Which medium was most effective in presenting ideas? Explain your answer. ....

....

....

D

Name _____ Date _____ Assignment _____

Evaluating Media

As you review a variety of sources to learn about a topic or idea, use the organizer below to evaluate the advantages and disadvantages of different mediums. Then answer the questions at the bottom of the page.

Topic: ....

Medium	Advantages	Disadvantages
Print or Digital Text		
Video		
Multimedia		

What information did each medium provide? ....

....

....

Which medium was most effective in presenting ideas? Explain your answer. ....

....

....

E

Name _____ Date _____ Assignment _____

Evaluating Media

As you review a variety of sources to learn about a topic or idea, use the organizer below to evaluate the advantages and disadvantages of different mediums. Then answer the questions at the bottom of the page.

Topic: ....

Medium	Advantages	Disadvantages
Print or Digital Text		
Video		
Multimedia		

What information did each medium provide? ....

....

....

Which medium was most effective in presenting ideas? Explain your answer. ....

....

....

F

Informational Text 8

> 8. Delineate and evaluate the argument and specific claims in a text, assessing whether the reasoning is sound and the evidence is relevant and sufficient; recognize when irrelevant evidence is introduced.

Explanation

You can follow an author's **argument** by reading the **claim,** or statement about what the author believes to be true. You can delineate the author's argument further by reading the **reasons** given to explain why the claim is true. Then review the **evidence,** or information supporting the reasons.

Evidence can consist of facts, examples, or statistics. When you read a persuasive argument, you should judge the reasoning and the evidence. Ask yourself whether the reasoning is sound—does it make sense? Judge whether the evidence is relevant to the argument—is the evidence about the same specific idea? You should ignore evidence that is not relevant. You should also judge whether the evidence is sufficient—are there enough examples to support the claim?

Examples

- An editorial writer proposed that people should not be allowed to talk on cell phones while driving. He reasoned that the act of talking to another person was distracting enough to make a driver too inattentive to drive safely. He cited statistics showing that a high proportion of accidents occurred while a driver was talking on a cell phone. He also stated that people talking on cell phones disturb those around them. While his reasoning is sound and his statistics support his reasoning, his statement about disturbing other people is not relevant and thus weakens his editorial. Readers need to ignore this part of his argument.

- A school board member wrote an essay urging parents to stop their children from playing video games. Her argument claimed that children who play video games excessively don't do as well in school as other children. She cited a study that showed the grades of children who played video games and those who did not. Her essay pointed out that children who spend large amounts of time playing video games are not using that time for study or reading, which would improve their grades. Her reasoning is sound and her evidence is relevant, although one study may not be enough to convince people that her claim is true.

Academic Vocabulary

argument writing that expresses a position on an issue and supports it with evidence

claim the statement of an argument

evidence information that supports an author's reasons

Apply the Standard

Use the worksheet that follows to help you apply the standard as you read informational text selections. Several copies of the worksheet have been provided for you.

- Evaluate an Argument

Name _____ Date _____ Assignment _____

Evaluate an Argument

Use the organizer to evaluate an argument.

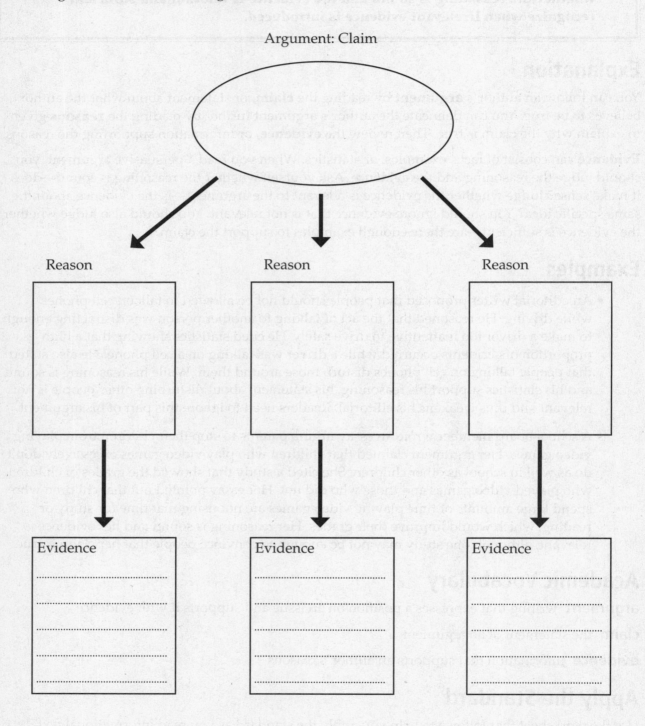

Argument: Claim

Reason

Reason

Reason

Evidence

· ·

· ·

· ·

· ·

· ·

Evidence

· ·

· ·

· ·

· ·

· ·

Evidence

· ·

· ·

· ·

· ·

· ·

A

Name ____________________ Date ______________ Assignment ______________

Evaluate an Argument

Use the organizer to evaluate an argument.

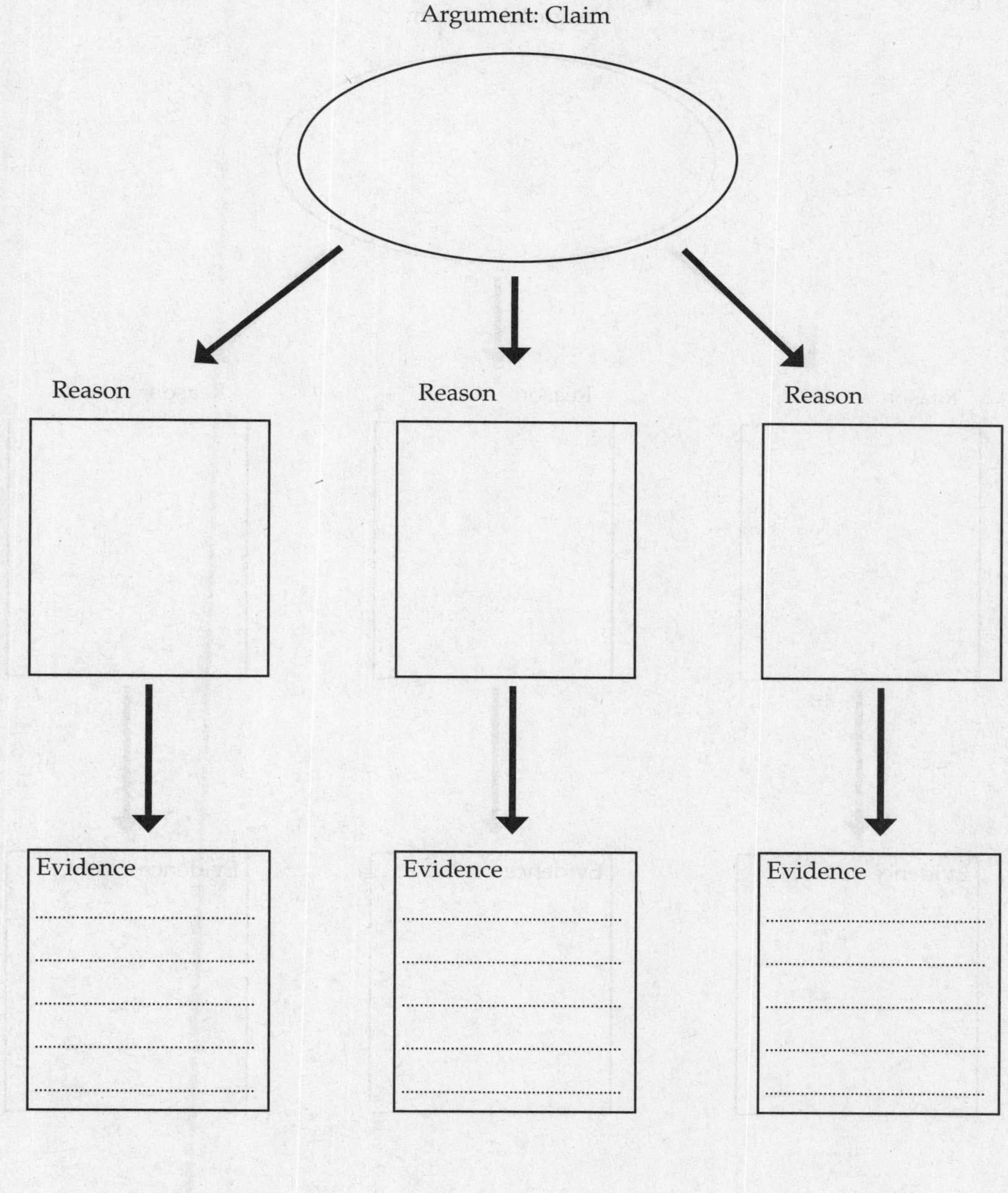

Argument: Claim
Reason
Reason
Reason
Evidence
Evidence
Evidence

B

For use with Informational Text 8

Name _____ Date _____ Assignment _____

Evaluate an Argument

Use the organizer to evaluate an argument.

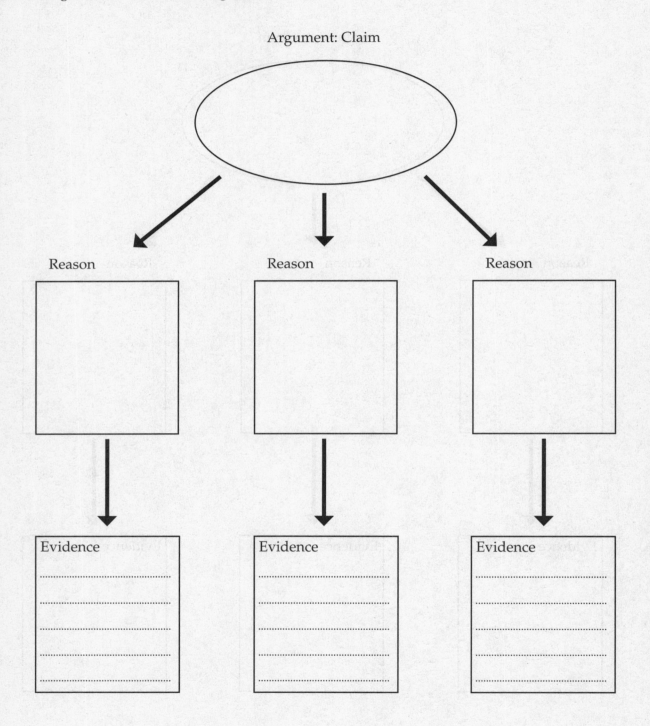

Argument: Claim

Reason

Reason

Reason

Evidence

Evidence

Evidence

C

Name _____ Date _____ Assignment _____

Evaluate an Argument

Use the organizer to evaluate an argument.

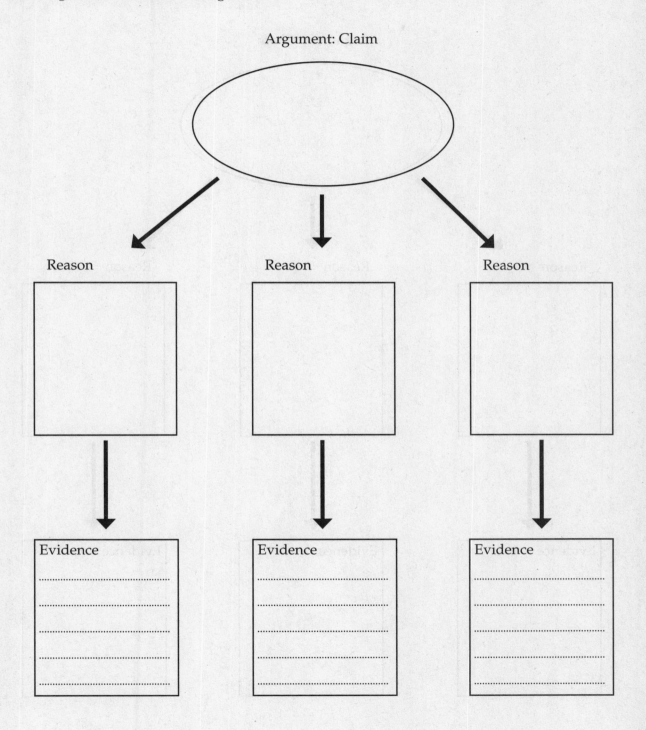

Argument: Claim

Reason

Reason

Reason

Evidence

Evidence

Evidence

D

For use with Informational Text 8

Name _____ Date _____ Assignment _____

Evaluate an Argument

Use the organizer to evaluate an argument.

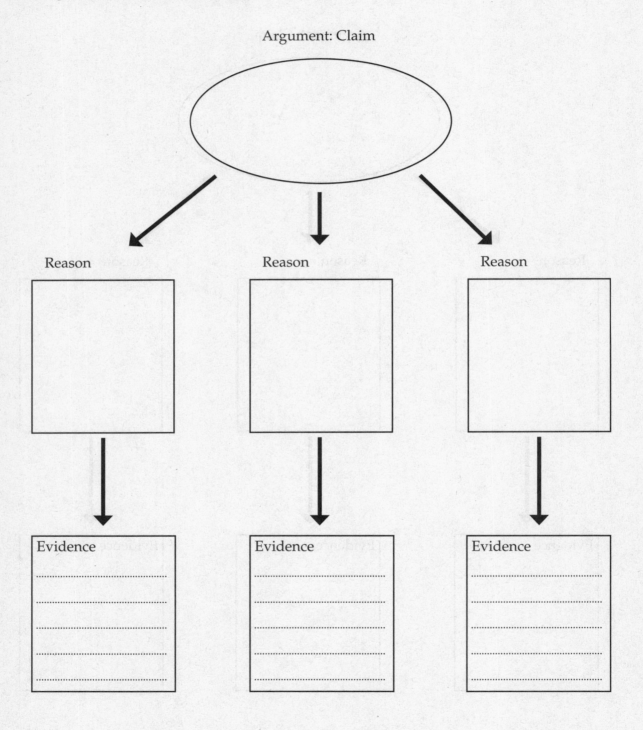

Argument: Claim

Reason

Reason

Reason

Evidence

Evidence

Evidence

E

Name _____ Date _____ Assignment _____

Evaluate an Argument

Use the organizer to evaluate an argument.

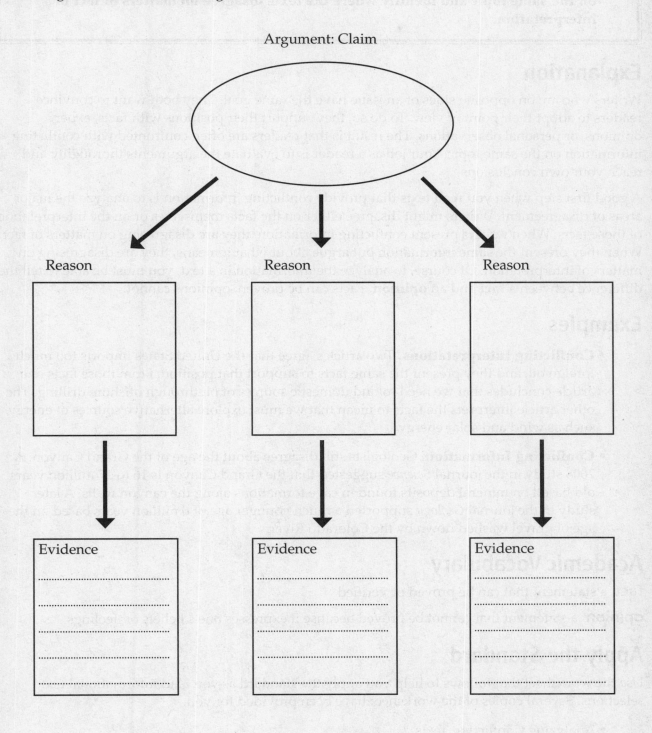

Argument: Claim

Reason

Reason

Reason

Evidence

....
....
....
....
....

Evidence

....
....
....
....
....

Evidence

....
....
....
....
....

F

Informational Text 9

9. **Analyze a case in which two or more texts provide conflicting information on the same topic and identify where the texts disagree on matters of fact or interpretation.**

Explanation

Writers who are on opposite sides of an issue have the same goal. They both want to convince readers to adopt their point of view. To do so, they support their positions with facts, expert opinions, or personal observations. The result is that readers are often confronted with conflicting information on the same topic. Your job as a reader is to evaluate the arguments thoroughly and reach your own conclusions.

A good first step when you read texts that provide conflicting information is to analyze the major areas of disagreement. Writers might disagree either on the facts themselves or on the interpretation of those facts. When writers present conflicting information, they are disagreeing on matters of fact. When they present the same information but argue about what it means, they are disagreeing on matters of interpretation. Of course, to analyze the information in a text, you must be able to tell the difference between a **fact** and an **opinion**. Facts can be proven; opinions cannot.

Examples

- **Conflicting Interpretations.** Two articles agree that the United States imports too much foreign oil, and they present the same facts to support that position. From those facts one article concludes that we need to find domestic sources of oil through offshore drilling. The other article interprets the facts to mean that we must explore alternative sources of energy, such as wind and solar energy.

- **Conflicting Information.** Geologists still disagree about the age of the Grand Canyon. A 2008 study in the journal *Science* suggested that the Grand Canyon is 16 to 17 million years old based on mineral deposits found in cave formations along the canyon walls. A later study in the journal *Geology* supported a much younger age of 6 million years based on the age of gravel washed down by the Colorado River.

Academic Vocabulary

fact a statement that can be proved or verified

opinion a statement that cannot be proved because it expresses one's beliefs or feelings

Apply the Standard

Use the worksheet that follows to help you apply the standard as you read informational text selections. Several copies of the worksheet have been provided for you.

- Analyzing Conflicting Texts

Name _____ Date _____ Assignment _____

Analyzing Conflicting Texts

Use the organizer below to analyze how two texts approach same subject. List the facts presented in each text and the way in which the facts are interpreted in each.

Text 1	Text 2
Writer's position	Writer's position
Fact	Fact
Writer's Interpretation of the Fact	Writer's Interpretation of the Fact
Fact	Fact
Writer's Interpretation of the Fact	Writer's Interpretation of the Fact
Fact	Fact
Writer's Interpretation of the Fact	Writer's Interpretation of the Fact

Major Areas of Disagreement Between the Two Texts

A

Name _____ Date _____ Assignment _____

Analyzing Conflicting Texts

Use the organizer below to analyze how two texts approach same subject. List the facts presented in each text and the way in which the facts are interpreted in each.

Text 1	Text 2
Writer's position	Writer's position
Fact	Fact
Writer's Interpretation of the Fact	Writer's Interpretation of the Fact
Fact	Fact
Writer's Interpretation of the Fact	Writer's Interpretation of the Fact
Fact	Fact
Writer's Interpretation of the Fact	Writer's Interpretation of the Fact

Major Areas of Disagreement Between the Two Texts

B

Name _____ Date _____ Assignment _____

Analyzing Conflicting Texts

Use the organizer below to analyze how two texts approach same subject. List the facts presented in each text and the way in which the facts are interpreted in each.

Text 1	Text 2
Writer's position	Writer's position
Fact	Fact
Writer's Interpretation of the Fact	Writer's Interpretation of the Fact
Fact	Fact
Writer's Interpretation of the Fact	Writer's Interpretation of the Fact
Fact	Fact
Writer's Interpretation of the Fact	Writer's Interpretation of the Fact

Major Areas of Disagreement Between the Two Texts

C

Name _____ Date _____ Assignment _____

Analyzing Conflicting Texts

Use the organizer below to analyze how two texts approach same subject. List the facts presented in each text and the way in which the facts are interpreted in each.

Text 1	Text 2
Writer's position	Writer's position
Fact	Fact
Writer's Interpretation of the Fact	Writer's Interpretation of the Fact
Fact	Fact
Writer's Interpretation of the Fact	Writer's Interpretation of the Fact
Fact	Fact
Writer's Interpretation of the Fact	Writer's Interpretation of the Fact

Major Areas of Disagreement Between the Two Texts

For use with Informational Text 9

Name _____ Date _____ Assignment _____

Analyzing Conflicting Texts

Use the organizer below to analyze how two texts approach same subject. List the facts presented in each text and the way in which the facts are interpreted in each.

Text 1	Text 2
Writer's position	Writer's position
Fact	Fact
Writer's Interpretation of the Fact	Writer's Interpretation of the Fact
Fact	Fact
Writer's Interpretation of the Fact	Writer's Interpretation of the Fact
Fact	Fact
Writer's Interpretation of the Fact	Writer's Interpretation of the Fact

Major Areas of Disagreement Between the Two Texts

E

Name _____ Date _____ Assignment _____

Analyzing Conflicting Texts

Use the organizer below to analyze how two texts approach same subject. List the facts presented in each text and the way in which the facts are interpreted in each.

Text 1	Text 2
Writer's position	Writer's position
Fact	Fact
Writer's Interpretation of the Fact	Writer's Interpretation of the Fact
Fact	Fact
Writer's Interpretation of the Fact	Writer's Interpretation of the Fact
Fact	Fact
Writer's Interpretation of the Fact	Writer's Interpretation of the Fact

Major Areas of Disagreement Between the Two Texts

F

Informational Text 10

> **10.** By the end of the year, read and comprehend literary nonfiction at the high end of the grades 6–8 text complexity band independently and proficiently.

Explanation

Complexity refers to the degree of difficulty of a work. Works of literary nonfiction can vary widely in their complexity. For example, essays and editorials can use familiar subjects that are easy to understand. However, they can also use unfamiliar subjects and present concepts that are difficult to understand. Some works use a simple style with conversational vocabulary and short sentences, while others use advanced vocabulary with figurative language and long sentences. Similar variations in difficulty exist for other types of literary nonfiction, such as journals, letters, memoirs, biographies, and autobiographies.

You will be expected to **comprehend**, or understand the meaning and importance of, more complex texts as you read more works of literary nonfiction. To comprehend complex texts, use reading strategies, such as monitoring comprehension, paraphrasing, summarizing, using context, connecting, and visualizing, some of which are described below.

Examples

- **Monitor** your comprehension by asking yourself questions about what you have just read. Do this whenever something happens that you might not have understood. For example, at the beginning of the excerpt from John Steinbeck's *Travels with Charley*, ask yourself what he and Charley are arguing about. Reread the beginning section until you understand what Steinbeck really wants.

- In the same essay, you can use **context** to understand all the vocabulary. When Steinbeck discusses a feeling he has and calls the experience inexplicable, he also points out that such things are "strange to me" and "mysterious," clues to the meaning of *inexplicable*.

- **Summarizing** sections help you understand what is going on. If you summarize the section of Steinbeck's excerpt dealing with his meeting a stranger in the Bad Lands, you will begin to understand not only the episode but also the feeling and mood that the Bad Lands instilled in Steinbeck. The stranger is silent and not at all friendly, a typical Badlander, Steinbeck concludes.

Academic Vocabulary

complexity the degree to which a work is difficult to understand

comprehend understand the meaning and importance of something

Apply the Standard

Use the worksheet that follows to help you apply the standard as you read. Several copies of the worksheet have been provided for you to use

- Comprehending Complex Texts

Name _____ Date _____ Selection _____

Comprehending Complex Texts

Explain what makes the literary nonfiction selection you are reading complex. Then explain how the strategy on the left in the chart helps you comprehend the selection.

What makes this selection complex?

....

....

Strategy	How the Strategy Helped Me Comprehend the Selection
monitoring comprehension	
using context	
summarizing	

A

Name _____ Date _____ Selection _____

Comprehending Complex Texts

Explain what makes the literary nonfiction selection you are reading complex. Then explain how the strategy on the left in the chart helps you comprehend the selection.

What makes this selection complex?

....

....

Strategy	How the Strategy Helped Me Comprehend the Selection
monitoring comprehension	
using context	
summarizing	

B

Name _____ Date _____ Selection _____

Comprehending Complex Texts

Explain what makes the literary nonfiction selection you are reading complex. Then explain how the strategy on the left in the chart helps you comprehend the selection.

What makes this selection complex?

....

....

Strategy	How the Strategy Helped Me Comprehend the Selection
monitoring comprehension	
using context	
summarizing	

C

Name _____ Date _____ Selection _____

Comprehending Complex Texts

Explain what makes the literary nonfiction selection you are reading complex. Then explain how the strategy on the left in the chart helps you comprehend the selection.

What makes this selection complex?

....

....

Strategy	How the Strategy Helped Me Comprehend the Selection
monitoring comprehension	
using context	
summarizing	

D

Name _____ Date _____ Selection _____

Comprehending Complex Texts

Explain what makes the literary nonfiction selection you are reading complex. Then explain how the strategy on the left in the chart helps you comprehend the selection.

What makes this selection complex?

....

....

Strategy	How the Strategy Helped Me Comprehend the Selection
monitoring comprehension	
using context	
summarizing	

E

Name _____ Date _____ Selection _____

Comprehending Complex Texts

Explain what makes the literary nonfiction selection you are reading complex. Then explain how the strategy on the left in the chart helps you comprehend the selection.

What makes this selection complex?

....

....

Strategy	How the Strategy Helped Me Comprehend the Selection
monitoring comprehension	
using context	
summarizing	

F

Writing Standards

Writing 1

> **1. Write arguments to support claims with clear reasons and relevant evidence.**

Writing Workshop: Argument

When you construct a written argument, you make a claim that states your position on an issue. Once you have established your position, you present logical reasons and relevant evidence to back up your claim. The reasons and evidence that you use to support your claim are the basis of the argument. If the reasons are logical and the evidence is specific, then the argument will be strong.

Assignment

Write an argumentative essay about an issue that concerns people in your community or school. Include these elements:

✓ a claim, or clear opinion statement that defines your position on an issue

✓ logical reasons and relevant evidence that support your position

✓ the use of reliable sources to give your argument accuracy and credibility

✓ evidence to distinguish between opposing points of view

✓ clear and effective organization

✓ the use of persuasive techniques, such as repetition and parallelism

✓ the use of transitions to create cohesion and clarify the relationships

✓ a consistent, formal style and correct use of language convention

*Additional Standards

1. Write arguments to support claims with clear reasons and relevant evidence.

1.a. Introduce claim(s), acknowledge and distinguish the claim(s) from alternate or opposing claims, and organize the reasons and evidence logically.

1.b. Support claim(s) with logical reasoning and relevant evidence, using accurate, credible sources and demonstrating an understanding of the topic or text.

1.c. Use words, phrases, and clauses to create cohesion and clarify the relationships among claim(s), counterclaims, reasons, and evidence.

1.d. Establish and maintain a formal style.

1.e. Provide a concluding statement or section that follows from and supports the argument presented.

Language

1. Demonstrate command of the conventions of standard English grammar and usage when writing or speaking.

Name _____ Date _____ Assignment _____

Prewriting/Planning Strategies

Choose a topic. Engage in a group discussion with classmates about issues in your school or community. List specific problems and two or three opposing points of view on how to solve these problems. For your topic, choose the issue that interests you the most.

You can also turn to the media to find a topic. Read local newspapers, including editorial and opinion columns, to find current controversial issues in your community. Watch or listen to local news on television and radio, especially to the editorial comments that often come at the end of a news broadcast. Choose an issue that sparks your interest.

Define your position. Before you can write, you need to define your position on the issue. Initially, you may support one side of an issue. After some quick research, however, you may discover that your position has changed. Once you have defined your position, write a strong thesis statement that summarizes your claim. Use the graphic organizer below to define your position and to write a thesis statement. When you write, use your thesis statement to keep you focused on your position.

Topic	
Freewrite Jot down thoughts, feelings, arguments, and your position on the issue.	
Quick Research Jot down a few factual details that address more than one position on the issue.	
Combine Ideas Choose ideas from your freewrite and from your research notes that go together.	
Write a Thesis Statement Use the ideas above to construct a powerful thesis statement that defines your position.	 _____ (Identify your specific topic) + (State your position)

Name _____ Date _____ Assignment _____

Supporting a Claim

Consider all sides of an issue. Collect evidence—including facts and statistics, examples, expert opinions, surveys and interviews—from accurate, credible up-to-date sources. Try to find a minimum of two sources for each fact. Consult books on your topic, and take time to check the background of the authors. Professionals in a field will be more knowledgeable and objective than amateurs or writers paid by self-interest groups. Gather evidence related to counterarguments so that you can acknowledge and respond to them in your essay. Once you have completed your chart, review the evidence to make sure it is specific and relevant to the claim in your thesis statement.

- If any idea you list is not **clear** and **specific,** look for more facts and details to clarify and strengthen your ideas.

- If any evidence contradicts another piece of evidence, delete it, or put a question mark next to it until you can confirm which evidence is **accurate**.

- If any idea is not **relevant,** or directly related to your topic, delete it.

Reasons and Evidence That Support My Claim	Sources Used
Reasons and Evidence That Address Counterarguments	

Name _____ Date _____ Assignment _____

Drafting Strategies

Create a structure for your draft. Make an organizational plan for your essay that is both logical and persuasive.

- Use the graphic organizer below to construct a sound argument. Copy the thesis statement that you developed during prewriting.

- Review the reasons and evidence you have gathered to support your claim. Rank reasons in order of importance, starting with number 1 for least important. List reasons in this order in the organizer. Choose one counterargument to address.

Claim **Thesis Statement:**	
Supporting Reason #1 (least important):	**Evidence** **A.** **B.**
Supporting Reason #2:	**Evidence** **A.** **B.**
Supporting Reason #3 (most important):	**Evidence** **A.** **B.**
Counterargument:	**Evidence** **A.** **B.**

For use with Writing 1

Name _____ Date _____ Assignment _____

Developing and evaluating your claim. Keep your task, purpose, and audience in mind as you draft your essay.

1. Write an introduction that includes your thesis statement. Use precise words and phrases that your audience will understand.

2. As you draft your claim, continue to make your position clear. Take readers step-by-step through your argument, emphasizing the strength of your position.

3. Use your notes as a guide. Include transitions to create a cohesive argument and to make the relationships among your claims, reasons, and evidence clear.

4. Address counterarguments fairly and reasonably. Give factual evidence that reveals the weaknesses of these counterarguments.

5. Conclude with a strong statement that summarizes your argument. Give readers something new to think about or challenges them to take action.

My Claim	Evaluating the Claim, Reasons, and Evidence
	❏ Is the claim clearly stated?
	❏ Is there any doubt which side of the issue my argument supports?
	❏ Are the reasons logical and serious?
	❏ Is all the evidence specific, accurate, and relevant?
	❏ Does the argument consider the audience's age and knowledge?
Counterarguments	
	❏ Have I addressed a counterargument fairly and reasonably?

Style

Establish and maintain a formal style
When you write an argumentative essay, you want readers to trust your ideas and agree that your position on the issue has value. To build that trust with readers, maintain a formal style as you write. Below are some guidelines for establishing and maintaining a formal style in your essay.

A formal style

- maintains a distance between the writer and the reader.

- uses a matter-of-fact, unemotional tone; any emotion is presented with dignity, in an impersonal manner.

- expresses ideas clearly and logically.

- backs up claims and important ideas with specific facts, reasons, and evidence.

- uses precise language and powerful images.

- uses standard English and avoids contractions, dialect, and slang.

Examples:
Claim: The government cannot promote healthier eating habits by placing a higher tax on fatty, less nutritious foods.

> **Informal:** Obviously, most Americans don't have the smarts to figure out for themselves what foods are healthy and what's junk.

> **Formal:** Increased taxes might stop some consumers from purchasing fatty foods, but educating the public on nutrition would have widespread, longer lasting effect.

Clarify the relationships among ideas.
A cohesive argument holds together because all the ideas relate logically to one another. You can create cohesion in several ways:

- Clarify connections between claims, reasons or evidence by connecting clauses that express those claims and reasons with such conjunctions as *and, but, or, so, yet, although, because,* and *whenever: Physical education benefits the mind and the body <u>so</u> it should be mandatory in schools.*

- Show the connections between ideas using phrases that begin with prepositions, such as *despite, because of,* and *due to: <u>Because of</u> its benefits to mind and body, physical education should be mandatory in schools.*

- Use transitional words, phrases, and clauses, such as *consequently, for this reason,* and *however* to clarify connections between sentences. *Physical education benefits the mind and the body. <u>For this reason</u>, it should be mandatory in schools.*

Name _____ Date _____ Assignment _____

Conclusion

Provide a strong conclusion. Your written argument should end with a strong conclusion that flows logically from and supports the argument in the body of the essay. Use the strategies shown below to write a strong conclusion.

- Begin with a summary statement of the claim: *As I have shown, a grading system that uses encouraging words to assess students' progress is more beneficial to students than a grading system of letters or number scores.*

- Then review the main points of the argument: *Students agree that, without the worry of passing or failing, they feel more relaxed and at the same time more motivated to learn. They also feel free to concentrate on learning ideas rather than memorizing facts to pass a test.*

- End by restating the claim in a memorable way. *Give readers something more to think about or encourage them to take action. Grading without grades is good for all students. Parents, teachers, and students should encourage the school board to change the grading system in all Montvale schools.*

My Conclusion	Evaluating My Conclusion
	❏ Does it begin with a restatement of my claim?
	❏ Does it review the main points of my argument?
	❏ Does it end with a memorable statement that gives readers something new to think about or asks them to take action?

Name _____ Date _____ Assignment _____

Revising Strategies

Put a checkmark beside each question as you revise.

	Questions to Ask as You Revise
Writing Task	❏ Have I written an essay that clearly defines my position on an issue? ❏ Does my topic have at least two sides? ❏ Does my essay have a clear and effective introduction, body, and conclusion?
Purpose	❏ Does my introduction contain a thesis statement that clearly states my claim or position? ❏ Do I give reasons and accurate, relevant evidence to support my claim? ❏ Are the reasons clear and logical? ❏ Do I have enough facts, quotations, expert opinions, examples, and other evidence to support my claim? ❏ Do I use only relevant evidence to strengthen my argument? ❏ Does my conclusion follow logically from ideas presented in my argument?
Audience	❏ Do I use precise language and details that are appropriate for the age and knowledge level of my readers? ❏ Is my argument cohesive? ❏ Do I use transitions to clarify relationships among ideas? ❏ Do I combine sentences to clarify relationships among ideas? ❏ Do I address questions and concerns my readers might have about my topic? ❏ Can readers distinguish my claim from alternate or opposing claims? ❏ Does my argument appeal to reason and not just to emotion? ❏ Will my audience be persuaded to agree with my position?

For use with Writing 1

Revising

Revise for repetition and parallel structure. Repetition and parallelism are techniques that you can use to strengthen your argument and make it more cohesive. When used correctly, repetition and parallelism add rhythm and balance to your writing. They also help clarify the relationships between claims, reasons, and evidence. As you revise, look for places where you can use repetition and parallel construction effectively.

Repetition

As the word suggests, repetition refers to the repeating of the same words and phrases within sentences, and from sentence to sentence.

Within a sentence: <u>At</u> work, <u>at</u> school, or <u>at</u> home, we have a right to privacy.

From sentence to sentence: <u>Eventually</u>, gender will not matter in an election. <u>Eventually</u>, voters will elect the best person for the job. <u>Eventually</u>, we will have a female president.

Use repetition for emphasis, but be careful. Too much repetition will make your writing sound monotonous.

Parallel Construction

Parallel constructions repeat identical patterns of words, phrases, and clauses within sentences. In parallel constructions all words in a series should be the same parts of speech, such as nouns, verbs, adjectives, or adverbs. All phrases and clauses in a series should be the same type, such as prepositional phrases or adverb or adjective clauses.

Not parallel: Locker searches are <u>inconvenient, invasive, and they can be embarrassing</u>.

Parallel: Locker searches are <u>inconvenient, invasive, and embarrassing</u>.

Identifying and Correcting Nonparallel Constructions

To revise sentences with nonparallel construction, use this strategy:

1. Identify similar or equal ideas within a sentence.

2. Determine whether the ideas are expressed in the same grammatical form—for example, all nouns or all prepositional phrases.

3. Rewrite the sentence using the best grammatical pattern to express the equal ideas. The best forms produce the smoothest rhythms and use the fewest words.

Revision Checklist

❑ Are there places where repetition can stress relationships between ideas?

❑ Are words in a series (e.g., *for him, for her, for all of them*) in parallel structure?

❑ Are there equal ideas within a sentence that should be in parallel structure?

Editing and Proofreading

Review your draft to correct errors in capitalization, spelling, grammar, and punctuation.

Focus on Capitalization: Review your draft carefully to find and correct capitalization errors. If your argumentative essay names places, people, or official groups and organizations, be sure that you have capitalized the proper name correctly.

Incorrect capitalization	**Correct capitalization**
mayor Janet Lewis	Mayor Janet Lewis

Focus on Spelling: An argumentative essay that includes spelling errors conveys a careless attitude toward your topic and your readers. Check the spelling of each word, especially words you misspell often. If you have used a computer to type your draft, run the spell-check feature to double-check for errors. Remember that spell-checkers will not find words that are typed incorrectly but spell a word, for example, *there* instead of *their*. Proofread carefully, even after you run spell-check.

Focus on Grammar: Proofread your essay to find and correct grammar errors. Check for double negatives, or the use of two negative words when only one is required.

Double Negative: There is *no* acceptable reason for drivers to *not* text while driving.

Correction 1: There is no acceptable reason for drivers to text while driving

Correction 2: There is not *any* acceptable reason for drivers to text while driving.

Focus on Punctuation: Proofread your writing to find and correct punctuation errors. In particular, look for words and phrases in a series. Be sure that you use serial commas and semicolons correctly.

Rule: Use a comma to separate three or more words, phrases, or clauses in a series: *The study showed that video games improve spatial awareness, visual attention skills, and problem-solving abilities.*

Rule: Use semicolons to avoid confusion when independent clauses or items in a series already contain commas: *The playground equipment is old, broken, and dangerous; the grounds are littered and dirty; and the fence has fallen down.*

Revision Checklist

❏ Have you checked that proper nouns are capitalized?

❏ Have you checked that all of the words are spelled correctly?

❏ Do you avoid creating confusion with double negatives?

❏ Do you use commas or semicolons in items in a series?

Name _____ Date _____ Assignment _____

Publishing and Presenting

Consider one of the following ways to present your writing:

Organize a forum. Present your argument in a panel of classmates. Read your arguments aloud to the rest of the class. Allow time for panel members and classmates to ask questions and to debate the merits of your argument. Then have the class vote on whether students agree or disagree with your position.

Publish in a newspaper. Send your argument to a local newspaper with a brief letter requesting that the paper publish it. Provide a brief summary of your argument in your request. Many newspapers have both print and online editions. For online editions, submit your essay and request by email. Use polite, formal language in your letter or email.

Rubric for Self-Assessment

Find evidence in your writing to address each category. Then use the rating scale to grade your work.

Evaluating Your Argument	not very					very
Focus: How clearly is your position stated?	1	2	3	4	5	6
Organization: How cohesive is your argument and how effectively does it build to a conclusion?	1	2	3	4	5	6
Support/Elaboration: How specific, accurate, relevant, and persuasive is your evidence?	1	2	3	4	5	6
Style: How well have you maintained a formal, objective style throughout your argument?	1	2	3	4	5	6
Conventions: How free of errors in grammar, usage, spelling, and punctuation is your argument?	1	2	3	4	5	6

For use with Writing 1

Writing 2

> **2. Write informative/explanatory texts to examine a topic and convey ideas, concepts, and information through the selection, organization, and analysis of relevant content.**

Writing Workshop: Comparison-and-Contrast Essay

In a comparison-and-contrast essay, a writer analyzes the similarities and differences between two or more subjects. The purpose of a comparison-and-contrast essay may be to enlighten an audience about the subjects. It may be to change the audience's perspective on a subject. Or, it may be to influence a choice members of the audience will make, such as where to go on vacation.

Assignment

Write a comparison-and-contrast essay that analyzes the similarities and differences between two or more subjects. Include these elements:

✓ a topic, involving two or more subjects that are different in some ways and similar in other ways

✓ an introduction that presents the *thesis*, or main point

✓ a body that develops the similarities and differences between the subjects with facts, descriptions, and examples

✓ a coherent, parallel structure that emphasizes key comparisons and contrasts

✓ a conclusion that follows from and supports the comparison and contrast

✓ a formal style

✓ correct use of language conventions

*Additional Standards

Writing
2. Write informative/explanatory texts to examine a topic and convey ideas, concepts, and information through the selection, organization and analysis of relevant content.

2.a. Introduce a topic clearly, previewing what is to follow; organize ideas, concepts, and information into broader categories; include formatting (e.g., headings), graphics (e.g., charts, tables), and multimedia when useful to aiding comprehension.

2.b. Develop the topic with relevant, well-chosen facts, definitions, concrete details, quotations, or other information and examples.

2.c. Use appropriate and varied transitions to create cohesion and clarify the relationships among ideas and concepts.

2.d. Use precise language and domain-specific vocabulary to inform about or explain the topic.

2.e. Establish and maintain a formal style.

2.f. Provide a concluding statement or section that follows from and supports the information or explanation presented.

4. Produce clear and coherent writing in which the development, organization, and style are appropriate to task, purpose, and audience.

6. Use technology, including the Internet, to produce and publish writing and link to and cite sources as well as to interact and collaborate with others, including linking to and citing sources.

Language
2. Demonstrate command of the conventions of standard English capitalization, punctuation, and spelling when writing.

6. Acquire and use accurately grade-appropriate general academic and domain-specific words and phrases; gather vocabulary knowledge when considering a word or phrase important to comprehension or expression.

Name _____ Date _____ Assignment _____

Prewriting/Planning Strategies

Choose a topic. Discuss current events with classmates, using a newspaper or news magazine for discussion ideas. As you discuss people, places, and events in the news, consider how they compare to people, places, and events in the past. For example, how does a political leader of today compare to a leader from a century ago? Use one of these comparisons as a topic for your essay.

If you prefer, you can fill in this timeline that shows how your preferences, attitudes, and perspectives have changed over time. List your feelings about clothes, foods, entertainment, family, friends, school, sports, or other topics at different ages on the timeline. Choose two entries—your feelings about one subject at two different ages—that are alike in some ways and different in other ways as a topic for your essay.

Preschool	Kindergarten	Grade 2	Grade 4	Grade 6	Grade 8

Narrow your topic. Some topics are too broad to discuss fully. A topic such as "The Best Movies of All Time," for example, is much too broad in scope to be addressed fully in a short essay. You might narrow it to *"Star Wars vs. Star Trek*—Which Has the Most Interesting Characters?" To make a broad topic more manageable, divide it into separate parts, or subtopics. Then focus your essay on one of these narrowed topics.

Name _____ Date _____ Assignment _____

Prewriting/Planning Strategies

Gather details. Use the diagram below to gather facts, definitions, descriptions, quotations, and examples related to your two subjects. Use the middle section where the circles overlap to record details that show how the subjects are alike. Record details that show how each subject is different in the outside sections. Look for interesting points of comparison that will engage your audience and may also surprise them. Try to find an equal number of points for each subject so that your comparison and contrast essay will be balanced.

Subject 2. ....

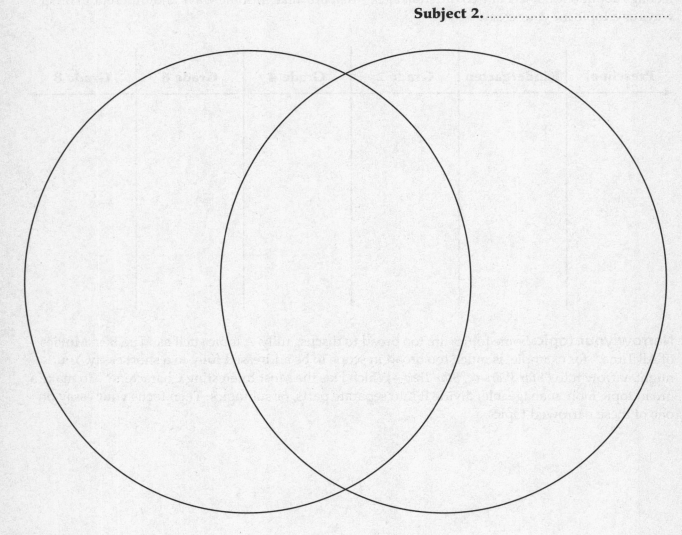

Subject 1. ....

Name _____ Date _____ Assignment _____

Drafting Strategies

Choose an appropriate organizational pattern. Most comparison-and-contrast essays are organized in one of two ways.

- **Block Method:** Present all of your details about one subject first. Then, present all of your details about the second subject. This method works well if you are writing about more than two things, or if your topic is very complex.

- **Point-by-Point Method:** Discuss one similarity or difference between your subjects, then another similarity or difference, and so on.

Use the following organizers to help you decide whether the block method or the point-by-point method is more appropriate for your essay.

Block Method

List all details about **Subject 1:**

List all details about **Subject 2:**

Point-by-Point Method

Subject 1   Subject 2

Name _____ Date _____ Assignment _____

Develop your comparison and contrast essay.

1. **Start with a strong introduction.** Write a lead sentence that captures your readers' attention and imagination. Introduce the subjects of your comparison with a clear thesis statement. Preview what will follow in the rest of your essay.

2. **Use specific details.** Support your comparison with well-chosen facts, concrete details, quotations, and examples. Do not include any details that do not directly support your thesis.

3. **Use parallel structure.** Keep the paragraphs in the body **parallel**, or consistent in structure and style. For example, if you describe the education and achievements of one person, then you should discuss the education and achievements of the second person in that same order. Keep your paragraphs parallel whether you are using the block method or point-by-point method of organization.

4. **Use transitions.** Use transitional words and phrases that clearly show the relationships between features. Transitions that show comparisons and contrasts include *similarly*, *likewise*, *but*, *however*, *nevertheless*, and *on the other hand*.

5. **Note formatting ideas.** Include a variety of elements such as headings for key ideas; bulleted or numbered items; bold or italic print for key terms; charts and diagrams; and multimedia elements such as photographs, illustrations, and video. Choose elements that help readers better understand your ideas.

My Comparison-Contrast	Formatting Notes

Style

Establish and maintain a formal style. A formal style communicates respect for your audience by maintaining a distance between the writer and readers. They will give your ideas more serious consideration if you use a formal style in your essay. Here are some guidelines for establishing and maintaining a formal style as you write.

- Establish a direct, matter-of-fact, unemotional tone. You may express strong opinions, but do so in general terms and an impersonal manner.

- Express ideas clearly and logically.

- Use concrete details and examples to support your ideas.

- Use precise language and higher-level vocabulary.

- Use standard English and avoid contractions, dialect, and slang.

Examples:

Informal: Moving when you're a little kid isn't nearly as rough as moving when you're a teen, that's for sure.

Formal: For children under the age of four or five, home is wherever their parents are. They are not likely to be as traumatized by moving as young adults often are.

Use precise language and domain-specific vocabulary. Precise language and domain-specific vocabulary contribute to a formal style and give your writing a knowledgeable voice. In addition, they can help answer questions such as *What kind?* or *In what way?*

Precise language can evoke clear images and clarify concepts for your audience.

Not precise: Walking is better for you than running.

Precise: Walking is a less stressful on your joints and less likely to cause injury than running. (Answers the question, *Better in what way?*)

Domain-specific terms are words and phrases that are specific to a subject area. If you think your audience may not be familiar with a specific term, provide a definition or clear example.

Not Domain Specific: Some people prefer less difficult exercise.

Domain Specific: Some people prefer low-impact aerobics, which involves making large movements and keeping one foot on the floor at all times. (*Uses a health and fitness term, and explains the term for readers.*)

Name _____ Date _____ Assignment _____

Conclusion

Provide a strong conclusion. Your comparison-and-contrast essay should end with a strong conclusion that follows from and supports the ideas developed in body of the essay. Use the following strategy to construct your conclusion.

- Begin with a summary statement that restates your thesis, or main idea: *Running, jogging, and walking are popular outdoor activities, but some people are not convinced that walking is a good form of exercise.*

- Sum up the main points for the reader: *Like running and jogging, walking burns calories, strengthens bones, and improves cardiovascular health. However, it provides these benefits without the risk of injury.*

- Conclude with a memorable statement or refer back to a point you introduced earlier in the essay. For example, you might answer a question asked in your introduction: *So, to answer the question as to whether walking is as beneficial as other, more strenuous exercises, the answer is a definite "Yes!"*

My Conclusion	Evaluating My Conclusion
	❏ Does it begin with a restatement of my thesis, or main idea?
	❏ Does it sum up the main points of my comparison and contrast?
	❏ Does it end with a memorable statement that gives readers something to think about?

Name _____ Date _____ Assignment _____

Revising

Evaluate organization and balance. Your essay should have a consistent organizational pattern and should give equal space to each subject. To check the balance and organization of your essay, review it point by point.

You can use different colored markers to underline or highlight details for each subject.

- If one color dominates, revise to add more details about the other subject.

- If the colors first appear in large chunks, and then the colors appear to alternate, you may have started your essay using a block organization pattern and then switched to a point-by-point pattern. Revise to make your organizational pattern consistent throughout the essay.

- If some paragraphs are not parallel, revise your essay to develop your comparison using parallel structures.

Use the chart to evaluate organization and balance in your essay. You may also ask a partner to review your essay and then revise based on your partner's comments.

	Subject 1	Subject 2
Point 1:		
Point 2:		
Point 3:		
Point 4:		

Name _____ Date _____ Assignment _____

Revising Strategies

Put a checkmark beside each question as you revise.

	Questions to Ask as You Revise
Writing Task	❑ Have I written an essay that compares and contrasts two or more subjects? ❑ Do I use specific details to analyze similarities between the subjects? ❑ Do I use specific details to analyze differences between the subjects?
Purpose	❑ Does my introduction identify my subjects and establish why the comparison is important? ❑ Do I develop the comparison with specific details? ❑ Do all the details directly support or elaborate on my main idea, or thesis? ❑ Are there an equal number of details for each subject? ❑ Do I use a consistent pattern of organization? ❑ Do the paragraphs in the body have consistently parallel structure? ❑ Does my conclusion follow logically from and support ideas presented in my essay?
Audience	❑ Do I use precise language and domain-specific terms that help readers understand my ideas? ❑ Is my comparison easy to follow and understand? ❑ Does my introduction grab readers' attention? ❑ Do I use transitions to signal similarity and difference? ❑ Is there anywhere that I can add concrete details to heighten interest? ❑ Does my conclusion emphasize my main point? ❑ Is there anywhere that I can add formatting to make my ideas clearer?

For use with Writing 2

Revising

Revise to vary sentences. To keep your writing lively, avoid writing sentences that follow a dull pattern. Many sentences begin with their subjects: *The waiter took our order.* To avoid beginning every sentence with its subject, consider these other options:

> **Adjective:** <u>Surprised</u>, the waiter rushed over.

> **Adverb:** <u>Running quickly</u>, he arrived at our table.

> **Prepositional Phrase:** <u>After a delay</u>, the food arrived.

Using Appositives and Appositive Phrases

To pack information into your sentences, use appositives, noun phrases that define or explain other words in the sentence.

> **Appositive:** The cat, <u>a tabby</u>, prowled the yard.

> **Appositive Phrase:** The dog, <u>my mother's longtime pet</u>, was happy to see us.

Fixing Repetitive Sentence Patterns

To fix a series of sentences that start the same way, follow the steps in the chart.

1. Identify the existing pattern of sentence beginnings.
• Draw a triangle around each subject that starts a sentence.
• Draw a box around each adjective or adverb that starts a sentence.
• Draw a circle around each prepositional phrase that stares a sentence.
2. Review your results.
• Count the number of triangles, boxes, and circles.
• If you have too many of one shape, rewrite the sentence beginnings to increase variety.
3. Consider using appositives to include more information.
• Identify key nouns in a sentence and write a brief noun phrase to define the word.
• Rewrite the sentence, using commas to set the new appositive off from the rest of the sentence.

Revision Checklist

❏ Are there a variety of sentence patterns?

❏ Is there a balanced mix of different sentence beginnings?

❏ Are appositives used to include more information in sentences?

Editing and Proofreading

Review your draft to correct errors in capitalization, spelling, and punctuation.

Focus on Capitalization: Review your draft carefully to find and correct capitalization errors. If your comparison-and-contrast essay names places, people, or official groups and organizations, be sure that you have capitalized the proper name correctly.

Incorrect capitalization	**Correct capitalization**
Dr. Martin Luther King, jr.	Dr. Martin Luther King, Jr.

Focus on Spelling: Take time to check the spelling of each word in your draft. Look for words that you frequently misspell and check that they are correct. If you used a computer to type your draft, run the spell-check feature to double-check for errors. Remember that spell-checkers will not find words that are typed incorrectly but that spell a word, such as *where* instead of *were*. For this reason, you should proofread carefully even after you run spell-check.

Check the spelling of domain-specific words in the dictionary. In some cases, you may have to consult a specialized dictionary.

Focus on Punctuation: Items in a Series and Lists Proofread your writing to find and address punctuation errors. Look for places where you list a series of details. Be sure you use serial commas, semicolons, and colons correctly.

Rule: Use commas to separate words, phrases, or clauses in a series. *Recycling is cheaper, easier, and cleaner than dumping.*

Rule: To avoid confusion, use semicolons when some items already contain commas. *We visited Moab, Utah; Lima, Ohio; and Bath, Maine.*

Rule: Use colons to introduce lists. *I will compare the following: beets, carrots, and celery.*

Revision Checklist

❑ Have you reviewed your essay for words that should be capitalized, including proper names?

❑ Have you read each sentence and checked that all of the words are spelled correctly?

❑ Do you have words, phrases or clauses in a series that should be separated by commas?

❑ Are there places where you should use a semicolon with items in a series that already contain commas?

❑ Are there places where you should use a colon to introduce a list?

Name _____ Date _____ Assignment _____

Publishing and Presenting

Consider one of the following ways to present your writing:

Publish a column. If your essay focuses on subjects of local interest, such as two restaurants or several stores in your community, submit your essay to your local newspaper. You can also post it on a community blog or Web site. Be sure to follow the proper protocol for posting on public sites.

Form a panel. If your essay contains information that is useful to consumers, such as a comparison of household products, form a consumer information panel with classmates. Read your essays to the class, using visual aids to enhance your presentations. You might also work with your teacher and classmates to create a Consumer Information Website so that other students and faculty at your school can benefit from your ideas.

Rubric for Self-Assessment

Find evidence in your writing to address each category. Then use the rating scale to grade your work. Circle the score that best applies for each category.

Evaluating Your Argument	not very					very
Focus: How clearly have you stated how two or more subjects are alike and different?	1	2	3	4	5	6
Organization: How effectively are points of comparison organized?	1	2	3	4	5	6
Support/Elaboration: How well do you use facts, descriptions, and examples to describe similarities and differences?	1	2	3	4	5	6
Style: How precise is your language and how well have you maintained a formal style?	1	2	3	4	5	6
Conventions: How free of errors in grammar, usage, spelling, and punctuation is your essay?	1	2	3	4	5	6

For use with Writing 2

Writing 3

> **3. Write narratives to develop real or imagined experiences or events using effective technique, relevant descriptive details, and well-structured event sequences.**

Writing Workshop

A **short story** is a brief fictional narrative with setting, characters, and a plot that develops around a conflict, or struggle between opposing forces. Because a short story is compact and concise, writing a good short story can be a challenge. You do not have space for characters or events that do not help move the plot forward. Every descriptive detail, every piece of dialogue, every action must be chosen carefully, with a thought to how it will convey the theme, or message of the story.

Assignment

Write a short story that has believable characters who face a realistic conflict. Include these elements:

✓ well-developed major and minor characters

✓ a clear setting—a time and place in which the action occurs

✓ a plot that develops the conflict through a series of sequential events

✓ a consistent point of view

✓ narrative techniques, including dialogue, pacing, and other literary elements

✓ precise vocabulary and sensory details

✓ effective use of transitions

✓ correct use of language conventions, especially subject-verb agreement

*Additional Standards

3. Write narratives to develop real or imagined experiences or events using effective technique, relevant descriptive details, and well-structured event sequences.

3.a. Engage and orient the reader by establishing a context and point of view and introducing a narrator and/or characters; organize an event sequence that unfolds naturally and logically.

3.b. Use narrative techniques, such as dialogue, pacing, description, and reflection to develop experiences, events, and/or characters.

3.c. Use a variety of transition words, phrases, and clauses to convey sequence, signal shifts from one time frame or setting to another, and show the relationships among experiences and events.

3.d. Use precise words and phrases, relevant descriptive details, and sensory language to capture the action and convey experiences and events.

3.e. Provide a conclusion that follows from and reflects on the narrated experiences or events.

6. Use technology, including the Internet, to produce and publish writing and present the relationships

between information and ideas efficiently as well as to interact and collaborate with others.

Language
2. Demonstrate command of the conventions of standard English capitalization, punctuation, and spelling when writing.

Name _____ Date _____ Assignment _____

Prewriting/Planning Strategies

Gather Details to Find a Focus. Follow the steps to find a focus for your short story. Write your choices in the chart below. Then list **sensory details** that you might use in your story to portray the main character, capture the action, and describe the setting. **Sensory details** are descriptive words and phrases that appeal to sight, sound, smell, touch, and taste—for example, *salty breeze* (taste, touch) and *low, gruff* (sound). Circle details that are not only vivid but that may also be relevant to the plot.

1. **Begin with a character:** Choose a character for your story. Base it on someone you know, a character from literature, or someone from your imagination.

2. **Invent a situation:** Use a "what if" strategy to focus on the action and conflict your character will face. Complete the following sentences in several different ways.

   • What if .... (*person*) wanted .... but .... (*name problem*)?

   • What if .... (*person*) suddenly........................ (*name problem*)?

3. **Picture the setting:** Choose a time and place for the story action to take place.

Character:	Problem:	Setting: ....
Sensory Details:	**Sensory Details:**	**Sensory Details:**

Explore conflict. Answer the questions to pinpoint the problem, or conflict, your story will develop.

What is the problem or conflict?	
How will the problem reveal itself	
How will the problem intensify?	
How will each of the characters react to the problem?	
How will the problem reach resolution or be solved?	

For use with Writing 3

Name _____ Date _____ Assignment _____

Understand your main character. Get to know your main character better before you write. Complete the web to explore your character's unique personality. Describe gestures, behaviors, facial expressions, ways of speaking, as well as physical appearance and personality traits that will help your readers know and connect with your character. Feel free to add additional categories as you develop your character.

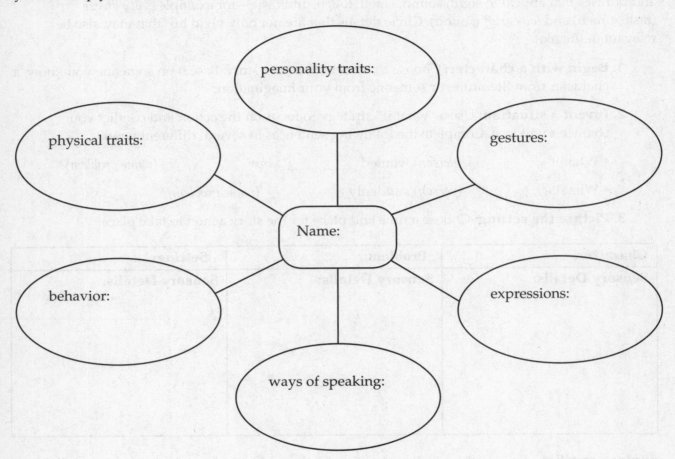

Identify minor characters. List two other minor, or less important, characters in your story. Explain their relationship to the main character and how that might affect the plot. Note descriptive details you can use to bring these characters to life for readers.

Minor Character 1:	**Minor Character 2:** ....

Name _____ Date _____ Assignment _____

Drafting Strategies

Determine a point of view. Every story has a narrator who tells the story from a particular point of view. Besides revealing how the story unfolds, the narrator also provides important background information and reflections, or thoughts, about setting, characters, and events. Read the descriptions of the types of point of view. Then put a check mark next to the one that you will use to tell your story.

	first person: The narrator is also a character in the story; the narrator refers to him- or herself as *I*.
	third person omniscient: The narrator is not a character in the story and can relate details about any of the characters' experiences and perceptions. Most stories are told from this point of view.
	third person limited: The narrator is not a character in the story, but the narrator focuses on the experiences and perceptions of the main character, showing story events from that character's point of view only.

Develop a plot outline. Use the plot diagram below to organize events in your short story. In the beginning, or **exposition,** provide information about the characters, setting, and conflict. In the **rising action,** develop the conflict event by event, until you reach the **climax,** or turning point, in the story. In the **falling action,** list one or two events that lead to the **resolution,** where the problem is solved.

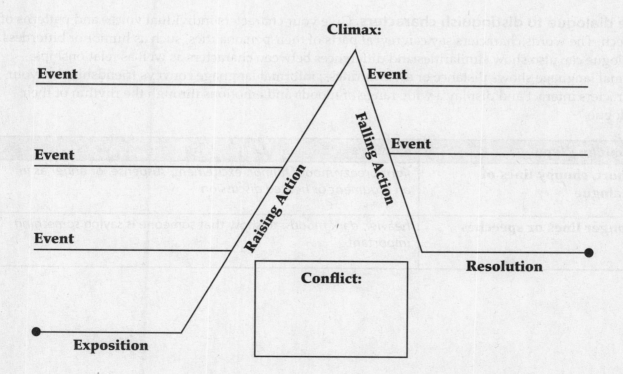

Narrative Techniques

A good story builds naturally and logically to a single exciting moment. To accomplish this, use a variety of narrative techniques.

Let the narrator set the pace. As you draft, consider the role of your narrator in setting the pace of the story. To ensure that you do not slow down the development of the plot and lose your readers' attention, narrate background information briefly, giving only necessary details. If, however, you want to emphasize the importance of a scene or maximize suspense, slow down the pace by "stretching out" the narration with vivid, descriptive details.

Use precise language and sensory details. Precise language, including strong action verbs, and sensory details can help you show readers setting, characters, and events instead of just telling about them. Good writers know to choose descriptive details that are not only vivid but that are also relevant to the story. For example, a descriptive detail that helps to reveal a character's personality, convey a particular setting or mood, or move the plot forward would be particularly relevant.

> **Vague and Dull:** I *was* surprised when he suddenly appeared.
> **Strong and Vivid:** I *gasped* when he suddenly appeared.
>
> **Vague and Dull:** There was mail for Fran in the kitchen.
> **Precise, Vivid, and Relevant:** A thick, white envelope with no return address and Fran's name scribbled in black crayon on the front lay on the kitchen table.

Use plot devices. You can enhance mood, add suspense, and maintain your readers' interest by using various plot devices. For example, **foreshadowing** can set the stage for a surprising event later in the story, and **flashback** can help explain a character's mysterious background.

Use dialogue to distinguish characters. Give your characters individual voices and patterns of speech. The words characters say can reveal parts of their personalities, such as humor or bitterness. Dialogue can also show similarities and differences between characters as well as relationships. Formal language shows distance or awkwardness; informal language conveys friendship. Let your characters interact and display a wide range of moods and emotions through the rhythm of their dialogue.

Dialogue Type	Conveys
Short, choppy lines of dialogue	*light breezy mood; humor, excitement, suspense,* or *anger as in an argument or heated discussion*
Longer lines or speeches	*heavier, dark moods;* to show that someone is saying *something important*

Name _____ Date _____ Assignment _____

Organize your narrative. Use the graphic organizer to organize events in your narrative. As you write, use a variety of transitional words, phrases, and clauses to convey sequence, to signal shifts from one time frame or setting to another, and to show the relationships among events.

- **Transitional words:** *first, next, then, meanwhile, before, during, now, yesterday, finally*

- **Transitional phrases:** *at the same time, last week, a month ago, some years back*

- **Transitional clauses:** *Before this event took place, While he was sleeping, When I was a child, After she left, As I walked into another room*

.... **(Title)**	1. Give your story a title. It should convey the real meaning of your story and capture your readers' interest. 2. Introduce your main characters, the setting, and the conflict. 3. Describe what happens up to and including the climax of the story. Remember to - maintain a consistent point of view. - use vivid, precise language, sensory details, and dialogue. - use flashbacks to shift back to an earlier time. - use foreshadowing to give hints about future events. - include the narrator's reflections about characters, events, and setting. - use a variety of transitions.

Name _____ Date _____ Assignment _____

Conclusion

Provide a strong, satisfactory conclusion. Write an effective resolution, or conclusion to your story that leaves your readers satisfied. Use these tips.

- End with emphasis, not abruptly or vaguely by trailing off. The last event you narrate or scene you describe should help to summarize and reflect on the narrative by clearly showing the results of what has happened. For example, if through the events in the story, the main character has changed in some significant way, then the last scene should show this change. If the character has learned a specific lesson, then the last scene should show how the character applies or plans to apply this lesson to his or her life in the future.

- Tie up loose ends. Unless you are planning to write a sequel to your story, you should not leave readers wondering what happened to an important character or whether an important problem was solved.

- Be careful not to cram details about every unresolved little matter into the resolution. The most significant problems or conflicts should be fully developed and explored as the story unfolds. The resolution is where you give the final outcome, not tell a whole story in a sentence or two.

My Conclusion	Evaluating My Conclusion
	❑ Does my conclusion show what happens to the main character after the conflict is resolved?
	❑ Does it flow naturally and logically from story events?
	❑ Does it flow reflect on the main character's experiences or story events?
	❑ Does it wrap up all the loose ends in the story?

Name _____ Date _____ Assignment _____

Revising Strategies

Use the organizer to explain how you plan to revise and edit your story to make it better.
If you wish you can give a partner a copy of your draft and this graphic organizer and have your partner suggest ways to improve your story.

Focus on Character Development	
Do my characters react realistically and appropriately to events and other characters?	Yes .... No ....
What gestures, words, facial expressions, thoughts, memories, or actions can I add or change to make characters' reactions more realistic?	
What gestures, words, facial expressions, thoughts, memories, or actions can I add or change to make characters' reactions more appropriate to the situation?	

Focus on Dialogue	
Does my dialogue feel natural and convey appropriate emotions? Does it help reveal character and move the plot forward?	Yes .... No ....
Where can I shorten dialogue to quicken the pace and add drama?	
Where can I lengthen dialogue to slow the pace and build tension?	
What words and phrases can I add to the dialogue to add excitement and realism? For example, are there places where I can add interjections, such as "Wow!" and "Unbelievable" to show strong emotion?	
Where can I add or revise dialogue to highlight differences between characters?	

Revising

Revising for subject-verb agreement.

A verb must agree with its subject in number. In grammar, the number of a word can be either *singular* (indicating *one*) or *plural* (indicating *more than one*). Unlike nouns, which usually become plural when *–s* or *–es* is added, verbs with *–s* or *–es* added to them are singular. Problems often arise with subject verb agreement when sentences are inverted and when interrupters—for example, phrases and clauses—come between the subject and the verb.

Nouns and Pronouns	
Singular	**Plural**
bus, goose, I, you, it	buses, geese, we, you, them
Verbs	
Singular	**Plural**
runs, reds, sleeps, writes	run, read, sleep, write

Here are some examples of correct subject-verb agreement. In each case, subjects are underlined and verbs are set in italics.

Singular: The <u>child</u> *goes* to sleep at eight o'clock.

Plural: The <u>children</u> *go* to sleep at eight o'clock.

Singular, with an Interrupter: The <u>girl</u> with the red sneakers *runs* fast.

Plural, with Interrupters: The <u>boys</u> on the sled at the front of the line *go* next.

Compound, Plural: <u>George and Martha</u> *agree* with our idea.

Fixing Faulty Subject–Verb Agreement

As you revise your draft, check subject-verb agreement in your sentences. To fix problems with subject-verb agreement, use the following methods:

1. **First identify the subject, then check its number.** For singular subject, use singular verbs. For plural subjects, use plural verbs.

2. **If the subject comes after the verb, rephrase the sentence.** This makes it easier to determine the number of the subject.
   Faulty Inverted Sentence: There *was* many <u>girls</u> in the store.
   Rephrased: Many <u>girls</u> *were* in the store.

3. **Check for interrupters between the subject and the verb.** Make sure that the verb agrees with the subject and not with a noun that is part of a phrase or clause.

4. **Check the context.** The subject *you* can be singular or plural. Read surrounding sentences or the rest of the paragraph to determine the correct number.

Editing and Proofreading

Review your draft to correct errors in capitalization, spelling, and punctuation.

Focus on Capitalization: Review your draft carefully to find and correct capitalization errors. Make sure you have capitalized the title of your story correctly. Remember that the first and last word of a title are always capitalized. Articles *(a, an, the)* and short prepositions *(in, on, at)* are not capitalized.

Incorrect capitalization:	Taking the Long way Home
Correct capitalization:	Taking the Long Way Home

Focus on Spelling: Check the spelling of each word in your story. Look for words that you frequently misspell and make sure that they are correct. Pay particular attention to the spelling of the irregular plurals. Check a dictionary if you are not sure of the spelling of an irregular plural. The correct spellings of irregular plurals are usually listed right after the pronunciation of the word. If you have typed your draft on a computer, use the spell-check feature to double-check for errors. Proofread carefully even after you run spell-check. Spell checkers will not find words that are used incorrectly, such as *your* instead of *you're* when the incorrect word is spelled correctly.

Focus on Punctuation: Proofread your writing to find and correct punctuation errors. Specifically, make sure you have punctuated dialogue correctly. Enclose a character's exact words in quotation marks. If dialogue comes *before* the speech tag (the words announcing speech), use a comma, question mark, or exclamation point at the end of the quotation—not a period. If dialogue comes *after* the speech tag, use a comma before the quotation. Always place a period at the end of a sentence inside the quotation marks.

Examples:

"Wait here," Dan said.

Maria looked around and whispered, "Well, what are your waiting for?"

Mike replied, "I don't want to go first."

Revision Checklist

❑ Have you reviewed your story to make sure your title, names, and other proper nouns are capitalized?

❑ Have you read each sentence and checked that all of the words are spelled correctly, especially irregular plurals?

❑ Have you punctuated dialogue correctly?

Name _____ Date _____ Assignment _____

Publishing and Presenting

Consider one of the following ways to present your writing:

Tell your story aloud. Hold a story telling events at which several students tell their stories. Hang posters announcing the event. You can also place an announcement on school and community Websites. Ask your teacher to record your readings. After the event, place print and audio copies of your stories in the school library, or upload them to the school Website.

Submit your story. Submit your story to a national magazine, an online journal, or a contest that solicits student writing. Read the submission guideline for each outlet, and be sure to follow the guidelines exactly to increase your chances of having your story published. Ask your teacher for advice and additional help if necessary.

Rubric for Self-Assessment

Find evidence in your writing to address each category. Then use the rating scale to grade your work.

Evaluating Your Short Story	not very					very
Focus: How clearly does the story show the conflict faced by the main character?	1	2	3	4	5	6
Organization: How effectively do you introduce the conflict, use plot devices, and develop the plot?	1	2	3	4	5	6
Support/Elaboration: How well do you use details to describe the setting?	1	2	3	4	5	6
Style: How well does your dialogue reveal character and further the plot?	1	2	3	4	5	6
Conventions: How correct is your grammar, especially your use of subject-verb agreement?	1	2	3	4	5	6

Writing 4

---

4. Produce clear and coherent writing in which the development, organization, and style are appropriate to task, purpose, and audience.

Explanation

Readers appreciate writing that is presented clearly and coherently. To produce writing that grabs your readers' attention and holds it, you must identify your task, purpose, and audience *before* you write. You also need to consider task, purpose, and audience *as* you write.

- Your **task** is the specific reason you are writing. For example, your task may be to write a multimedia report or a short story. The purpose of the report might be to explain; the purpose of a story is to entertain.

- Your **purpose** is your main goal for writing or the effect you want your writing to produce. For example, your purpose may be to write a report about the growth and development of an American city, using a variety of media; or it may be to tell a realistic story with odd characters and bizarre events that will make readers laugh. Whatever your purpose is, keep it in mind as you write. It should affect the choices you make as a writer on everything from word choice to sentence length.

- Your **audience** is the people for whom you are writing. Usually, you will write for your teachers and classmates. You could also write for family members, friends, or a wider audience, such as your school or community. You may also have an audience of web followers who read your postings. Whoever your audience is, they will affect the style and tone of your writing.

Your specific task, purpose, and audience will determine nearly every choice you make as a writer. For example, if you are writing a cause-and-effect essay for your teacher, you will likely use formal language to introduce your thesis in the first paragraph. Then you might show cause-and effect relationships that support your thesis in the body paragraphs and conclude with a paragraph that summarizes your ideas. But imagine your task is to write a letter to apply for a job, an email to a close relative, or a book review for a young readers' magazine. The **organization,** development, and **style** of your writing will be different in each case. To produce clear and coherent writing, always consider the relationship of the organization, development, and style of your writing to your task, purpose, and audience.

Academic Vocabulary

organization the way in which details are arranged in a piece of writing

style specific language a writer uses to connect ideas and make an impression on readers

Apply the Standard

Use the worksheet that follows to help you apply the standard as you write. Several copies of the worksheet have been provided for you to use with different assignments.

- Writing to a Specific Task, Purpose, and Audience

Name _____ Date _____ Assignment _____

Writing to a Specific Task, Purpose, and Audience

Use the organizer to identify the task, purpose, and audience of your writing assignment. Then note how each will affect your choice of organization, development, and style.

Assignment:	
Writing Task	**Note:**
Purpose	**Note:**
Audience	**Note:**

A

Name _____ Date _____ Assignment _____

Writing to a Specific Task, Purpose, and Audience

Use the organizer to identify the task, purpose, and audience of your writing assignment. Then note how each will affect your choice of organization, development, and style.

Assignment:	
Writing Task	**Note:**
Purpose	**Note:**
Audience	**Note:**

B

Name _____ Date _____ Assignment _____

Writing to a Specific Task, Purpose, and Audience

Use the organizer to identify the task, purpose, and audience of your writing assignment. Then note how each will affect your choice of organization, development, and style.

Assignment:	
Writing Task	**Note:**
Purpose	**Note:**
Audience	**Note:**

C

Name _____ Date _____ Assignment _____

Writing to a Specific Task, Purpose, and Audience

Use the organizer to identify the task, purpose, and audience of your writing assignment. Then note how each will affect your choice of organization, development, and style.

Assignment:	
Writing Task	**Note:**
Purpose	**Note:**
Audience	**Note:**

D

For use with Writing 4

Name _____ Date _____ Assignment _____

Writing to a Specific Task, Purpose, and Audience

Use the organizer to identify the task, purpose, and audience of your writing assignment. Then note how each will affect your choice of organization, development, and style.

Assignment:	
Writing Task	**Note:**
Purpose	**Note:**
Audience	**Note:**

E

Name _____ Date _____ Assignment _____

Writing to a Specific Task, Purpose, and Audience

Use the organizer to identify the task, purpose, and audience of your writing assignment. Then note how each will affect your choice of organization, development, and style.

Assignment:	
Writing Task	**Note:**
Purpose	**Note:**
Audience	**Note:**

F

Writing 5

> 5. With some guidance and support from peers and adults, develop and strengthen writing as needed by planning, revising, editing, rewriting, or trying a new approach, focusing on how well purpose and audience have been addressed.

Explanation

A well-constructed writing plan can help you stay on track as you compose a first draft. To be successful, you must show a clear understanding of your purpose and audience and that you intend to write with that purpose and audience in mind. Yet, even with sufficient planning, most writers should expect their first draft to need some revisions. Your teacher and **peers** can offer you advice on how to improve your writing. Here are some ideas on how to get guidance and support from your teacher and peers:

- After reviewing the comments on your first draft, meet with your teacher to discuss why you agree or disagree with his or her ideas for **revising**.

- Post a copy of your draft on the class website (or place a copy in the school library or classroom writing center) for peer review. Provide a checklist to help your peers focus on the main goals of the assignment.

- Read aloud your draft to a partner and ask for feedback. Provide a checklist that will help your partner focus on the main goals of the assignment.

- During a peer group session, discuss ideas for strengthening your writing, focusing on how well you address purpose and audience.

- Ask a peer to review your writing for errors in **conventions** and to check for varied sentence patterns, the use of transitions, and consistency in style and tone.

Your teacher or peers may suggest that you rewrite or rethink your approach to a piece of writing. Be open to their suggestions. Discuss and weigh their ideas to decide if they are valid. If you agree, go back to the prewriting stage and make a new plan. Be sure to discuss a revised schedule for turning in your work with your teacher.

Academic Vocabulary

peer a person who is the same age or has the same status as another person

revising rewriting to improve and strengthen writing

conventions correct use of punctuation, capitalization, grammar, and spelling

Apply the Standard

Use the worksheets that follow to help you apply the standard as you write. Several copies of each worksheet have been provided for you to use with different assignments.

- Evaluating Writing with Peers

- Revising and Editing

Name _____ Date _____ Assignment _____

Evaluating Writing with Peers

Work with a partner to evaluate one another's first drafts of a writing assignment. Use the organizer below to focus your evaluation. 1 is *not very* and 6 is *very*.

Focus Questions	Comments and Suggestions for Revision
How clear is my purpose? 1 2 3 4 5 6	
How well do my choice of details, vocabulary, and overall style show a consideration of my audience? 1 2 3 4 5 6	
How clear is my thesis statement or main idea? 1 2 3 4 5 6	
How effective are my details at clarifying and elaborating each important idea? 1 2 3 4 5 6	
How clear is the organizational plan? 1 2 3 4 5 6	
How clear is the relationship between ideas in sentences and paragraphs? 1 2 3 4 5 6	
How effectively do I use transitions, and how smoothly does the writing flow? 1 2 3 4 5 6	
How well do I use precise nouns and vivid adjectives, adverbs, and verbs to create clear, strong images? 1 2 3 4 5 6	
How well do I use the active voice and vary sentence patterns and length? 1 2 3 4 5 6	

A

Name _____ Date _____ Assignment _____

Evaluating Writing with Peers

Work with a partner to evaluate one another's first drafts of a writing assignment. Use the organizer below to focus your evaluation. 1 is *not very* and 6 is *very*.

Focus Questions	Comments and Suggestions for Revision
How clear is my purpose? 1 2 3 4 5 6	
How well do my choice of details, vocabulary, and overall style show a consideration of my audience? 1 2 3 4 5 6	
How clear is my thesis statement or main idea? 1 2 3 4 5 6	
How effective are my details at clarifying and elaborating each important idea? 1 2 3 4 5 6	
How clear is the organizational plan? 1 2 3 4 5 6	
How clear is the relationship between ideas in sentences and paragraphs? 1 2 3 4 5 6	
How effectively do I use transitions, and how smoothly does the writing flow? 1 2 3 4 5 6	
How well do I use precise nouns and vivid adjectives, adverbs, and verbs to create clear, strong images? 1 2 3 4 5 6	
How well do I use the active voice and vary sentence patterns and length? 1 2 3 4 5 6	

B

For use with Writing 5

Name _____ Date _____ Assignment _____

Evaluating Writing with Peers

Work with a partner to evaluate one another's first drafts of a writing assignment. Use the organizer below to focus your evaluation. 1 is *not very* and 6 is *very*.

Focus Questions	Comments and Suggestions for Revision
How clear is my purpose? 1 2 3 4 5 6	
How well do my choice of details, vocabulary, and overall style show a consideration of my audience? 1 2 3 4 5 6	
How clear is my thesis statement or main idea? 1 2 3 4 5 6	
How effective are my details at clarifying and elaborating each important idea? 1 2 3 4 5 6	
How clear is the organizational plan? 1 2 3 4 5 6	
How clear is the relationship between ideas in sentences and paragraphs? 1 2 3 4 5 6	
How effectively do I use transitions, and how smoothly does the writing flow? 1 2 3 4 5 6	
How well do I use precise nouns and vivid adjectives, adverbs, and verbs to create clear, strong images? 1 2 3 4 5 6	
How well do I use the active voice and vary sentence patterns and length? 1 2 3 4 5 6	

C

For use with Writing 5

Name _____ Date _____ Assignment _____

Evaluating Writing with Peers

Work with a partner to evaluate one another's first drafts of a writing assignment. Use the organizer below to focus your evaluation. 1 is *not very* and 6 is *very*.

Focus Questions	Comments and Suggestions for Revision
How clear is my purpose? 1 2 3 4 5 6	
How well do my choice of details, vocabulary, and overall style show a consideration of my audience? 1 2 3 4. 5 6	
How clear is my thesis statement or main idea? 1 2 3 4 5 6	
How effective are my details at clarifying and elaborating each important idea? 1 2 3 4 5 6	
How clear is the organizational plan? 1 2 3 4 5 6	
How clear is the relationship between ideas in sentences and paragraphs? 1 2 3 4 5 6	
How effectively do I use transitions, and how smoothly does the writing flow? 1 2 3 4 5 6	
How well do I use precise nouns and vivid adjectives, adverbs, and verbs to create clear, strong images? 1 2 3 4 5 6	
How well do I use the active voice and vary sentence patterns and length? 1 2 3 4 5 6	

D

For use with Writing 5

Name _____ Date _____ Assignment _____

Evaluating Writing with Peers

Work with a partner to evaluate one another's first drafts of a writing assignment. Use the organizer below to focus your evaluation. 1 is *not very* and 6 is *very*.

Focus Questions	Comments and Suggestions for Revision
How clear is my purpose? 1 2 3 4 5 6	
How well do my choice of details, vocabulary, and overall style show a consideration of my audience? 1 2 3 4 5 6	
How clear is my thesis statement or main idea? 1 2 3 4 5 6	
How effective are my details at clarifying and elaborating each important idea? 1 2 3 4 5 6	
How clear is the organizational plan? 1 2 3 4 5 6	
How clear is the relationship between ideas in sentences and paragraphs? 1 2 3 4 5 6	
How effectively do I use transitions, and how smoothly does the writing flow? 1 2 3 4 5 6	
How well do I use precise nouns and vivid adjectives, adverbs, and verbs to create clear, strong images? 1 2 3 4 5 6	
How well do I use the active voice and vary sentence patterns and length? 1 2 3 4 5 6	

E

For use with Writing 5

Name _____ Date _____ Assignment _____

Evaluating Writing with Peers

Work with a partner to evaluate one another's first drafts of a writing assignment. Use the organizer below to focus your evaluation. 1 is *not very* and 6 is *very*.

Focus Questions	Comments and Suggestions for Revision
How clear is my purpose? 1 2 3 4 5 6	
How well do my choice of details, vocabulary, and overall style show a consideration of my audience? 1 2 3 4 5 6	
How clear is my thesis statement or main idea? 1 2 3 4 5 6	
How effective are my details at clarifying and elaborating each important idea? 1 2 3 4 5 6	
How clear is the organizational plan? 1 2 3 4 5 6	
How clear is the relationship between ideas in sentences and paragraphs? 1 2 3 4 5 6	
How effectively do I use transitions, and how smoothly does the writing flow? 1 2 3 4 5 6	
How well do I use precise nouns and vivid adjectives, adverbs, and verbs to create clear, strong images? 1 2 3 4 5 6	
How well do I use the active voice and vary sentence patterns and length? 1 2 3 4 5 6	

F

For use with Writing 5

Name _____ Date _____ Assignment _____

Revising and Editing

Use the organizer to explain how you plan to revise and edit your writing.

Beginning/Introduction:

How successful is it?

How will I revise or edit to improve and strengthen my writing?

↓

Middle/Body:

How well does it work?

How will I revise or edit to improve and strengthen my writing?

↓

End/Conclusion:

How effective is it?

How will I revise or edit to improve and strengthen my writing?

A

Name _____ Date _____ Assignment _____

Revising and Editing

Use the organizer to explain how you plan to revise and edit your writing.

Beginning/Introduction:

How successful is it?

How will I revise or edit to improve and strengthen my writing?

↓

Middle/Body:

How well does it work?

How will I revise or edit to improve and strengthen my writing?

↓

End/Conclusion:

How effective is it?

How will I revise or edit to improve and strengthen my writing?

B

For use with Writing 5

Name _____ Date _____ Assignment _____

Revising and Editing

Use the organizer to explain how you plan to revise and edit your writing.

Beginning/Introduction:

How successful is it?

How will I revise or edit to improve and strengthen my writing?

↓

Middle/Body:

How well does it work?

How will I revise or edit to improve and strengthen my writing?

↓

End/Conclusion:

How effective is it?

How will I revise or edit to improve and strengthen my writing?

C

Name _____ Date _____ Assignment _____

Revising and Editing

Use the organizer to explain how you plan to revise and edit your writing.

Beginning/Introduction:

How successful is it?

How will I revise or edit to improve and strengthen my writing?

↓

Middle/Body:

How well does it work?

How will I revise or edit to improve and strengthen my writing?

↓

End/Conclusion:

How effective is it?

How will I revise or edit to improve and strengthen my writing?

D

For use with Writing 5

Name _____ Date _____ Assignment _____

Revising and Editing

Use the organizer to explain how you plan to revise and edit your writing.

Beginning/Introduction:

How successful is it?

How will I revise or edit to improve and strengthen my writing?

↓

Middle/Body:

How well does it work?

How will I revise or edit to improve and strengthen my writing?

↓

End/Conclusion:

How effective is it?

How will I revise or edit to improve and strengthen my writing?

E

Name _____ Date _____ Assignment _____

Revising and Editing

Use the organizer to explain how you plan to revise and edit your writing.

Beginning/Introduction:

How successful is it?

How will I revise or edit to improve and strengthen my writing?

↓

Middle/Body:

How well does it work?

How will I revise or edit to improve and strengthen my writing?

↓

End/Conclusion:

How effective is it?

How will I revise or edit to improve and strengthen my writing?

F

For use with Writing 5

Writing 6

> **6. Use technology, including the Internet, to produce and publish writing and present the relationships between information and ideas efficiently as well as to interact and collaborate with others.**

Explanation

The technology of today offers an unprecedented opportunity for ordinary people to produce and publish their own writing. The Internet also makes it easy to interact and collaborate with other writers. For example, you can collaborate with classmates to create a website or publish your thoughts on social media sites and blogs. You can also use peer-editing software to review one another's work, or use email to seek advice from other writers. For more formal writing outcomes, technology can simplify the writing process, allowing you to work efficiently and to clearly present the relationships between information and ideas.

- You can use computer software to create a graphic organizer. Fill it in with notes related to your writing topic, and then cut and paste to group ideas that are related.

- You can save multiple drafts of your paper or alternate introductions and conclusions to ensure that your best ideas end up in the final draft.

- You can do research online to discover how other writers relate information and ideas about your topic.

- You can use the outline tool found in many word processing programs to create an outline, easily adding to or deleting information from the outline.

- After getting feedback from your teacher and peers on how to improve and strengthen the relationships between ideas in your writing, you can easily insert or delete facts and information or move sentences and paragraphs around by cutting and pasting.

- You can emphasize the relationships between information and ideas by incorporating photographs, charts, graphs, videos, and audio into an online presentation.

Using technology enormously expands what you can do as a writer.

Academic Vocabulary

technology advanced electronic tools, such as computers, scanners, printers, word-processing and design programs, and the Internet

collaborate work with others for one purpose

Apply the Standard

Use the worksheets that follow to help you apply the standard as you write. Several copies of each worksheet have been provided for you to use with different assignments.

- Using Technology

- Collaborating with Others

Name _____ Date _____ Assignment _____

Using Technology

Use the organizer below to plan how you will use technology during each stage of the writing process. Focus on how technology can help you work more efficiently.

| **Prewriting** |
| What technology can you use? |
| How will it help? |

| **Drafting** |
| What technology can you use? |
| How will it help? |

| **Writing** |
| What technology can you use? |
| How will it help? |

| **Revising and Editing** |
| What technology can you use? |
| How will it help? |

| **Publishing** |
| What technology can you use? |
| How will it help? |

A

Name _____ Date _____ Assignment _____

Using Technology

Use the organizer below to plan how you will use technology during each stage of the writing process. Focus on how technology can help you work more efficiently.

Prewriting

What technology can you use?

How will it help?

Drafting

What technology can you use?

How will it help?

Writing

What technology can you use?

How will it help?

Revising and Editing

What technology can you use?

How will it help?

Publishing

What technology can you use?

How will it help?

For use with Writing 6

Name _____ Date _____ Assignment _____

Using Technology

Use the organizer below to plan how you will use technology during each stage of the writing process. Focus on how technology can help you work more efficiently.

| **Prewriting** |
| What technology can you use? |
| |
| How will it help? . |

| **Drafting** |
| What technology can you use? |
| |
| How will it help? |

| **Writing** |
| What technology can you use? |
| |
| How will it help? |

| **Revising and Editing** |
| What technology can you use? |
| |
| How will it help? |

| **Publishing** |
| What technology can you use? |
| |
| How will it help? |

C

For use with Writing 6

Name _____ Date _____ Assignment _____

Using Technology

Use the organizer below to plan how you will use technology during each stage of the writing process. Focus on how technology can help you work more efficiently.

Prewriting
What technology can you use?
How will it help?

Drafting
What technology can you use?
How will it help?

Writing
What technology can you use?
How will it help?

Revising and Editing
What technology can you use?
How will it help?

Publishing
What technology can you use?
How will it help?

D

For use with Writing 6

Name _____ Date _____ Assignment _____

Using Technology

Use the organizer below to plan how you will use technology during each stage of the writing process. Focus on how technology can help you work more efficiently.

| **Prewriting** |
| What technology can you use? |
| How will it help? |

| **Drafting** |
| What technology can you use? |
| How will it help? |

| **Writing** |
| What technology can you use? |
| How will it help? |

| **Revising and Editing** |
| What technology can you use? |
| How will it help? |

| **Publishing** |
| What technology can you use? |
| How will it help? |

E

For use with Writing 6

Name _____ Date _____ Assignment _____

Using Technology

Use the organizer below to plan how you will use technology during each stage of the writing process. Focus on how technology can help you work more efficiently.

| **Prewriting** |
| What technology can you use? |
| |
| How will it help? |
| |
| |

| **Drafting** |
| What technology can you use? |
| |
| How will it help? |
| |
| |

| **Writing** |
| What technology can you use? |
| |
| How will it help? |
| |
| |

| **Revising and Editing** |
| What technology can you use? |
| |
| How will it help? |
| |
| |

| **Publishing** |
| What technology can you use? |
| |
| How will it help? |
| |
| |

F

Name _____ Date _____ Assignment _____

Collaborating with Others

Use the organizer to plan how you will use technology to collaborate with other students.
After you complete the assignment, use the organizer to evaluate your efforts.

Plan

What technology will you use to interact and collaborate with others for this assignment?

❏ E-mail

❏ Group chat

❏ Web page

❏ Blog

❏ Peer editing software

❏ Other (Explain) ....

Review

For each item you utilized, circle a number to rate how well you used technology to collaborate with other students. 1 is poor, and 6 is excellent.

Gathering information	1	2	3	4	5	6
Organizing details	1	2	3	4	5	6
Sharing feedback for drafts	1	2	3	4	5	6
Revising to improve	1	2	3	4	5	6
Editing	1	2	3	4	5	6
Publishing	1	2	3	4	5	6

Choose one item from the rating scale. Explain why you gave it the rating that you did.

A

For use with Writing 6

Name _____ Date _____ Assignment _____

Collaborating with Others

Use the organizer to plan how you will use technology to collaborate with other students.
After you complete the assignment, use the organizer to evaluate your efforts.

Plan

What technology will you use to interact and collaborate with others for this assignment?

❏ E-mail

❏ Group chat

❏ Web page

❏ Blog

❏ Peer editing software

❏ Other (Explain) ....

Review

For each item you utilized, circle a number to rate how well you used technology to collaborate with other students. 1 is poor, and 6 is excellent.

Gathering information	1	2	3	4	5	6
Organizing details	1	2	3	4	5	6
Sharing feedback for drafts	1	2	3	4	5	6
Revising to improve	1	2	3	4	5	6
Editing	1	2	3	4	5	6
Publishing	1	2	3	4	5	6

Choose one item from the rating scale. Explain why you gave it the rating that you did.

B

Name _____ Date _____ Assignment _____

Collaborating with Others

Use the organizer to plan how you will use technology to collaborate with other students. After you complete the assignment, use the organizer to evaluate your efforts.

Plan

What technology will you use to interact and collaborate with others for this assignment?

❑ E-mail

❑ Group chat

❑ Web page

❑ Blog

❑ Peer editing software

❑ Other (Explain) ....

Review

For each item you utilized, circle a number to rate how well you used technology to collaborate with other students. 1 is poor, and 6 is excellent.

Gathering information	1	2	3	4	5	6
Organizing details	1	2	3	4	5	6
Sharing feedback for drafts	1	2	3	4	5	6
Revising to improve	1	2	3	4	5	6
Editing	1	2	3	4	5	6
Publishing	1	2	3	4	5	6

Choose one item from the rating scale. Explain why you gave it the rating that you did.

C

Name _____ Date _____ Assignment _____

Collaborating with Others

Use the organizer to plan how you will use technology to collaborate with other students.
After you complete the assignment, use the organizer to evaluate your efforts.

Plan

What technology will you use to interact and collaborate with others for this assignment?

- ❑ E-mail
- ❑ Group chat
- ❑ Web page
- ❑ Blog
- ❑ Peer editing software
- ❑ Other (Explain) ....

Review

For each item you utilized, circle a number to rate how well you used technology to collaborate with other students. 1 is poor, and 6 is excellent.

Gathering information	1	2	3	4	5	6
Organizing details	1	2	3	4	5	6
Sharing feedback for drafts	1	2	3	4	5	6
Revising to improve	1	2	3	4	5	6
Editing	1	2	3	4	5	6
Publishing	1	2	3	4	5	6

Choose one item from the rating scale. Explain why you gave it the rating that you did.

D

Name _____ Date _____ Assignment _____

Collaborating with Others

Use the organizer to plan how you will use technology to collaborate with other students.
After you complete the assignment, use the organizer to evaluate your efforts.

Plan

What technology will you use to interact and collaborate with others for this assignment?

- ❏ E-mail
- ❏ Group chat
- ❏ Web page
- ❏ Blog
- ❏ Peer editing software
- ❏ Other (Explain) ....

Review

For each item you utilized, circle a number to rate how well you used technology to collaborate with other students. 1 is poor, and 6 is excellent.

Gathering information	1	2	3	4	5	6
Organizing details	1	2	3	4	5	6
Sharing feedback for drafts	1	2	3	4	5	6
Revising to improve	1	2	3	4	5	6
Editing	1	2	3	4	5	6
Publishing	1	2	3	4	5	6

Choose one item from the rating scale. Explain why you gave it the rating that you did.

E

For use with Writing 6

Name _____ Date _____ Assignment _____

Collaborating with Others

Use the organizer to plan how you will use technology to collaborate with other students.
After you complete the assignment, use the organizer to evaluate your efforts.

Plan

What technology will you use to interact and collaborate with others for this assignment?

- ❏ E-mail
- ❏ Group chat
- ❏ Web page
- ❏ Blog
- ❏ Peer editing software
- ❏ Other (Explain) ....

Review

For each item you utilized, circle a number to rate how well you used technology to collaborate with other students. 1 is poor, and 6 is excellent.

Gathering information	1	2	3	4	5	6
Organizing details	1	2	3	4	5	6
Sharing feedback for drafts	1	2	3	4	5	6
Revising to improve	1	2	3	4	5	6
Editing	1	2	3	4	5	6
Publishing	1	2	3	4	5	6

Choose one item from the rating scale. Explain why you gave it the rating that you did.

F

Writing 7

> 7. Conduct short research projects to answer a question (including a self-generated question), drawing on several sources and generating additional related, focused questions that allow for multiple avenues of exploration.

Explanation

A short research project answers focused, closely related questions about a specific topic. Often your teacher will suggest the topic and ask you to generate, or come up with, two or three questions to research. For example, after reading a selection by Mark Twain about his experiences on the Mississippi, you might generate these questions to research:

- What is a steamboat?

- When did steamboats become a common means of transportation in the United States?

- What were the advantages and disadvantages of steamboats?

After completing your initial research, use the information you have gathered to generate additional related, focused questions that allow for multiple **avenues of exploration:**

- Who developed the first steamboat in the United States?

- Why were steamboats important for American business?

- What caused the decline of the steamboat?

To research your initial questions, consult several different sources, such as online encyclopedia articles, books, and reliable websites. As you investigate your additional questions, you may need to expand your research to include your library's online databases, interviews with experts on the topic, and a wide variety of reliable print and online sources, including magazines, newspapers, and other periodicals. When you have finished your research, **synthesize** related ideas from all the sources to draw conclusions and answer your questions.

Academic Vocabulary

self generated a thought or idea you come up with on your own

avenues of exploration separate sources and research processes

synthesize to put together information from different sources and present it in a new way

Apply the Standard

Use the worksheets that follow to help you apply the standard as you write. Several copies of each worksheet have been provided for you to use with different assignments.

- Researching to Answer a Question

- Synthesizing Information from Different Sources

Name _____ Date _____ Assignment _____

Researching to Answer a Question

Use the organizer to gather information for each question you asked about your topic. Identify your topic, and write your questions at the top of the organizer. Then identify each source, and note any information related to the topic that you found in each source.

Topic: ....

	Initial Question:	**Additional Question 1:**	**Additional Question 2:**
Source:			
Source:			
Source:			
Source:			

A

Name _____ Date _____ Assignment _____

Researching to Answer a Question

Use the organizer to gather information for each question you asked about your topic. Identify your topic, and write your questions at the top of the organizer. Then identify each source, and note any information related to the topic that you found in each source.

Topic: ....

	Initial Question:	**Additional Question 1:**	**Additional Question 2:**
Source:			
Source:			
Source:			
Source:			

B

Name _____ Date _____ Assignment _____

Researching to Answer a Question

Use the organizer to gather information for each question you asked about your topic. Identify your topic, and write your questions at the top of the organizer. Then identify each source, and note any information related to the topic that you found in each source.

Topic: ....

	Initial Question:	**Additional Question 1:**	**Additional Question 2:**
Source:			
Source:			
Source:			
Source:			

C

Name _____ Date _____ Assignment _____

Synthesizing Information from Different Sources

Use the organizer to synthesize information from different sources. Write only the most helpful information from each source—facts that directly answer your questions. Then put it all together to write a paragraph about your topic.

Initial Question:

Additional Questions:

Information from Source 1:

Information from Source 2:

Information from Source 3:

Information from Source 4:

↓

Synthesis Paragraph:

A

Name _____ Date _____ Assignment _____

Synthesizing Information from Different Sources

Use the organizer to synthesize information from different sources. Write only the most helpful information from each source—facts that directly answer your questions. Then put it all together to write a paragraph about your topic.

Initial Question:

Additional Questions:

Information from Source 1:

Information from Source 2:

Information from Source 3:

Information from Source 4:

↓

Synthesis Paragraph:

B

Name _____ Date _____ Assignment _____

Synthesizing Information from Different Sources

Use the organizer to synthesize information from different sources. Write only the most helpful information from each source—facts that directly answer your questions. Then put it all together to write a paragraph about your topic.

Initial Question:

Additional Questions:

Information from Source 1:

Information from Source 2:

Information from Source 3:

Information from Source 4:

↓

Synthesis Paragraph:

C

For use with Writing 7

Writing 8

> **8. Gather relevant information from multiple print and digital sources, using search terms effectively; assess the credibility and accuracy of each source; and quote or paraphrase the data and conclusions of others while avoiding plagiarism and following a standard format for citation.**

Writing Workshop

A research report brings together information gathered from several sources in order to prove a central point, or thesis. When you engage in the process of writing a research report, you begin a quest to find answers to questions you have about a topic. In your quest, you explore and investigate multiple sources to find the answers to your questions. Often, your investigation will lead you to ask more specific questions that in turn lead you to additional resources. At the end of your quest, you will have gained an abundance of knowledge about your topic that you can share with others.

Assignment

Write a research report based on information from a variety of sources. Include these elements:

✓ a specific focus, or main idea, expressed in a thesis statement

✓ supporting evidence collected from a variety of reliable primary and secondary sources, with appropriate citations

✓ a clear organization and smooth transitions

✓ accurate, relevant facts and details to support the thesis

✓ a bibliography or "Works Cited" list

✓ correct use of language conventions, including the correct use of subordinate clauses

*Additional Standards

Speaking and Listening
8. Gather relevant information from multiple print and digital sources, using search terms effectively; assess the credibility and accuracy of each source; and quote or paraphrase the data and conclusions of others while avoiding plagiarism and following a standard format for citation.

2. Write informative/explanatory texts to examine a topic and convey ideas, concepts, and information through the selection, organization, and analysis of relevant content.

6. Use technology, including the Internet, to produce and publish writing and present the relationships between information and ideas efficiently as well as to interact and collaborate with others

9. Draw evidence from literary or informational texts to support analysis, reflection, and research.

Language
2. Demonstrate command of the conventions of standard English capitalization, punctuation, and spelling when writing.

Name _____ Date _____ Assignment _____

Prewriting/Planning Strategies

Choose a general idea. To find topic ideas, flip through recent magazines or newspapers, listen to the news, and review your notebooks. Tune in to television and radio news broadcasts. Surf the Internet for ideas, creating and organizing bookmarks in your Internet browser to identify possible topics. List subjects (for example, *politicians, entertainers, scientists*) as well the names of people, places, events, and current issues that you want to investigate. Choose a possible topic from among these ideas.

Use a topic web to narrow your topic. After you have a general idea for a topic, do some quick research. If you find an enormous amount of information, your topic is too broad. Narrow your topic to make it more specific and more manageable for a research report. Use the topic web to narrow your topic. Each row should contain smaller and smaller aspects of your general topic. For example, "educational toys" is probably too broad a topic for a research paper. A narrower, more focused topic could be "electronic readers."

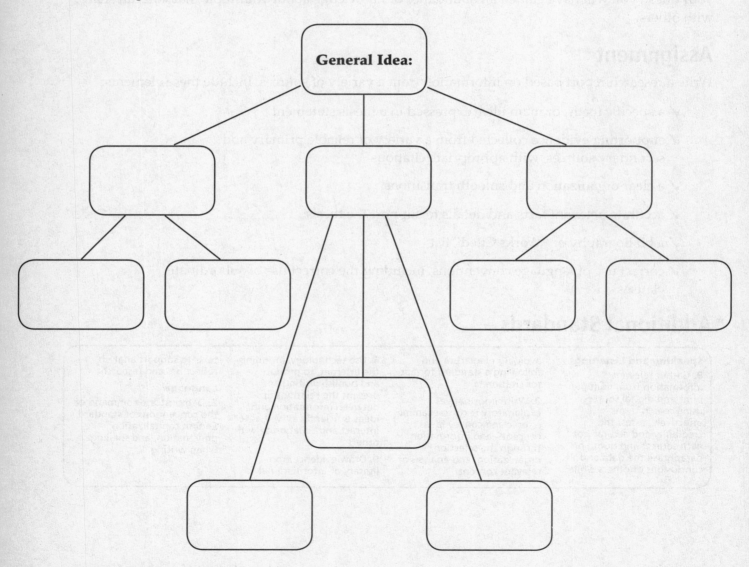

Write your narrowed topic: ....

For use with Writing 8

Name _____ Date _____ Assignment _____

Ask questions about your topic. Thoughtful, interesting questions can help focus your topic and your research. Make a list of several broad-based questions about your topic. Use these questions as a starting point to guide your research. As you continue your research, delete unwanted questions and add questions that are more specific and closer to the focus of your report.

Use a variety of primary and secondary sources. Use both **primary sources** (firsthand or original accounts, such as interview transcripts and personal observations recorded in news reports, journals, diaries, and letters) and **secondary sources** (accounts that are not first hand or original, such as encyclopedia entries, the Internet, books, television, and magazine articles.) A secondary source often contains a bibliography or list of works cited. You can use these citations to find additional sources.

Use the graphic organizer to write your focused research questions and sources that contain answers to those questions. List both primary and secondary sources.

Topic:				
	Question 1:	**Question 2:**	**Question 3:**	**Question 4:**
Source 1				
Source 2				
Source 3				
Source 4				

Evaluating Sources

You will consult a wide variety of print and digital sources as you research your report. However, just because something is in print or online does not mean it is true or unbiased. Often you will find articles written by unreliable authors, articles with a bias or agenda, or articles that lack factual evidence to support their claims.

Print Sources. You can usually find accurate information in encyclopedia articles; textbooks; nonfiction books; autobiographies; interview transcripts; and in magazines published by respected organizations, such as the Smithsonian. Nonfiction books and articles in specialized magazines, such as science journals, are often more reliable than articles in popular magazines; however, the information in some books may be less up-to-date than that of recent periodicals or Internet Web sites.

Digital Sources You can use a variety of digital sources for your research. These include CDs; radio and television documentaries; videos and slide programs; and the Internet.

When doing research on Internet Web sites, check the credentials of the person(s) responsible for the content on the site before accepting that the facts on that site are true. Do not automatically accept as true information on sites sponsored by companies or special interest groups. Facts on these sites may be skewed to suit the purpose of these sponsors. Internet sources sponsored by the government (ending in *.gov*) or educational institutions (ending in *.edu*) are generally more credible than those established by businesses (ending in *.com*). Check that university sites are actually sponsored by the university and are not private sites of students enrolled in the university.

Learn to conduct efficient Internet searches. Use highly specific terms, such as a person's full name, or use slightly less general terms. For example, "slavery" is too general a search term. It will generate too many hits that are unrelated to your focus. "Underground Railroad routes" is more targeted and should yield more relevant hits.

Evaluate your sources. To ensure that your information is current, accurate, and balanced, evaluate your sources. Use the following checklist.

- Does the source go into enough depth to cover the subject?

- Does the publisher have a good reputation?

- Do at least two other sources agree with this source?

- What are the author's credentials? Is he or she is an authority on the topic?

If three or more sources disagree, consider mentioning this disagreement in your report.

Name _____ Date _____ Assignment _____

Record source information. At the end of your report, you will provide a bibliography or "Works Cited" page of every source you cite in your report. Keep accurate details about your sources as you conduct your research to facilitate this task.

Use the **source cards** to record details for each book, article, or Web site you use. For print sources, list the title, author, publisher, place and date of publication, and page numbers. For Internet sources, list the page name, the sponsor, date of last revision, the date you accessed the site, and the Web address. Use the "Other" line, to list any other notes about the source, for example, if it is a CD or an interview transcript. Use as many source cards as you need. Be sure to record information carefully and accurately.

Title:	
Author:	
Publisher and Publication Date and Place:	
Page Numbers:	
Other:	

Page Name:	
Sponsor:	
Date of Last Revision:	Date Accessed:
Web Address:	
Other:	

For use with Writing 8

Name _____ Date _____ Assignment _____

Taking Notes. Follow these guidelines for taking notes efficiently.

- Take complete and accurate notes. This will save you from having to go back and verify every source when you draft and revise.

- Keep your notes organized and focused. Write one of your focused research questions at the top of each card. Use different colored markers to highlight each question. Then write only facts and details that answer that question on the note card. If your note cards get mixed up, you can see at a glance by the color which notes go together.

- Use a new note card for each new source. Go back and number your source cards. Then write that source number on the note card. If you prefer, you can write an abbreviated form of the title of the source or the author's last name.

- Use quotation marks when you copy words exactly. Indicate the author's last name and page number on which the quotation appears in parenthesis after the quotation. This will be helpful if you have go back to check the quotation when you draft, and if you decide to use the exact quotation in your report.

- In most cases, you should take notes in your own words. This will help you to avoid accidentally **plagiarizing**, or copying someone else's ideas and words, when you write your draft.

Record fact, details, examples, and explanations about your topic on note cards like this. Use as many note cards as you need.

Research Question:
Source notation:

Name _____ Date _____ Assignment _____

Drafting Strategies

Create an outline to organize information: When your notes are complete, use the graphic organizer to create an outline for your draft. A detailed and complete outline will keep you focused when you write your draft.

- First, (I) write a strong thesis statement that expresses the main point you want to make about your topic. Refer to your thesis frequently as you draft your report.

- Next, group your notes by category and turn these categories into subtopics, or main points. You can also turn your prewriting questions into subtopics. Use Roman Numerals (I, II, III, IV) to number your subtopics. Use capital letters (A, B, C) for the supporting details.

- For the conclusion, write a sentence that restates your main idea.

Thesis Statement ....

(Subtopic 1)   I. ....

(Detail)   A. ....

(Detail)   B. ....

(Detail)   C. ....

(Subtopic 2)   II. ....

(Detail)   A. ....

(Detail)   B. ....

(Detail)   C. ....

(Subtopic 3)   III. ....

(Detail)   A. ....

(Detail)   B. ....

(Detail)   C. ....

Conclusion   IV. ....

For use with Writing 8

Creating Unity

Draft your report. Follow your outline as you write your draft. Write a strong introduction. Begin with an intriguing question, a surprising fact or statistic, or an interesting quotation. Write two or three sentences that preview the main points that you will make about your topic in the body of your and end with your thesis statement.

Write the body of your report: Carefully construct and organize your paragraphs to create a smooth flow of ideas within and between paragraphs. Each paragraph in the body of your report, should contain a clear topic sentence that expresses the main idea of that paragraph. Every other sentence in the paragraph should contain facts, examples, and details that illustrate or expand the idea expressed in the topic sentence. All paragraphs should explain the thesis, expressed in the introduction.

To smooth the flow between paragraphs and between ideas, use transitions such as *next, finally, although, as a result of, therefore, despite, and however.* Another effective way to create smooth transitions between the paragraphs is to repeat a word or phrase from one paragraph at the beginning of the next paragraph.

Reference sources as you draft. As you continue to draft, choose the most relevant and interesting facts, details, examples, and explanations from your notes. Strive to achieve a balance between research-based information and your own original ideas. You can summarize, paraphrase, or use a direct quotation to incorporate research information into your report. Whichever method you choose, you must credit another writer's ideas within your report and with a full bibliography to avoid plagiarism. Plagiarism is the act of stealing someone else's ideas and words and trying to pass them off as one's own.

- For *summarized or paraphrased information,* insert in parentheses the author's last name and the page number(s) from which the information came.

- For a *direct quotation,* use quotation marks to enclose the sources exact words. After the end quotation mark, insert in parentheses the author's last name and the page number(s) from which the quotation came. If the quotation is more than four lines, introduce the quotation with a colon. Set the quotation off from your text by starting a new line and indenting the quotation. *Do not use* quotation marks.

Use visuals to support key ideas. Use photographs, diagrams maps, charts, graphs, and tables to organize and display information in a way that visually illustrates your main points. Visuals can make complex ideas easier for readers to grasp.

Crediting Sources

When you finish drafting, provide full information about your sources in a bibliography at the end of your report or in a separate alphabetical "Works Cited" list.

This chart shows the Modern Language Association (MLA) format for crediting sources. Most likely, your teacher will ask you to apply this style to your bibliography or "Works Cited" list.

MLA Style for Listing Sources

Book with one author	Pyles, Thomas. *The Origins and Development of the English Language.* 2nd ed. New York: Harcourt Brace Jovanovich, Inc., 1971.
Book with two or three authors	McCrum, Robert, William Cran, and Robert MacNeil. *The Story of English.* New York: Penguin Books, 1987.
Book with an editor	Truth, Sojourner: *Narrative of Sojourner Truth.* Ed. Margaret Washington. New York: Vintage Books, 1993.
Signed article in a weekly magazine	Wallace, C. (2000, February 14). A Vodacious Deal. *Time,* 155, 63.
Signed article in a Monthly magazine	Gustatitis, Joseph. The Sticky History of Chewing Gum." *American History* Oct. 1998: 30–38.
Unsigned editorial or story	"Selective Silence" Editorial. *Wall Street Journal* 11 Feb. 2000: A14.
Filmstrips, slide programs, videocassettes, DVDS	*The Diary of Anne Frank.* Dir. George Stevens. Perf. Millie Perkins, Shelly Winters, Joseph Schildkraut, Lou Jacobi, and Richard Beymer. Twentieth Century Fox, 1959.
Internet	"Fun Facts About Gum." NACGM site. National Association of Chewing Gum Manufacturers. 19 Dec. 1999 <http://www.nacgm.org/consumer/funfacts.html>
Newspaper	Thurow, Roger. "South Africans Who Fought for Sanctions Now Scrap for Investors." *Wall Street Journal* 11 Feb. 2000: A1+
Personal Interview	Smith, Jane. Personal interview. 10 Feb. 2000.
CD(with multiple publishers)	Simms, James, ed. *Romeo and Juliet.* By William Shakespeare. CD-ROM. Oxford: Attica Cybernetics Ltd.; London: BBC Education; London: HarperCollins Publishers, 1995.

Name _____ Date _____ Assignment _____

Create a bibliography or a "Works Cited" list. Use the graphic organizer to create a bibliography or a "Works Cited" list for your research report. Use the entries in the MLA style sheet on the previous page as a model. If you are creating a bibliography, arrange your sources in the order that you cited them for the first time in your report. If you are creating a "Works Cited" page, arrange entries in alphabetical order.

Bibliography/Works Cited

Name _____ Date _____ Assignment _____

Revising Strategies

Revise for effective paragraph structure. Review each paragraph in your draft to make sure it has a clear topic sentence that expresses the main idea of the paragraph. Check that all the other sentences support the topic sentence. Follow the steps in the chart to revise for effective paragraph structure.

1. Circle each topic sentence.
2. Underline supporting sentences.
3. Cross out any sentence that does not elaborate on the topic sentence.
4. Cross out any sentence that does not contain a fact, detail, or example that illustrates the topic sentence.
5. If you discover that a paragraph does not have a topic sentence, write one now.
6. If you have only one or two sentences left in a paragraph after deleting irrelevant details, add new details; or combine the remaining sentences with another paragraph.

Revise for unity and organization. A research report that has unity is focused on one central idea. It covers that idea completely, without introducing any irrelevant ideas about the topic. A unified research report is organized clearly and logically. Ideas flow smoothly from one paragraph to the next, from the introduction through the conclusion. Use the following questions to evaluate your research report for unity and organization. Make revisions based on your responses.

Does every paragraph develop the thesis statement in my introduction?	Yes	No
Does every paragraph have a main idea that helps explain my thesis?	Yes	No
Do all of my paragraphs contain topic sentences that express the main idea of the paragraph?	Yes	No
Do I introduce any ideas that are not related to my thesis statement?	Yes	No
Do I repeat words and phrases at the end of one paragraph and the beginning of the next to show how ideas are connected?	Yes	No
Do I use transitions such as *first, then,* and *finally* between paragraphs to create a smooth flow of ideas?	Yes	No
Does the conclusion sum up ideas in the body of my essay and restate my thesis? Does it leave readers with something new to think about?	Yes	No

Revising to Combine Sentences Using Clauses

As you revise your draft, look for places where your draft sounds choppy and disconnected. To eliminate choppiness and to show connections between ideas, use subordinate clauses to combine sentences.

Identifying subordinate clauses. A clause is any group of words with a subject and a verb. A subordinate clause cannot stand alone.

> **Subordinate clause:** <u>Although Rosa Parks said she was simply tired</u>, she became a symbol of strength.

Combining short sentences. Writers often combine two short sentences by converting one into a subordinate clause that establishes a specific relationship between the two ideas.

> **Time:**   *After soccer practice*, we will eat pizza.
>
> **Cause and effect:**   *If the temperature drops*, winds may pick up.
>
> **Contrast:**   *Although the sun shone*, it was still raining.

Combining sentences using subordinate clauses To combine sentences by using subordinate clauses, follow these steps

1. **Identify two sentences whose ideas are connected.**

2. **Rewrite the less important idea as a subordinate clause.**

3. **Use punctuation and subordinating conjunctions to combine the two sentences:**

   • Use a comma after most introductory clauses. *When he arrived back in Missouri, he visited his family.*
   Do no use a comma if the subordinate clause follows the main clause. *He visited his family when he got to Missouri.*

   • A list of subordinating conjunctions is shown here. Use these conjunctions to join the clause with the rest of the sentence.

Frequently Used Subordinating Conjunctions			
after	as though	in order that	until
although	because	since	when
as long as	before	than	where
as soon as	even though	unless	while

Editing and Proofreading

Review your draft to correct errors in capitalization, spelling, and punctuation.

Focus on Capitalization: Review your draft carefully to find and correct capitalization errors. Make sure every sentence begins with a capital letter. Focus on the citations in your report and bibliography. Check your draft against your notes to make sure you have copied titles and names correctly.

Focus on Spelling: Check the spelling of each word in your report. Pay particular attention to the spelling of author's names and domain-specific words. When in doubt, go back to source materials to double check for accuracy, or use a dictionary. Proofread carefully after you run spell check. Remember that a spell checker will not find words that are spelled correctly but used incorrectly, such as *affect* and *effect, and already and all ready*. In addition, a spell checker will not find words that are typed incorrectly but still spell a word, such as *form* instead of *from*.

Focus on Punctuation: Proofread your writing to find and correct punctuation errors. Make sure every sentence has correct end punctuation. If you are using the MLA style, citations should appear in parentheses directly after the information cited. Check that you have used quotation marks around direct quotations and short works, and that you have underlined or italicized long written works or periodicals. Make sure that all the entries in your bibliography or "Works Cited" list are punctuated correctly.

Revision Checklist

❑ Have you reviewed your research report for correct capitalization?

❑ Have you read each sentence and checked that all of the words are spelled correctly?

❑ Have you punctuated all your sentences and your bibliography or "Works Cited" list correctly?

Name _____ Date _____ Assignment _____

Publishing and Presenting

Consider one of the following ways to present your writing:

Share your report with a large audience. Find out which organizations (historical societies, fan clubs, or other groups) might be interested in your topic. Submit the manuscript for your report to one of these groups for publication in a newsletter or on a Web site. Include a cover sheet explaining why you think your report will be of interest to the group. Be sure to include with your contact information, including your name, address, phone number, and email address.

Deliver an impromptu speech. Now that you are knowledgeable about your topic, give an impromptu (unrehearsed) speech to your classmates. Describe your initial questions, your thesis, and what you discovered as a result of your research. After you finish, answer questions from the audience. If you cannot answer a question from a classmate or are not sure that an answer is accurate, share your list of reliable reference sources so that interested students can find the answers themselves.

Rubric for Self-Assessment

Find evidence in your writing to address each category. Then use the rating scale to grade your work.

Evaluating Your Research Report	not very					very
Focus: How clearly do you state your main idea?	1	2	3	4	5	6
Organization: How clear and logical is your organization?	1	2	3	4	5	6
Support/Elaboration: How well do you use evidence to support your statements?	1	2	3	4	5	6
Style: How clearly and accurately do you present the sources you used for research?	1	2	3	4	5	6
Conventions: Did you use subordinate clauses effectively?	1	2	3	4	5	6

Writing 9a

> **9a. Draw evidence from literary or informational texts to support analysis, reflection, and research**
>
> - Apply *grade 8 Reading standards to literature* (e.g., "Analyze how a modern work of fiction draws on themes, patterns of events, or character types from myths, traditional stories, or religious works such as the Bible, including describing how the material is rendered new").

Explanation

Many modern works of fiction draw on themes, patterns of events, and character types from **myths,** traditional stories, and religious works such as the Bible. You can write an essay to compare and contrast a modern fictional story that draws on traditional elements to stories from other cultures and times. When you write such an essay, you examine how a writer makes the traditional material new and relevant for a modern audience.

For your essay, select a modern story that draws on traditional elements and one or two traditional stories that share the same elements. The stories may share

- **a universal theme** (such as the destructiveness of greed)

- a traditional narrative pattern (such as a long journey with many obstacles)

- a traditional character type, or **archetype** (such as the trickster)

Before you write, gather details about each story. Be sure to note how the author of the modern story makes the traditional material feel fresh and new. When you write, begin with an introduction that identifies the works being compared and has a clear thesis statement explaining why you are comparing the works. Then, use your notes to elaborate your thesis with specific examples from the texts. Finally write a conclusion that restates your thesis and leaves readers with something new to think about.

Academic Vocabulary

myths legends, folk tales, and other stories that reflect the traditional customs and beliefs of a culture

universal theme message about life and human nature expressed regularly in many cultures and periods of time

archetype a plot, character, symbol, image, setting, or idea that recurs in the literature, mythology, and folklore of many different cultures

Apply the Standard

Use the worksheet that follows to help you apply the standard as you write. Several copies have been provided for you to use with different assignments.

- Comparing and Contrasting

Name _____ Date _____ Assignment _____

Comparing and Contrasting

Use the organizer below to gather details for an essay comparing and contrasting a modern work of fiction to two traditional works of fiction with a similar theme, pattern of events, or character type. Then, answer the questions.

Title of modern story:

Author:

Summary:

↕↑

Title of traditional story:

Author (if known):

Type (e.g., myth, fable, folktale, religious narrative):

Summary:

↕↑

Title of traditional story:

Author (if known):

Type (e.g., myth, fable, folktale, religious narrative):

Summary:

How does the modern story draw on the theme, pattern of events, or character type in the traditional stories? Be specific. ....

....

....

How does the author of the modern story make the material seem fresh? ....

....

....

A

Name _____ Date _____ Assignment _____

Comparing and Contrasting

Use the organizer below to gather details for an essay comparing and contrasting a modern work of fiction to two traditional works of fiction with a similar theme, pattern of events, or character type. Then, answer the questions.

Title of modern story:

Author:

Summary:

↓↑

Title of traditional story:

Author (if known):

Type (e.g., myth, fable, folktale, religious narrative):

Summary:

↓↑

Title of traditional story:

Author (if known):

Type (e.g., myth, fable, folktale, religious narrative):

Summary:

How does the modern story draw on the theme, pattern of events, or character type in the traditional stories? Be specific. ....

....

....

How does the author of the modern story make the material seem fresh? ....

....

....

B

Name _____ Date _____ Assignment _____

Comparing and Contrasting

Use the organizer below to gather details for an essay comparing and contrasting a modern work of fiction to two traditional works of fiction with a similar theme, pattern of events, or character type. Then, answer the questions.

Title of modern story:

Author:
Summary:

↓↑

Title of traditional story:

Author (if known):
Type (e.g., myth, fable, folktale, religious narrative):
Summary:

↓↑

Title of traditional story:

Author (if known):
Type (e.g., myth, fable, folktale, religious narrative):
Summary:

How does the modern story draw on the theme, pattern of events, or character type in the traditional stories? Be specific. ....

....

....

How does the author of the modern story make the material seem fresh? ....

....

....

C

For use with Writing 9a

Writing 9b

> **9b.** Draw evidence from literary or informational texts to support analysis, reflection, and research.
>
> - Apply *grade 8 Reading standards* to literary nonfiction (e.g., "Delineate and evaluate the argument and specific claims in a text, assessing whether the reasoning is sound and the evidence is relevant and sufficient; recognize when irrelevant evidence is introduced").

Explanation

Persuasive writing argues a position on an issue. When you write an evaluation of an **argument,** you examine in detail how the writer supports his or her **claim.** You discuss whether supporting evidence is relevant and sufficient, and you point out any examples of irrelevant evidence. Based on your thoughtful analysis, you tell whether the writer has built a successful argument.

Select an editorial, speech, opinion column, or other persuasive text to evaluate. Then take notes for your essay. Use these points as a guide.

- A sound argument contains a clearly stated opinion or **claim.**

- The claim is supported by relevant and sufficient **evidence,** such as facts, statistics, anecdotes, quotations from authorities, and examples.

- The evidence always leads to the writer's conclusion about the issue.

- The writer addresses opposing arguments, using evidence that reveals their weaknesses.

- The writer maintains a polite and reasonable tone throughout.

When writers lack sufficient evidence to support their opinions, they may introduce evidence that is irrelevant. For example, they might include an anecdote about a celebrity who supports the issue; or writers make outrageous claims about what will happen if their position is not supported. They may appeal to the reader's emotions instead of logic. In your essay, point out any evidence that is weak or irrelevant. Then explain how it weakens the development and success of the argument.

Academic Vocabulary

claim a writer's position on an issue

evidence factual details that support a claim

Apply the Standard

Use the worksheet that follows to help you apply the standard as you write. Several copies have been provided for you to use with different assignments.

- Evaluating an Argument

Name _____ Date _____ Assignment _____

Evaluating an Argument

Use the organizer to take notes for your essay evaluating an argument. Use specific details from the text to explain your responses.

Title:	Form (e.g. editorial, speech):

Author's position:

What does the author want readers to believe or do?

Evaluation Questions	Response	Explain
Is an opinion clearly stated?	❏ Yes ❏ No	
Is the claim supported by sound reasons and factual evidence?	❏ Yes ❏ No	
Are the reasons and evidence relevant?	❏ Yes ❏ No	
Does the evidence lead to the writer's conclusion about the issue?	❏ Yes ❏ No	
Are transitions used to make the argument easy to follow?	❏ Yes ❏ No	
Does the writer maintain a reasonable tone throughout the argument and avoid overly emotional language?	❏ Yes ❏ No	
Does the writer give evidence against an opposing point of view?	❏ Yes ❏ No	
Are readers likely to agree or disagree with the writer's position?	❏ Yes ❏ No	

A

For use with Writing 9b

Name _____ Date _____ Assignment _____

Evaluating an Argument

Use the organizer to take notes for your essay evaluating an argument. Use specific details from the text to explain your responses.

Title:	Form (e.g. editorial, speech):	
Author's position:		
What does the author want readers to believe or do?		
Evaluation Questions	**Response**	**Explain**
Is an opinion clearly stated?	❏ Yes ❏ No	
Is the claim supported by sound reasons and factual evidence?	❏ Yes ❏ No	
Are the reasons and evidence relevant?	❏ Yes ❏ No	
Does the evidence lead to the writer's conclusion about the issue?	❏ Yes ❏ No	
Are transitions used to make the argument easy to follow?	❏ Yes ❏ No	
Does the writer maintain a reasonable tone throughout the argument and avoid overly emotional language?	❏ Yes ❏ No	
Does the writer give evidence against an opposing point of view?	❏ Yes ❏ No	
Are readers likely to agree or disagree with the writer's position?	❏ Yes ❏ No	

B

For use with Writing 9b

Name _____ Date _____ Assignment _____

Evaluating an Argument

Use the organizer to take notes for your essay evaluating an argument. Use specific details from the text to explain your responses.

Title:	Form (e.g. editorial, speech):	
Author's position:		
What does the author want readers to believe or do?		
Evaluation Questions	**Response**	**Explain**
Is an opinion clearly stated?	❑ Yes ❑ No	
Is the claim supported by sound reasons and factual evidence?	❑ Yes ❑ No	
Are the reasons and evidence relevant?	❑ Yes ❑ No	
Does the evidence lead to the writer's conclusion about the issue?	❑ Yes ❑ No	
Are transitions used to make the argument easy to follow?	❑ Yes ❑ No	
Does the writer maintain a reasonable tone throughout the argument and avoid overly emotional language?	❑ Yes ❑ No	
Does the writer give evidence against an opposing point of view?	❑ Yes ❑ No	
Are readers likely to agree or disagree with the writer's position?	❑ Yes ❑ No	

C

Writing 10a

> **10a. Write routinely over extended time frames (time for research, reflection, and revision) and shorter time frames (a single sitting or a day or two) for a range of discipline-specific tasks, purposes, and audiences.**

Explanation

Writing plays a central role in every student's education. Some writing assignments extend over a long period of time to allow for the student to reflect on a topic, gather research, write, and revise. A research report is an example of a long-term writing assignment. Other assignments are short term and require only a single class period or a day or two to complete. A friendly letter, for example, can be completed in a short time frame.

Although a friendly letter has the same basic parts as a business letter, it is less formal and more personal in tone than a business letter. Friendly letters are usually written to close friends and relatives. However, your class assignment might be to write a letter from a story's narrator to its main character or from one character to another. Use these strategies to plan and write a friendly letter:

- Identify your task, purpose, and audience. Ask yourself: Who will receive this letter? What do I want this person to know? If you have been given a **writing prompt**, read the prompt carefully and highlight its key ideas.

- Plan how to use the time available. If you have 50 minutes, you might use 15 minutes to plan, 25 minutes to write, and 10 minutes to revise and edit.

- Take some time to write down the main points you want to make in the body of your letter. Then number your ideas in the order that you will present them.

- Draft your letter. Remember that a friendly letter has all the same parts as a business letter: the heading, the salutation or greeting, the body, the closing, and the signature. Maintain a friendly, polite, conversational tone. Avoid using slang.

- Reread your letter to make sure it is complete and your ideas make sense.

- Correct any errors in punctuation, capitalization, spelling, and grammar. Check that your heading contains an address and a date, that each paragraph is indented, and that your greeting and your closing are capitalized and followed by commas.

Academic Vocabulary

writing prompt a sentence or sentences that provide a specific writing idea

Apply the Standard

Use the worksheet that follows to help you apply the standard as you write.

- Writing a Friendly Letter

Name _____ Date _____ Assignment _____

Writing a Friendly Letter

Use the organizer to plan and organize your friendly letter.

Task:	Purpose:	Audience: ....
Plan your time Prewrite: .... minutes	Draft: .... minutes	Revise and Edit: .... minutes
Organize Ideas		
....	← address ← date	
greeting ➞	.... '	
message ➞	....	
closing ➞	.... '	
signature ➞	....	

Writing 10b

> **10b. Write routinely over extended time frames (time for research, reflection, and revision) and shorter time frames (a single sitting or a day or two) for a range of discipline-specific tasks, purposes, and audiences.**

Explanation

In social studies, science, language arts, and other classes, students are often asked to write descriptions. For example, in social studies, you might be asked to write an essay or report describing a significant historic event. In science, you could write a one or two paragraph description of something you observed in nature. For language arts, you might have to describe a memorable character from a literary selection.

Successful writers use precise language, **sensory details,** and vivid **imagery** to make a person, place, thing, or event come alive for readers. Look at the descriptions below. The first uses vague, empty language. The second contains rich sensory language that appeals to readers' senses and helps them "see" what is happening.

Vague: *The streetlight was dim. The alley was dark and scary.*

Vivid: *The streetlight's feeble glow only heightened the menacing gloom of the alley.*

When writing a description, first identify your task, purpose, and audience and determine how much time you have to spend on each stage of the writing process. Once you know your topic, gather enough sensory details to complete your task. The kinds of sensory details you gather depend on the impression you want to create. Before you begin writing, decide on a logical order to present your details. In revising, make sure that you have used details effectively so that readers can clearly imagine what you are describing.

Academic Vocabulary

imagery vivid mental pictures created with figurative language and sensory details

sensory details language that describes how something looks, sounds, feels, tastes, or smells

Apply the Standard

Use the worksheet that follows to help you apply the standard as you write. Several copies have been provided for you to use with different assignments.

- Writing a Description

Name _____ Date _____ Assignment _____

Writing a Description

Use the organizer below to plan and write a description.

Task:	Purpose:	Audience: ....
Plan your time Prewrite: .... minutes	Draft: .... minutes	Revise and Edit: .... minutes

Topic:

Gather Sensory Details

Sound	Sight	Feel/Touch	Smell	Taste

Choose a General Organizational Pattern (You may end up using more than one pattern in a long essay or report)

❑ Chronological Order: works well for descriptions of events; use transition words such as *first, next, then,* and *finally.*

❑ Spatial Order: works well for descriptions of places and people; use transition words such as *near, far, above,* and *below.*

❑ Order of Importance: works well for descriptions of significant events and people; use transition words, such as *first of all, especially,* and *most importantly.*

❑ Other: ....Transition words:

....

A

Name _____ Date _____ Assignment _____

Writing a Description

Use the organizer below to plan and write a description.

Task:	Purpose:	Audience: ....
Plan your time Prewrite: .... minutes	Draft: .... minutes	Revise and Edit: .... minutes
Topic:		

Gather Sensory Details				
Sound	Sight	Feel/Touch	Smell	Taste

Choose a General Organizational Pattern (You may end up using more than one pattern in a long essay or report)

❑ Chronological Order: works well for descriptions of events; use transition words such as *first, next, then,* and *finally.*

❑ Spatial Order: works well for descriptions of places and people; use transition words such as *near, far, above,* and *below.*

❑ Order of Importance: works well for descriptions of significant events and people; use transition words, such as *first of all, especially,* and *most importantly.*

❑ Other: ....Transition words:

....

B

Name _____ Date _____ Assignment _____

Writing a Description

Use the organizer below to plan and write a description.

Task:	Purpose:	Audience:
Plan your time Prewrite: ...... minutes	Draft: ...... minutes	Revise and Edit: ...... minutes
Topic:		

Gather Sensory Details

Sound	Sight	Feel/Touch	Smell	Taste

Choose a General Organizational Pattern (You may end up using more than one pattern in a long essay or report)

❑ Chronological Order: works well for descriptions of events; use transition words such as *first, next, then,* and *finally.*

❑ Spatial Order: works well for descriptions of places and people; use transition words such as *near, far, above,* and *below.*

❑ Order of Importance: works well for descriptions of significant events and people; use transition words, such as *first of all, especially,* and *most importantly.*

❑ Other: ....Transition words:

....

C

Writing 10c

> **10b. Write routinely over extended time frames (time for research, reflection, and revision) and shorter time frames (a single sitting or a day or two) for a range of discipline-specific task, purposes, and audiences.**

Explanation

Fiction writers often create brief sketches of the characters they plan to include in their stories. In a **character sketch,** the author jots down details of a character's appearance, behavior, peculiar habits, patterns of speech, and other characteristics. This exercise helps a writer develop a character's personality and imagine how the character is likely to behave in certain situations.

Frequently, students are given short-term assignments to write character sketches of people they know, characters from literature, or historical figures. A character sketch focuses on a person's key traits. It may contain biographical details, but it is not meant to chronicle a person's life. Instead, it provides basic details about a person's appearance and behavior so that readers can form a clear picture.

To write a character sketch, follow these steps.

- Identify the subject of your sketch. Your subject may be a friend or relative, a literary character, a figure from history, or a character you invent.

- Decide what impression you want your character to make on readers.

- Take notes about your subject that will help you accomplish your task. Ask and answer questions about your subject's age and appearance, behavior, and other **personality traits**. List evidence you might use to illustrate specific characteristics.

- Gather your notes and write a brief description of your subject. Remember to focus only on his or her most important or revealing traits.

Academic Vocabulary

character sketch a brief description of a person that highlights key traits

personality traits basic characteristics or qualities of a person

Apply the Standard

Use the worksheet that follows to help you apply the standard as you write.

- Writing a Character Sketch

Name _____ Date _____ Assignment _____

Writing a Character Sketch

Use the organizer below to gather ideas for a character sketch.

Task:	Purpose:	Audience: ....
Plan your time Prewrite: .... minutes	Draft: .... minutes	Revise and Edit: .... minutes

Gather ideas for a character sketch	
Who is the subject of the character sketch?	
What is your subject's age and gender?	
What do you want readers to understand most about your subject?	

Answer the questions to explore your subject in detail. When appropriate, give evidence from your subject's life that you can use in your sketch to illustrate a specific quality or trait.

Questions	Responses	Evidence
What does your subject look like? What is unique about your subject's appearance?		
What are your subject's most important beliefs and values?		
How does your subject treat other people?		
What adjectives would you and others use to describe your subject?		
What outstanding traits does your subject have? (Include traits that show your subject's strengths and weaknesses.)		

For use with Writing 10c

Writing 10d

> **10d. Write routinely over extended time frames (time for research, reflection, and revision) and shorter time frames (a single sitting or a day or two) for a range of discipline-specific task, purposes, and audiences.**

Explanation

A **how-to essay** is a short, focused piece of writing that explains a **process**. You encounter process writing every day in recipes, travel directions, technology manuals, game rules, and instruction booklets. If you have been assigned a how-to essay, select a topic that is interesting and familiar to you. Determine how much your audience already knows about your topic, and which terms and details will need elaboration. Plan to address any **factors** and **variables** that could change the outcome. Your paper should include these elements:

- a focused topic that can be fully explained in the essay

- a series of logical steps explained in chronological order

- an explanation of unfamiliar terms and materials

- a few transitional words and phrases to make the order clear; for example, *first, next, after a while, once you have, simultaneously, immediately after,* and *finally.*

- a visual aid, such as a diagram or chart, and special formatting such as bullets, numbers, and bold type to elaborate ideas and set off materials and steps

- a list of factors and variables that should be considered

Allow time for prewriting, drafting, revising, editing, and producing a clean copy. When you revise, check that your introduction and conclusion convey your enthusiasm and the value to be gained in completing the project. Then, review the steps to make sure that they are in order and that no vital piece of information is missing.

Academic Vocabulary

factors elements that influence the successful outcome of a process

how-to essay a short, focused piece of expository writing that explains a process

process a series of steps or actions that lead to a specific result

variables different conditions that can affect the outcome of a process

Apply the Standard

Use the worksheet that follows to help you apply the standard as you write.

- Writing a How-to Paper

Name _____ Date _____ Assignment _____

Writing a How-to Paper

Use the organizer below to gather and organize details for your how-to paper.

Task:	Purpose:	Audience: ....
Plan your time Prewrite: .... minutes	Draft: .... minutes	Revise and Edit: .... minutes

Steps	Materials needed to complete step	Elaboration (e.g., defining a term, adding formatting, or using a chart, diagram, or illustration)	Factors and Variables (e.g., the weather or use of a different ingredient)
Step 1:			
Step 2:			
Step 3:			
Step 4:			
Step 5:			

Speaking and Listening Standards

Speaking and Listening 1

> **1. Engage effectively in a range of collaborative discussions (one-on-one, in groups, and teacher-led) with diverse partners on *grade 8 topics, texts, and issues,* building on others' ideas and expressing their own clearly.***

Workshop: Deliver a Persuasive Speech

The purpose of a persuasive speech is to convince or persuade the listener to accept or adopt your point of view or idea. Your speech should have a clear, well-reasoned position statement, or thesis, and plenty of strong evidence to support the thesis. Illustrative, eye-catching multimedia—such as charts, diagrams, video, and even audio—can help emphasize key points in your speech and increase the persuasive effect on your audience. Once you have delivered the speech to your classmates, you will engage in a discussion and evaluation of the effectiveness of your argument.

Assignment

Deliver a persuasive speech to your classmates on a topic of your choosing. Include these elements:

- ✓ a clearly stated thesis, or position statement

- ✓ reasoned, logical organization of your ideas

- ✓ research that provides strong support for your main idea

- ✓ anecdotes, analogies, and illustrations that help demonstrate your thesis and key points

- ✓ multimedia, such as video, audio, charts, or diagrams

- ✓ appropriate eye contact, adequate volume, and clear pronunciation

- ✓ language that is formal, precise, and follows the rules of standard English

*Additional Standards

Speaking and Listening

1. Engage effectively in a range of collaborative discussions (one-on-one, in groups, and teacher-led) with diverse partners on *grade 8 topics, texts, and issues* building on others' ideas and expressing their own clearly.

1.a. Come to discussions prepared, having read or researched material under study; explicitly draw on that preparation by referring to evidence on the topic, text, or issue to probe and reflect on ideas under discussion.

1.b. Follow rules for collegial discussions and decision-making, track progress toward specific goals and deadlines, and define individual roles as needed.

1.c. Pose questions that connect the ideas of several speakers and respond to others' questions and comments with relevant evidence, observations, and ideas.

1.d. Acknowledge new information expressed by others, and, when warranted, qualify or justify their own views in light of the evidence presented.

4. Present claims and findings, emphasizing salient points in a focused, coherent manner with relevant evidence, sound valid reasoning, and well-chosen details; use appropriate eye contact, adequate volume, and clear pronunciation.

5. IIntegrate multimedia and visual displays into presentations to clarify information, strengthen claims and evidence, and add interest.

6. Adapt speech to a variety of contexts and tasks, demonstrating command of formal English when indicated or appropriate.

Language

L.7.3a. Choose language that expresses ideas precisely and concisely, recognizing and eliminating wordiness and redundancy.

Name _____ Date _____ Assignment _____

Research and Organize Your Persuasive Speech

After deciding on a specific topic, you need to gather information and conduct research. In small groups, discuss your topic with fellow students. Listen for good suggestions about your topic, and share your thoughts on their topics. These collaborative discussions may be helpful in planning your speech.

Research your topic. Use books, magazines, and the Internet to gather information. This will help you formulate a thesis statement and provide supporting evidence for your speech. To make sure the sources you use are valid and reliable, ask the following questions:

- Is the source generally considered reliable for its correct facts?

- Is the information current (within the past two years)?

- If using a web source, does it have *.org* or *.edu* at the end of the web address?

Write a strong thesis. State your position in one clear and specific thesis sentence. For example, if your topic is healthier school lunch choices, a strong thesis might be: "By offering students healthy lunches and snack foods, schools can help create good eating habits and reduce the national problem of teenage obesity." With a partner, take turns reading your thesis sentences aloud to be sure your positions are clear.

Engage your audience. To help persuade your audience, use strong research and rhetorical devices, such as:

- Anecdotes, or short true stories (often based on personal experience) that support your position

- Analogies, or comparisons between two things or ideas, that help the listener think about your topic in a new and different way

- Illustrations, either spoken or visual, that help the listener picture what you are talking about

Use precise and succinct language. Make sure your thesis, the body of your speech, and your conclusion are all clear and specific. Avoid using vague words that might confuse the reader or too many words because that might make it hard to follow the logic of your argument. Look at the following example:

Wordy, imprecise language: *Really sweet and sugary foods, like candy or cookies or chocolate or other sweets, all make the obesity problem of today's teenagers a bigger problem than it needs to be.*

Precise, succinct language: *Junk food with excessive sugar content, like candy and cookies, contributes greatly to teenage obesity.*

Conclusion End your speech with a strong and dramatic conclusion. You can restate your thesis in a new way, use an interesting and illustrative anecdote, or pose a question directly to your listeners—just be sure to leave an impression.

Name _____ Date _____ Assignment _____

Organize Your Persuasive Speech

Organize your speech so that your thesis and the key supporting points are easy to follow. Use the graphic organizer below to organize your main idea and support.

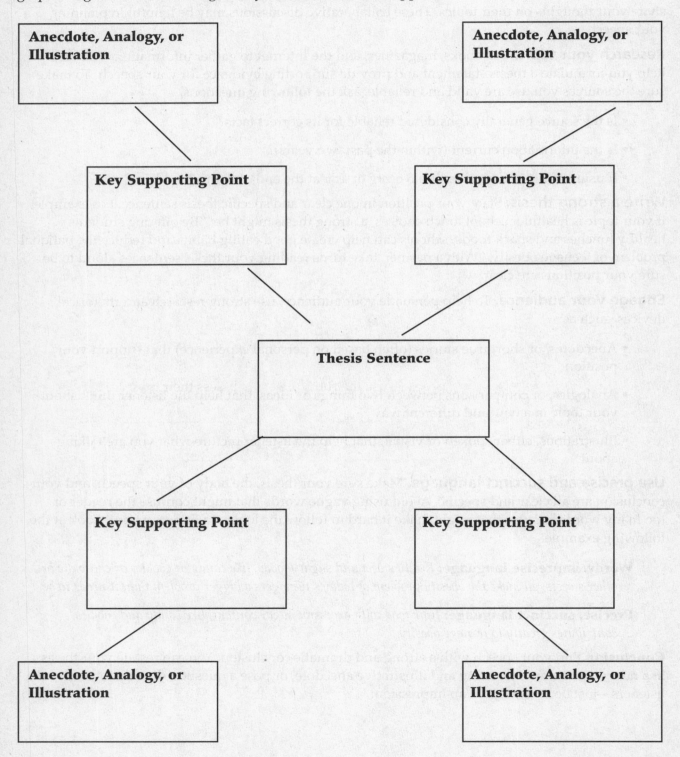

Anecdote, Analogy, or Illustration

Anecdote, Analogy, or Illustration

Key Supporting Point

Key Supporting Point

Thesis Sentence

Key Supporting Point

Key Supporting Point

Anecdote, Analogy, or Illustration

Anecdote, Analogy, or Illustration

Name _____ Date _____ Assignment _____

Presentation Techniques

The way you deliver your persuasive speech is almost as important as how well you have organized and written it. Rehearse your speech multiple times before delivering it to an audience. Practice in front of a mirror, and if possible, practice with friends or family members.

Use presentation techniques. Keep these tips in mind as you rehearse and eventually deliver your presentation:

- **Eye contact:** Make eye contact with members of the audience. You want them to feel like you are speaking directly to them.

- **Volume:** Vary the speed and volume of your delivery. When appropriate, increase or decrease your volume for dramatic effect. This is especially effective when making an important point.

- **Pronunciation:** Speak clearly and enunciate your words so your audience can understand what you are saying. If you have trouble pronouncing a word, practice it frequently so you won't stumble over it when delivering your speech.

- **Gestures and posture:** Face your audience and stand up straight as you deliver your speech. Avoid nervous or distracting gestures. Instead, use natural gestures to engage the audience and to help make salient points.

- **Language conventions:** Make sure the language you use in your presentation is proper and grammatically correct. Inappropriate slang or jargon can distract listeners from your message.

As you listen to your classmates' speeches, use the rubric below to assess their presentation techniques.

Presentation Technique	Listening Rubric
Eye contact	❑ Did the speaker maintain eye contact? ❑ Did you feel the speaker was speaking directly to you?
Speaking volume	❑ Was the speaker loud enough for everyone to hear? ❑ Did the speaker vary his or her tone for dramatic effect or to make an important point?
Pronunciation	❑ Was the speaker's delivery evenly paced and easy to understand? ❑ Did the speaker exhibit control over the language in his or her report?
Gestures	❑ Did the speaker use effective hand gestures to emphasize important points in the presentation?
Language conventions	❑ Did the speaker use standard English? ❑ Was the language clear and precise?

Name _____ Date _____ Assignment _____

Visuals and Multimedia

Use visually engaging charts, graphs, diagrams, and other multimedia to make your persuasive speech as effective as possible.

Use visual displays and multimedia components. You can grab an audience's attention with engaging visuals and multimedia, such as video and audio. Adding visuals and multimedia can also clarify complex information and ideas by presenting it in an easy to understand way. Choose media that will best support or reinforce the thesis or key points in your speech. Graphs and diagrams can illustrate how something works or the relationships between different ideas. Audio or video clips allow you to bring your ideas to life for the audience. Just try not to overdo the visuals and multimedia—they are most effective when used to emphasize important points. Also, make sure you introduce each element, and explain how it supports your central point.

Collaborate with a small group to brainstorm ideas for which visuals and multimedia to use in your speeches. Let everyone discuss their theses and major points so the group can generate ideas. Once you have decided which visuals and multimedia to use, complete this chart to help integrate them into your speech:

Visual or Multimedia Component	Main Point It Supports	Where to Include It and How to Introduce It

Name _____ Date _____ Assignment _____

Discuss and Evaluate

When you are finished with your speech, discuss the content and your delivery. Find out how persuasive your speech was with your classmates.

Discuss and evaluate the presentation. Ask your classmates to identify your thesis. Survey the class to see if they thought your speech was persuasive. How well did the supporting evidence reinforce the thesis? Ask your classmates to identify specific strengths and weaknesses in the speech. Listen for a consensus among your classmates' responses. Try to summarize the points where people agreed and disagreed. Refer to the guidelines below to make your discussion as productive as possible.

Guidelines for Discussion

To prepare for the discussion with your classmates, review the rubric for evaluating a persuasive speech.

- Help the group set goals for the discussion and assign specific roles, such as leader or notetaker, as necessary.

- Ask detailed questions and answer others' questions in a way that helps the group stay focused and meet its goals.

- Listen for new ideas suggested by others and, when appropriate, change your own thinking to take such ideas into account.

Guidelines for Group Discussion

Notes	Discussion Rubric
	❑ Did everyone in the group participate in the discussion? ❑ Was everyone able to express his or her opinion freely?
	❑ Was there a leader guiding the discussion? ❑ Was someone taking notes to share with the group at the end of the discussion?
	❑ Did participants ask detailed questions? ❑ Did participants answer and elaborate on questions asked by others? ❑ Did the group's questions and answers stay focused on the topic?
	❑ Were participants open to comments from others? ❑ Were people in the group open to new ideas and different perspectives?

Name _____ Date _____ Assignment _____

Self-Assessment

After you have completed the class discussion and evaluation, take a few moments to reflect on your speech. How do you think it went? How logical was the organization? How effective was your delivery? Did the media elements engage the listeners? Consider how your classmates reacted to the speech. To what extent did the group discussion help you to realize anything about your speech?

Using a rubric for self-assessment Consider how you felt your speech went, as well as what you learned from your classmates' responses to the speech, and fill out the rubric below. Imagine you were an audience member and assess your speech from a listener's point of view. Use the rating scale to grade your work. Circle the score that best applies for each category.

Criteria	Rating Scale					
	not very					very
Focus: How clearly did my speech state the thesis?	1	2	3	4	5	6
Focus: How clearly were the most important points explained?	1	2	3	4	5	6
Organization: To what extent was my speech logically organized so that listeners could easily follow it?	1	2	3	4	5	6
Research and Support: How effectively did I support the thesis and key points with strong research, clear visual displays, and engaging and appropriate multimedia components?	1	2	3	4	5	6
Delivery: To what extent was my tone relaxed yet formal? How often did I make eye contact with listeners? How effectively did I vary my delivery volume? Did I speak clearly?	1	2	3	4	5	6
Conventions: How free of errors in grammar, spelling, and punctuation was my speech?	1	2	3	4	5	6

Speaking and Listening 2

> **2. Analyze the purpose of information presented in diverse media and formats (e.g., visually, quantitatively, orally) and evaluate the motives (e.g., social, commercial, political) behind its presentation.**

Explanation

It is possible to find information about virtually any topic, text, or issue in an enormous variety of **media,** or forms of communication. If you are conducting research for a presentation, you might begin by looking at print media, such as books, magazines, newspapers, and other texts. You might also check a variety of non-print sources, including internet articles, television programs, documentary films, and even music CDs. Both print and non-print media contain information presented in a variety of **formats,** including: visual elements, such as pictures, films, and videos; quantitative information, such as charts and graphs; and oral elements, such as interviews, speeches, and lyrics.

Successful listeners and speakers are able to **analyze** and **evaluate** information that they find in all kinds of media and formats. When you analyze and evaluate information, you should be able to explain what purpose it serves: to address a social issue, to sell a product, or some other reason.

Examples

- Information can be presented in different media and formats for social motives. For example, a television program about community service may include statistics about problems in several communities, as well as pictures of volunteers helping people. The creators of the program probably included this information to encourage viewers to volunteer in their communities.

- Often information is presented for commercial motives. For example, an advertisement might include a graph showing how effective a brand of toothpaste is at fighting tooth decay. The purpose of the advertisement is to convince readers to purchase the toothpaste.

- Sometimes political motives are behind the information presented in different media and formats. For example, a mayor might give a speech explaining what he or she has done for the town or city. The motive is most likely to win the political support of listeners.

Academic Vocabulary

analyzes to examine a work closely in order to understand it better

evaluate to consider something to decide its value or worth

format the way in which something is presented and published

media various forms of mass communication (e.g., TV, radio, newspapers, Internet)

Apply the Standard

Use the worksheet that follows to help you apply the standard. Several copies of the worksheet have been provided for you to use with different assignments.

- Analyzing Information from Different Media

Name _____ Date _____ Assignment _____

Analyzing Information from Different Media

Use the organizer below to analyze information presented in your media source. Fill in three pieces of information from your source and analyze their purpose and motive. Then answer the questions that follow.

Source: ....

Type of Media: ....

1. Information:

Format	Purpose Served by Information	Motive for Including Information

2. Information:

Format	Purpose Served by Information	Motive for Including Information

3. Information:

Format	Purpose Served by Information	Motive for Including Information

Describe the most likely reason that the source was published or presented.

....

....

How successful is the source?

....

....

A

Name _____ Date _____ Assignment _____

Analyzing Information from Different Media

Use the organizer below to analyze information presented in your media source. Fill in three pieces of information from your source and analyze their purpose and motive. Then answer the questions that follow.

Source: ....

Type of Media: ....

1. Information:		
Format	**Purpose Served by Information**	**Motive for Including Information**

2. Information:		
Format	**Purpose Served by Information**	**Motive for Including Information**

3. Information:		
Format	**Purpose Served by Information**	**Motive for Including Information**

Describe the most likely reason that the source was published or presented.

....

....

How successful is the source?

....

....

B

Name _____ Date _____ Assignment _____

Analyzing Information from Different Media

Use the organizer below to analyze information presented in your media source. Fill in three pieces of information from your source and analyze their purpose and motive. Then answer the questions that follow.

Source: ....

Type of Media: ....

1. Information:

Format	Purpose Served by Information	Motive for Including Information

2. Information:

Format	Purpose Served by Information	Motive for Including Information

3. Information:

Format	Purpose Served by Information	Motive for Including Information

Describe the most likely reason that the source was published or presented.

....

....

How successful is the source?

....

....

C

Speaking and Listening 3

> 3. Delineate a speaker's argument and specific claims, evaluating the soundness of the reasoning and the relevance and sufficiency of the evidence and identifying when irrelevant evidence is introduced.

Explanation

The messages we encounter everyday—from speakers, on TV and radio, in web ads, newscasts, magazines, and newspapers—are crafted to influence, persuade, or affect us in some way. Analyzing and evaluating these messages and the reasoning behind them is an important skill.

Examples

- To delineate a speaker's argument, you need to identify the **thesis,** or main claim the speaker is asserting. The thesis usually appears early in a message—it is intended to grab the audience's attention with a specific claim worthy of discussion or debate. Once you've identified the thesis, listen for secondary or supporting claims. For example, if the thesis is about the need for a stricter rating system on electronic games, the speaker might include supporting claims, such as most electronic games depict too much graphic violence.

- After the thesis and supporting claims have been indentified, you can evaluate the soundness of the **reasoning,** or the arguments and proof used to support the thesis and claims. Each claim should be supported with facts, statistics, quotes from experts, or other reliable evidence. The argument should be logically organized, meaning one idea should lead to the next idea and make sense.

- The evidence the speaker uses should be relevant, which means it sensibly connects to the subject matter. Evidence that is not connected to the subject matter of the argument is considered irrelevant. For example:

Relevant:	Many games depict extremely gruesome and explicit violence, exposing kids to disturbing and distressing images.
Irrelevant:	These games are really popular and make lots of money for the companies that make them.

Academic Vocabulary

thesis the main claim or assertion

reasoning the arguments, proof, and analysis used to support an assertion or claim

Apply the Standard

Use the worksheets that follow to help you apply the standard. Several copies of the worksheet have been provided for you.

- Understanding a Speaker's Argument

- Evaluating Evidence and Reasoning

Name _____ Date _____ Assignment _____

Understanding a Speaker's Argument

Use the organizer to help delineate a speaker's argument and identify specific claims. Then answer the question.

Supporting Claim 1
Include the key evidence points

....

....

....

THESIS

....

....

....

Supporting Claim 2
Include the key evidence points

....

....

....

Supporting Claim 3
Include the key evidence points

....

....

....

Does the speaker provide sufficient support for the thesis?

....

....

....

....

....

A

Name _____ Date _____ Assignment _____

Understanding a Speaker's Argument

Use the organizer to help delineate a speaker's argument and identify specific claims. Then answer the question.

Supporting Claim 1
Include the key evidence points

....

....

....

THESIS

....

....

....

Supporting Claim 2
Include the key evidence points

....

....

....

Supporting Claim 3
Include the key evidence points

....

....

....

Does the speaker provide sufficient support for the thesis?

....

....

....

....

....

....

B

Name _____ Date _____ Assignment _____

Understanding a Speaker's Argument

Use the organizer to help delineate a speaker's argument and identify specific claims. Then answer the question.

Supporting Claim 1
Include the key evidence points

....

....

....

THESIS

....

....

....

Supporting Claim 2
Include the key evidence points

....

....

....

Supporting Claim 3
Include the key evidence points

....

....

....

Does the speaker provide sufficient support for the thesis?

....

....

....

....

....

....

C

Name _____ Date _____ Assignment _____

Evaluating Evidence and Reasoning

Use the organizer to evaluate the relevance and sufficiency of the evidence in a speaker's argument. Then answer the question.

Specific Evidence Cited	Relevant Or Irrelevant? (R or I)	How Does It Support the Thesis?

How well crafted and organized was the speaker's argument?

....

....

....

....

....

A

Name _____ Date _____ Assignment _____

Evaluating Evidence and Reasoning

Use the organizer to evaluate the relevance and sufficiency of the evidence in a speaker's argument. Then answer the question.

Specific Evidence Cited	Relevant Or Irrelevant? (R or I)	How Does It Support the Thesis?

How well crafted and organized was the speaker's argument?

....

....

....

....

....

B

Name _____ Date _____ Assignment _____

Evaluating Evidence and Reasoning

Use the organizer to evaluate the relevance and sufficiency of the evidence in a speaker's argument.
Then answer the question.

Specific Evidence Cited	Relevant Or Irrelevant? (R or I)	How Does It Support the Thesis?

How well crafted and organized was the speaker's argument?

....

....

....

....

....

....

C

Speaking and Listening 4

> **4. Present claims and findings, emphasizing salient points in a focused, coherent manner with relevant evidence, sound valid reasoning, and well-chosen details; use appropriate eye contact, adequate volume, and clear pronunciation.**

Explanation

When you speak to an audience, your goal is to focus on presenting your claim and findings about a topic. To ensure your presentation is focused and **coherent,** emphasize **salient,** or important points with relevant evidence, well-chosen details, and sound, **valid** reasoning. Effective speakers also use eye contact, appropriate volume, and clear pronunciation to keep their audiences engaged.

Examples

- Think about the best ways to organize your presentation. Your most important or salient points should stand out for your audience. For example, suppose your claim is that your community should provide free Internet access. Your most important points may be that residents will be better able to stay informed and that free Internet access will give local businesses a competitive advantage.

- Use relevant evidence, well-chosen details, and valid reasoning to support your claim. Your evidence—facts, statistics, expert testimony, or other details—should have a direct and obvious connection to your claim. For example, information about the cost of providing free Internet access is relevant, while a list of your favorite websites is not. Your presentation should feature only valid reasoning, so that your presentation has credibility.

- When delivering a presentation, keep your audience engaged. As you speak, look around the room, and make eye contact with people in the audience, especially those who show the most interest. Also, make sure your voice is clear and loud enough to be heard by everyone. Do not speak too quickly or too slowly. When making an important point, vary your tone and volume for dramatic effect. If there are words you have trouble pronouncing, practice them before delivering you presentation.

Academic Vocabulary

coherent clear and logical; connected in a way that makes sense

salient important, relevant

valid logical, reasonable, effective

Apply the Standard

Use the worksheets that follow to help you apply the standard. Several copies of each worksheet have been provided for you to use with different assignments.

- Organizing Information

- Presenting a Speech Effectively

Name _____ Date _____ Assignment _____

Organizing Information

Use the chart below to organize information for a presentation.

```
                    ┌──────────────────────────────────┐
                    │                                  │
                    │              Claim               │
                    │                                  │
                    │                                  │
                    └──────────────────────────────────┘
```

Important Point 1

Evidence, Reasoning, and Details:

Important Point 2

Evidence, Reasoning, and Details:

Important Point 3

Evidence, Reasoning, and Details:

A

For use with Speaking and Listening 4

Name _____ Date _____ Assignment _____

Organizing Information

Use the chart below to organize information for a presentation.

Claim

Important Point 1

Evidence, Reasoning, and Details:

Important Point 2

Evidence, Reasoning, and Details:

Important Point 3

Evidence, Reasoning, and Details:

B

For use with Speaking and Listening 4

Name _____ Date _____ Assignment _____

Organizing Information

Use the chart below to organize information for a presentation.

```
┌──────────────────────────┐
│                          │
│          Claim           │
│                          │
└──────────────────────────┘
```

Important Point 1

Evidence, Reasoning, and Details:

Important Point 2

Evidence, Reasoning, and Details:

Important Point 3

Evidence, Reasoning, and Details:

C

For use with Speaking and Listening 4

Name _____ Date _____ Assignment _____

Presenting a Speech Effectively

Use the organizer to help you prepare your presentation and to assess your delivery when you are finished. Then answer the question at the bottom of the page.

	Presentation Checklist
Preparation	❑ Does my speech clearly present my claim and findings? ❑ Is my speech organized effectively? ❑ Is my speech focused and coherent? ❑ Have I emphasized my salient points? ❑ Have I included enough relevant evidence and well-chosen details? ❑ Is my reasoning sound and valid?
Eye Contact	❑ Did I make and maintain eye contact? ❑ Did I look around at different people in the audience? ❑ Was my audience engaged?
Volume	❑ Did I speak loudly and clearly enough? ❑ Did I vary my tone and volume to emphasize important points in my speech? ❑ Did I maintain a steady pace in my delivery?
Pronunciation	❑ Was my delivery natural? ❑ Did I pronounce difficult words clearly and correctly?

How would you assess your overall presentation? Consider both your preparation and your delivery to

an audience. ....

....

A

Name _____ Date _____ Assignment _____

Presenting a Speech Effectively

Use the organizer to help you prepare your presentation and to assess your delivery when you are finished. Then answer the question at the bottom of the page.

	Presentation Checklist
Preparation	❏ Does my speech clearly present my claim and findings? ❏ Is my speech organized effectively? ❏ Is my speech focused and coherent? ❏ Have I emphasized my salient points? ❏ Have I included enough relevant evidence and well-chosen details? ❏ Is my reasoning sound and valid?
Eye Contact	❏ Did I make and maintain eye contact? ❏ Did I look around at different people in the audience? ❏ Was my audience engaged?
Volume	❏ Did I speak loudly and clearly enough? ❏ Did I vary my tone and volume to emphasize important points in my speech? ❏ Did I maintain a steady pace in my delivery?
Pronunciation	❏ Was my delivery natural? ❏ Did I pronounce difficult words clearly and correctly?

How would you assess your overall presentation? Consider both your preparation and your delivery to

an audience. ....

....

B

Name _____ Date _____ Assignment _____

Presenting a Speech Effectively

Use the organizer to help you prepare your presentation and to assess your delivery when you are finished. Then answer the question at the bottom of the page.

	Presentation Checklist
Preparation	❑ Does my speech clearly present my claim and findings? ❑ Is my speech organized effectively? ❑ Is my speech focused and coherent? ❑ Have I emphasized my salient points? ❑ Have I included enough relevant evidence and well-chosen details? ❑ Is my reasoning sound and valid?
Eye Contact	❑ Did I make and maintain eye contact? ❑ Did I look around at different people in the audience? ❑ Was my audience engaged?
Volume	❑ Did I speak loudly and clearly enough? ❑ Did I vary my tone and volume to emphasize important points in my speech? ❑ Did I maintain a steady pace in my delivery?
Pronunciation	❑ Was my delivery natural? ❑ Did I pronounce difficult words clearly and correctly?

How would you assess your overall presentation? Consider both your preparation and your delivery to

an audience. ....

....

C

Speaking and Listening 5

> **5. Integrate multimedia and visual displays into presentations to clarify information, strengthen claims and evidence, and add interest.**

Explanation

Effective speakers **integrate** multimedia and visual displays into their presentations to clarify information, strengthen claims and **evidence,** and add interest. Elements such as graphs, diagrams, photos, video clips, sound effects, and music can turn an average presentation into an outstanding one. These components can grab an audience's interest and provide strong support for your claims.

Examples

- When you plan a speech, consider how multimedia and visual elements can improve your presentation. Think about which key points or claims would benefit most from a visual or media display. Ask yourself: Are there complex points that a chart or graph could make clearer for the audience? Would a photograph or illustration add interest and prompt an emotional response? Might an audio clip, such as an interview, strengthen a claim? Evidence such as facts, statistics, and expert opinions can be translated into visuals that will help the audience quickly and easily understand a point. Where appropriate, video can provide additional support for a key point. Music can set a mood or be used for dramatic effect.

- Make sure the multimedia and visual components you want to integrate into your presentation support your claims. They should help make points clearer or provide additional evidence. Images, graphics, or sounds that do not explicitly apply to your subject and claims can be distracting and confusing to your audience. Consider the following questions when choosing multimedia:

  - How does this element apply directly and clearly to my subject matter?

  - How does this multimedia clarify and strengthen my claims and evidence?

  - How will the multimedia make my presentation more interesting?

- Practice delivering your presentation to ensure that your implementation of various media and visual elements is smooth and seamless.

Academic Vocabulary

evidence material or information that proves the validity of something

integrate to combine or incorporate different elements into a larger whole

Apply the Standard

Use the worksheet that follows to help you apply the standard.

- Using Multimedia and Visuals

Name _____ Date _____ Assignment _____

Using Multimedia and Visuals

Use the organizer to identify multimedia and visual components you will include in your presentation. Describe how you will integrate each component. Then tell how each component will clarify information or strengthen your claims and evidence.

Media/Visual Component (brief description)	How It Will Be Integrated Into Presentation	How It Clarifies or Strengthens Key Point

A

Speaking and Listening 6

> 6. Adapt speech to a variety of contexts and tasks, demonstrating command of formal English when indicated or appropriate.

Explanation

To be an effective speaker, you must know how to adapt your speech for the **context** and your speaking **task**. You may need to add explanations or delete information that is not of interest to your audience. Think about your purpose. Are you speaking to persuade, to entertain, to inform, or to describe? In most cases, you should use **formal English** when speaking to ensure that your audience can easily understand what you say and follow your logic. Avoid using casual, everyday language, including slang.

Examples

- Precise, engaging language is one of the keys to effective speaking. Unclear or confusing language can make even the strongest presentation difficult to understand. Consider the following when preparing a speech or presentation:

  Pronouns: Unclear pronoun references will confuse your audience. When you use pronouns, make sure they refer to nouns clearly and correctly. To be even more effective, use specific nouns and proper names to avoid confusion.

  Sentence Variety: Vary the length and tempo of your sentences. Repeating the same sentence patterns can make your speech boring. Use short, simple sentences to emphasize key points and longer, more complex sentences for detailed descriptions.

- The context in which you are speaking and your speaking task may affect what you say as well. For example, if you were speaking about climate to scientists, you would not need to explain basic facts. A scientific audience already knows this information. However, if you were speaking to fellow students, you should include additional explanations to help the audience understand your topic.

Academic Vocabulary

context the general situation in which a given thing happens

formal English language that strictly follows rules of grammar

task assignment; piece of work that someone is given to do

Apply the Standard

Use the worksheets that follow to help you apply the standard. Several copies of each worksheet have been provided for you to use with different assignments.

- Adapting a Speech to an Audience

- Using Appropriate Language

Name _____ Date _____ Assignment _____

Adapting a Speech to an Audience

Use the organizer to adapt your speech to different audiences. Then answer the question at the bottom of the page.

```
┌─────────────────────────────────────────────────────┐
│                      Audience                         │
│  Identify your audience.                              │
│                                                       │
│                                                       │
│                                                       │
│  What do you know about your audience?                │
│                                                       │
│                                                       │
│                                                       │
└─────────────────────────────────────────────────────┘
```

Adaptation / Change to Speech	Reason for Change
1.	
2.	
3.	

Which aspect of your speech needed the most adaptation and why? ....

....

....

....

....

A

Name _____ Date _____ Assignment _____

Adapting a Speech to an Audience

Use the organizer to adapt your speech to different audiences. Then answer the question at the bottom of the page.

Audience

Identify your audience.

What do you know about your audience?

Adaptation / Change to Speech	Reason for Change
1.	
2.	
3.	

Which aspect of your speech needed the most adaptation and why? ....

....

....

....

....

B

Name _____ Date _____ Assignment _____

Adapting a Speech to an Audience

Use the organizer to adapt your speech to different audiences. Then answer the question at the bottom of the page.

<table>
<tr><td>

Audience

Identify your audience.

What do you know about your audience?

</td></tr>
</table>

↓

Adaptation / Change to Speech	**Reason for Change**
1.	
2.	
3.	

Which aspect of your speech needed the most adaptation and why? ....

....

....

....

....

....

C

Name _____ Date _____ Assignment _____

Using Appropriate Language

Before you give a speech, use the checklist to evaluate your use of language. Then answer the question at the bottom of the page.

Audience: ....

Speaking Task: ....

	Speech Checklist
Language	❏ Is my language appropriate for the context and speaking task? ❏ Am I using formal English consistently? ❏ Is my language and word choice precise and engaging enough to keep the listeners interested?
Sentences	❏ Are my sentences varied enough? ❏ Can I change sentence lengths to vary my pace and tempo? ❏ Do I use short sentences for dramatic effect or to emphasize important points?
Pronouns	❏ Are there too many pronouns in my speech? ❏ Can I substitute proper names and specific nouns to avoid confusion? ❏ Is who or what my pronouns refer to absolutely clear?

Explain how you will adapt your language to make it appropriate for the context and writing task.

....

....

....

....

....

....

....

....

....

....

A

For use with Speaking and Listening 6

Name _____ Date _____ Assignment _____

Using Appropriate Language

Before you give a speech, use the checklist to evaluate your use of language. Then answer the question at the bottom of the page.

Audience: ....

Speaking Task: ....

	Speech Checklist
Language	❏ Is my language appropriate for the context and speaking task? ❏ Am I using formal English consistently? ❏ Is my language and word choice precise and engaging enough to keep the listeners interested?
Sentences	❏ Are my sentences varied enough? ❏ Can I change sentence lengths to vary my pace and tempo? ❏ Do I use short sentences for dramatic effect or to emphasize important points?
Pronouns	❏ Are there too many pronouns in my speech? ❏ Can I substitute proper names and specific nouns to avoid confusion? ❏ Is who or what my pronouns refer to absolutely clear?

Explain how you will adapt your language to make it appropriate for the context and writing task.

....

....

....

....

....

....

....

....

....

....

....

B

Name _____ Date _____ Assignment _____

Using Appropriate Language

Before you give a speech, use the checklist to evaluate your use of language. Then answer the question at the bottom of the page.

Audience: ....

Speaking Task: ....

	Speech Checklist
Language	❑ Is my language appropriate for the context and speaking task? ❑ Am I using formal English consistently? ❑ Is my language and word choice precise and engaging enough to keep the listeners interested?
Sentences	❑ Are my sentences varied enough? ❑ Can I change sentence lengths to vary my pace and tempo? ❑ Do I use short sentences for dramatic effect or to emphasize important points?
Pronouns	❑ Are there too many pronouns in my speech? ❑ Can I substitute proper names and specific nouns to avoid confusion? ❑ Is who or what my pronouns refer to absolutely clear?

Explain how you will adapt your language to make it appropriate for the context and writing task.

....

....

....

....

....

....

....

....

....

....

....

C

Language Standards

Language 1a

> **1a.** Demonstrate command of the conventions of standard English capitalization, punctuation, and spelling when writing.
>
> - Explain the function of verbals (gerunds, participles, infinitives) in general and their function in particular sentences.

Explanation

A **verbal** is a verb form that does not act as a true verb. For example, the word *thrilled* functions as a true verb in this sentence: *The fireworks <u>thrilled</u> onlookers.* In this sentence, however, *thrilled* is a verbal that functions as an adjective, not a verb: *The <u>thrilled</u> crowd cheered.* **Gerunds, participles,** and **infinitives** are all verbals.

Examples

Gerunds are verbals that end in *–ing.* Gerunds are used as nouns. They can function like any other noun in a sentence—as subjects, direct objects, or objects of prepositions.

> *<u>Pitching</u> was difficult for Maria.* (functions as the **subject** of the sentence)
>
> *She avoided <u>pitching</u>.* (functions as **direct object** of *avoided.*)
>
> *She disliked the pressure of <u>pitching</u>.* (functions as **object of the preposition** *of*)

Infinitives usually consist of the basic form of a verb preceded by the word *to.* An infinitive can function as a noun, an adjective, or an adverb.

> *The boys liked to <u>swim</u>.* (functions as a **noun**; direct object of *liked*)
>
> *The team had many laps <u>to go</u>.* (functions as an **adjective**; modifies *laps*)
>
> *The captain is always anxious <u>to win</u>.* (functions as an **adverb**; modifies *anxious*)

Participles are verbals that can act as adjectives. A present participle is formed by adding *–ing* to a verb. It describes an ongoing or present condition. A past participle is formed by adding *–ed* to a verb. It describes something that has already happened.

> *The <u>confusing</u> rules baffled him.* (**present participle**; modifies *rules*)
>
> *The <u>confused</u> team played badly.* (**past participle**; modifies *team*)

Name _____ Date _____ Assignment _____

Apply the Standard

A. Underline the infinitive in each sentence. On the line, write how the infinitive functions by writing **_n_** for _noun_, **_adj_** for _adjective_, or **_adv_** for _adverb_.

1. .... To skate is her one and only goal.

2. .... Coach Jackson is teaching her to spin.

3. .... At the beginning of the lesson, he begins to demonstrate the move to students.

4. .... To compete in the regional competition would make Kim happy.

5. .... Kim needs more time to practice.

B. Underline the gerund in each sentence. On the line, write how the gerund functions in the sentence by writing **_S_** for _subject_, **_DO_** for _direct object_, or **_OP_** _object of a preposition._

1. .... Diving is difficult for Andrew.

2. .... By practicing, he is improving his dives.

3. .... Soon Michela will start swimming on a team.

4. .... Good coaching from Miss Rodriguez is sharpening her technique.

5. .... Sergio is beginning his training next week.

C. Underline the verbal in each sentence. On the line, indicate if the verb is an _infinitive, gerund,_ or _participle._

1. .... Bowling is Reggie's favorite sport.

2. .... Personally, I like to watch.

3. .... He begins to worry before a tournament.

4. .... Excited players sometimes make mistakes.

5. .... An athlete's spirits are lifted by cheering fans.

For use with Language 1a

Language 1b

> **1b. Demonstrate command of the conventions of standard English grammar and usage when writing or speaking.**
> • **Form and use verbs in the active and passive voice.**

Explanation

The kinds of verbs that you choose can either make your writing lively or limp. Use active verbs, instead of passive verbs, whenever possible. They are active and give sentences a sense of movement and energy.

Examples

Voice is the form of a verb that shows whether the subject is performing the action or not. A verb is in **active voice** if its subject performs the action. Active verbs are used in these sentences:

Su Lin **removed** her boots at the doorway.	The subject *Su Lin* performs the action of removing boots.
Soon, crowds **filled** the stadium.	The subject *crowds* performs the action of filling the stadium.
The graceful skater **spun** at a dizzying speed.	The subject *skater* performs the action of spinning.

A verb is in **passive voice** if its action is performed upon the subject. A passive verb is made from a form of the verb *be (was, were, is, is being)* plus the past participle of a transitive verb. In general, it is best to use the active voice in your writing. During the editing process, look for places where you can change passive verbs to active verbs, as shown below.

Passive Verbs (Weaker)	Active Verbs (Stronger)
Piano lessons **were taken** by Juanita.	Juanita **took** piano lessons.
Suddenly James **was bitten** by the dog.	Suddenly, the dog **bit** James.
The player **was instructed** by the coach to play better defense.	The coach **instructed** the player on how to play better defense.

In at least two cases, it is appropriate to use the passive voice:

- To emphasize the receiver of the action, rather than the performer
  *Several eighth graders **were admitted** to the summer program.* (emphasizes the receivers)

- When the performer is not important or easily identified
  *The speaker **was interrupted** three times.* (the performer is not important)

Name _____ Date _____ Assignment _____

Apply the Standard

A. Underline the verb in each sentence. Write *active verb* or *passive verb* on the line provided to identify the voice of the verb.

1. The principal named all of the students on the honor roll. ....

2. The new rule was criticized by many members. ....

3. All the sweaters on sale were bought by early customers. ....

4. A dessert was added to the order at the last minute. ....

5. A thick fog covered the valley. ....

6. He renewed his library card last week. ....

7. The call to action was read aloud by Tanya in a loud voice. ....

8. Fire fighters hooked the heavy hose to the nearest hydrant. ....

9. The windows were rattled by sharp winds. ....

10. Holiday shoppers crowded the stores in search of good buys. ....

B. Rewrite the sentences below from passive to active voice. Write the new sentences on the lines.

1. The high fly ball was easily caught by the outfielder. ....

....

2. Tony was asked by the driving instructor to sit in the back seat. ....

....

3. Definitions for the key terms are provided in the glossary. ....

....

4. Twenty-row tractors are used by modern farmers to harvest crops. ....

....

5. The familiar carols are sung by the school choir in unison. ....

....

For use with Language 1b

Language 1c

1c. **Demonstrate command of the conventions of standard English grammar and usage when writing or speaking.**

- **Form and use verbs in the indicative, imperative, interrogative, conditional, and subjunctive mood.**

Explanation

The **mood** of a verb shows the attitude that a writer has to what is being written. The **indicative mood** is the most common. It is used to make a statement, such as *"I like to read"*. Most sentences are written in the indicative mood. The **imperative mood** is a command. It is used when the writer gives an order or a suggestion, such as *"Read often."* Other moods in English are the **interrogative mood, subjunctive mood,** and **conditional mood.**

Examples

- The indicative mood makes a statement:

    The man <u>rode</u> the subway.
    The children in his train car <u>were</u> loud.

- The **interrogative mood** asks a question. It is usually formed by using a helping verb as the first word in the sentence. The subject is placed between the helping verb and the main verb. However, when the main verb is a form of *be* (such as *is, are, were, was)*, no helping verb is added.

    <u>Did</u> the man <u>ride</u> the subway?
    <u>Are</u> the children in his train car loud?

- The **imperative mood** gives a command or makes a suggestion. The subject is usually dropped, but it is understood to be *you*. The imperative mood uses the verb in its base form.

    (You) <u>Tell</u> the children a story.
    (You) <u>Be</u> quiet!

- The **subjunctive mood** is used in dependent clauses. It is used to express a wish, a possibility, or other condition that is contrary to fact. A clause in the subjunctive mood often begins with the word *that*, such as in the first example below. In the present tense, it uses the base form of the verb:

    I demand that the train <u>stop</u> here.
    I wish I <u>had</u> earplugs with me.

When you use the subjunctive mood in the past tense with the verb *be*, always use *were* instead of *was*:

    If I <u>were</u> on that train, I would have a headache.

- The **conditional mood** expresses uncertainty about whether an action will occur. It is usually formed using the helping verbs *would, should, shall, could, can, might,* or *may.*

    They <u>might</u> <u>become</u> quiet if he told a story.

Name _____ Date _____ Assignment _____

Apply the Standard

A. Identify the mood of the underlined verbs in each of these sentences. On the line, write *indicative, interrogative, imperative, subjunctive,* or *conditional.*

1. <u>Did</u> the hurricane <u>cause</u> much damage? ....

2. Powerful winds <u>blew</u> the roofs off homes. ....

3. Help <u>clean</u> up this mess. ....

4. I wish that I <u>owned</u> a dump truck. ....

5. I <u>would haul</u> away the garbage if I could. ....

6. If they can <u>rebuild</u> their home, they will move it away from the shore. ....

7. <u>Look</u> at those overturned cars. ....

8. Hurricanes <u>draw</u> their power from warm, humid air. ....

9. <u>Are</u> hurricanes stronger near the shore? ....

10. Yes, hurricanes <u>get</u> weaker over land. ....

11. I hope that the water <u>is</u> safe to drink. ....

12. The mayor <u>should call</u> for emergency relief services. ....

13. Some people <u>could stay</u> at the city shelter. ....

14. If you <u>hear</u> shifting noises, leave the building immediately. ....

15. You <u>should wear</u> a hard hat and goggles for cleanup work. ....

B. Edit the verbs in the following sentences. Draw an **X** through incorrect verbs and write the correct form of the verb on the line. If a verb is used correctly, write **OK** on the line.

1. .... If I was you, I would watch the weather report.

2. .... He suggested that it might raining tonight.

3. .... I wish the weather would be better.

4. .... The newscaster say anything about tomorrow's weather?

5. .... Turn the TV off.

Language 1d

> **1d. Demonstrate command of the conventions of standard English grammar and usage when writing or speaking.**
>
>   • **Recognize and correct inappropriate shifts in verb voice and mood.**

Explanation

A verb shift is a change within a sentence. For example, the voice of verbs may shift from active to passive, but unnecessary shifts are confusing. You should try to avoid or correct unnecessary shifts in verb mood and voice.

Shifts in Voice

The voice of a verb refers to whether it is active or passive. In the **active voice,** the subject is the doer of the action. In the **passive voice,** the subject is the receiver of the action. Avoid shifting voices within a sentence.

> *Incorrect*: We <u>went</u> (*active*) to the movie, and all our money <u>was spent</u> (*passive*).
>
> *Correct*: We <u>went</u> to the movie and <u>spent</u> all our money. [Here both verbs are active.]

Shifts in Mood

A verb's mood refers to the writer's attitude toward the subject. Verbs can have these moods:

> **Indicative:** I like scary movies.
> **Interrogative:** Do you like them?
> **Imperative:** Look up the movie times.
> **Subjunctive:** I wish I could go right now.
> **Conditional:** I would bring you along.

In sentences with more than one verb, avoid shifting from one **mood** to another. Correcting a mood shift often involves a change in wording.

> **Incorrect:** Look at the schedule, and you will tell me the show times.
> (*shifts from imperative to indicative*)
> **Correct:** Look at the schedule and tell me the show times.
> **OR**
> **Correct:** You will look at the schedule and you will tell me the show times.

> **Incorrect:** I would like to see the next show and why don't you come, too?
> (*shifts from subjunctive to interrogative*)
> **Correct:** I would like to see the next show and have you come, too.
> **OR**
> **Correct:** Why don't you and I see the next show?

Name _____ Date _____ Assignment _____

Apply the Standard

A. Write **active** or **passive** on the lines to identify the voice of the underlined verbs.

1. Some people <u>like</u> (..........................) nature shows, but comedies <u>are preferred</u>
(..........................) by others.

2. I <u>watched</u> (..........................) a nature show and my knowledge of migration <u>was</u> greatly
<u>increased</u> (..........................).

3. Some animals <u>leave</u> (..........................) their seasonal homes and later the homes <u>are</u>
<u>returned</u> (..........................) to.

4. Sea turtles <u>swim</u> (..........................) for hundreds of miles to <u>have</u> their eggs <u>laid</u>
(..........................) at their own birthplace.

5. One and a half million wildebeest <u>go</u> (..........................) on the Great Migration, and about
500,000 gazelle <u>follow</u> (..........................) behind.

6. As wildebeest <u>migrate</u> (..........................), serious dangers <u>are</u> <u>faced</u>
(..........................) by them.

B. Find the five sentences above that have unnecessary shifts in voice. Rewrite them correctly on the lines below.

1. ....

2. ....

3. ....

4. ....

5. ....

C. An unnecessary shift of mood is underlined in each sentence below. Rewrite the underlined part.

1. Turn on the show on the Great Migration and <u>could you watch it with me?</u> ....
....

2. Sit on the couch, but <u>you should not sit too close to the TV.</u> ....
....

Language 2a

> **2a.** Demonstrate command of the conventions of standard English capitalization, punctuation, and spelling when writing.
>
> • Use punctuation (comma, ellipsis, dash) to indicate a pause or break.

Explanation

As you know, a period indicates a full stop at the end of a sentence. Several other punctuation marks, however, indicate shorter, brief pauses: the comma (,), ellipsis (. . .), and dash (—).

Examples

A **comma** is a punctuation mark that indicates a brief pause. Use a comma

- before a conjunction to separate two independent clauses in a compound sentence.
  The marathon runners took their places, <u>and</u> the starting whistle blew.

- between items in a series.
  The crowd <u>clapped, cheered, and shouted</u> encouragement.

- between adjectives.
  The <u>hot, tired</u> runners kept going.

- after an introductory phrase or clause
  <u>After 26.2 miles,</u> the race was over.

- with parenthetical expressions.
  The runners were, <u>without a doubt</u>, relieved to cross the finish line.

- to set off appositives, participial phrases, or adjective clauses.
  The winner, <u>a 25-year-old from California</u>, set a record.

A **dash** signals a longer and more abrupt pause. Usually a dash sets off information that interrupts the sentence to take it for a moment in another direction.

> *The kids played board games——chess and checkers were their favorites—and read books when it rained.*

A dash is also used to set off an important explanatory statement, especially when it contains commas.

> *Beetles—such as ladybugs, weevils, and June bugs—contain more insects than any other species.*

A dash looks something like a hyphen, but it is wider. When you are handwriting, make a dash that is about as wide as two letters. At the computer, make two hyphens. Many word processing programs automatically convert two hyphens to a dash.

An **ellipsis** can be used to signal a pause that is caused by confusion or uncertainty. Using an ellipsis is something like saying "err" or "hmmm" in speech.

> *"I think . . . well, I'm not sure what I think," she said.*

An ellipsis usually consists of three periods with spaces between them. If the ellipsis follows a complete sentence, however, first place the period after the sentence and then follow it with the three periods of the ellipsis.

Name _____ Date _____ Assignment _____

Apply the Standard

A. Rewrite the sentences. Insert commas, dashes, or ellipses where they are needed.

1. P.T. Barnum who was born in 1810 was a true showman. ....

....

2. He was also an author publisher and politician. ....

....

3. In 1854 he hired Charles Stratton. ....

....

4. Stratton who was only 2 feet 3 inches became known as Tom Thumb. ....

....

5. At age sixty-one Barnum opened his famous circus. ....

....

6. It was fun original and popular. ....

....

7. Barnum you could never say he was shy called it "The Greatest Show on Earth." ....

....

8. His circus by the way made $400,000 in one year. ....

....

B. Write a sentence for each phrase or clause below. Set the words off with the punctuation marks that appear in parentheses.

1. which is a great book (commas) ....

....

2. mostly seventh and eighth graders (dashes) ....

....

3. on the other hand, let's not (ellipsis) ....

....

Language 2b

> **2b.** Demonstrate command of the conventions of standard English capitalization, punctuation, and spelling when writing.
> - Use an ellipsis to indicate an omission.

Explanation

When you write a research report or a response to literature, you often use direct quotations to support your ideas. A **direct quotation** is the exact text from a source. You copy it word-for-word from the original text and enclose it in quotation marks. However, some quotations are simply too long to include, or they include passages that do not apply to your subject. In those cases, you can remove words from the original source and replace them with an ellipsis. An **ellipsis** is a punctuation mark made of three evenly spaced dots (. . .). It indicates that text was omitted from the quotation.

Examples

The most common use of the ellipsis is to show that words have been taken out of a direct quotation. Writers may omit words because they do not have enough space to quote the entire text. Writers may also omit parts of a quotation because they are unimportant or unnecessary. An ellipsis usually has three periods with spaces between them. In the example below, the words replaced by an ellipsis are underlined in the original source.

Original Source: "The parade honored ten heroic soldiers who had just arrived <u>on a jet plane several hours late</u> from Iraq."

Shortened Text: "The parade honored ten heroic soldiers who had just arrived . . . from Iraq."

If the text that is left out comes after a full sentence, place the ellipses after the period. As usual, there should be no space between the period and the sentence. However, there should be spaces between the dots of the ellipsis.

Original Source: "Few writers find it easy to face the blank page. <u>I've been writing for years and I still find it hard to do.</u> The best advice is to just start writing."

Shortened Text: "Few writers find it easy to face the blank page. . . . The best advice is to just start writing."

REMEMBER: It is acceptable to shorten a long quotation by using an ellipsis to omit unnecessary words. However, you should never use the ellipsis to leave out important words. Doing so might change the *meaning* of the quotation.

Name _____ Date _____ Assignment _____

Apply the Standard

A. On the lines, write a direct quotation from the original source. Use ellipses to replace any text that is underlined in the original.

1. *Original Source (a science textbook):* "Nine million Americans—<u>not a small number by anyone's count</u>—suffer hearing loss from exposure to noise."

   Direct quotation: According to a science textbook, ...

   ....

2. *Original Source ("The Gettysburg Address," by Abraham Lincoln, 1863):* "We here highly resolve that <u>these dead shall not have died in vain—that this nation, under God, shall have a new birth of freedom—and that</u> government of the people, by the people, for the people, shall not perish from the earth. "

   Direct Quotation: President Lincoln dedicated the country to democracy when he said, ...

   ....

3. *Original Source (The President's Council on Physical Fitness and Sports):* "Walking is easily the most popular form of exercise. <u>Other activities generate more conversation and media coverage, but none of them approaches walking in number of participants.</u> Approximately half of the 165 million American adults <u>(18 years of age and older)</u> claim they exercise regularly, and the number who walk for exercise is increasing every year."

   Direct Quotation: One government publication promotes walking. It says, ...

   ....

4. *Original Source (A safety expert):* "We need laws against driving with cell phones. <u>In my opinion, we need them immediately.</u> Even the use of hands-free cell phones is dangerous. <u>The problem is not just holding the phone to your ear.</u> Distraction at the wheel is what causes accidents."

   Direct Quotation: One safety expert argued, ...

   ....

B. On the lines, write a direct quotation from the original source. Shorten the quotation by omitting words. Make sure your omission does not change the meaning of the quotation.

1. *Original Source:* ("A Woman's Right to Suffrage," by Susan B. Anthony, 1872): "It shall be my work this evening to prove to you that in thus voting, I not only committed no crime, but, instead, simply exercised my *citizen's rights,* guaranteed to me and all United States citizens by the National Constitution, beyond the power of any State to deny."

   Direct Quotation: Susan B. Anthony was arrested for voting at a time when women were not allowed to vote. In protest, she said: ....

   ....

Language 2c

2c. Demonstrate command of the conventions of standard English capitalization, punctuation, and spelling when writing.

- **Spell correctly.**

Explanation

Correct spelling helps readers understand what you have written. A compelling story, a strong persuasive essay, or a vivid description could become confusing if you fail to catch and correct spelling errors. Here are some guidelines to help you prevent—or catch—spelling errors.

Examples

Homophones are words that sound alike and have similar spellings, which can sometimes cause people to use the wrong spelling. If you write on a computer, even the spell checker cannot help you catch this type of error, because you aren't spelling the word incorrectly—you are using the *wrong* word! This chart shows some commonly confused homophones. Learn their definitions and differences.

allowed—"permitted" *Mom allowed me to stay up late.*	**aloud**—"with the speaking voice" *We read important passages aloud.*
threw—"propelled through the air" *The pitcher threw a fast ball.*	**through**—"by way of" *We drove through the Holland Tunnel.*
presence—"the fact of being there, or present" *The presence of her big sister calmed the child.*	**presents**—"gifts" *When will you open your birthday presents?*
whose—pronoun, relating to the possessor *Whose hat is this?*	**who's**—contraction, meaning "who is" *Who's coming to the party?*
accept—"receive willingly" *The director accepted her as a choir member.*	**except**—"with the exception of" *The store is open daily, except Mondays.*

Irregular plurals are unlike most plural nouns because they are not formed by simply adding *–s*. Here are some rules to keep in mind.

- Change a final *f* to *v* and add *–es*: *wife/wives; knife/knives; wolf/wolves*

- Add *–es* to words ending in *–sh, -ss,* or *–ch*: *brush/brushes; mess/messes; church/churches*

- Use the same form for both singular and plural: *one sheep/two sheep; one species/two species*

- Change the vowel structure: *tooth/teeth; woman/women; mouse/mice*

Words with Unstressed Vowel Sounds are tricky because the unstressed sound can be spelled different ways. These four groups show examples:

*mount**ain** eros**ion** black**en** heal**er** tail**or** expos**ure** pock**et** benef**it** ador**able** aud**ible***

REMEMBER: Always use a dictionary if you are unsure of the spelling of a difficult or confusing word.

Name _____ Date _____ Assignment _____

Apply the Standard

A. Each sentence contains two or more misspelled or misused words. Circle them, and write the correct spellings on the line.

1. Chickins and goats are exampuls of odd pets that people sometimes keep.

....

2. Have you evor herd of goats living write in the middel of the city?

....

3. Actually, goats can be agreeible pets, even though they may eat anything in site that's chewuble.

....

4. Our neighbors had a pet goat that nibbled at the cornor of there guest's hat.

....

5. "Feed that animel some hey, would you, pleas?" she said.

....

6. In some citys, citizens are aloud to keep chickens in there yards.

....

7. Oh well, theifs will probably never steal them, and the hens ley fresh eggs almost daily.

....

8. We ourselfs have often thought about raising chickens, accept we're afraid others may object.

....

9. Some peopul fear that chickens have a bad sent, but a coop doesn't smell if its kept clean.

....

10. Some prefir that goats and chickens stay on farms, along with horses, sheeps, and cattle.

....

B. Use each of these pairs of easily confused words in a sentence. Make sure your sentences clearly show the different meanings of the words.

1. allowed, aloud ....

2. threw, through ....

Language 3a

> 3a. **Use knowledge of language and its conventions when writing, speaking, reading, or listening.**
>
> - **Use verbs in the active and passive voice and in the conditional and subjunctive mood to achieve particular effects (e.g., emphasizing the actor or the action; expressing uncertainty or describing a state contrary to fact).**

Explanation

The kinds of verbs you use can either strengthen or weaken your writing. Good writers know how to use the active and passive voice and the conditional and subjunctive moods to achieve particular effects.

Examples

Active and Passive Voices

The **active voice** is more dynamic because it stresses the doer, or the subject, of the action. In the **passive voice** the action is performed upon the subject. When you write, try mostly to write in the active voice.

> **Active Voice:** *Tanya <u>hit</u> a home run.*
>
> **Passive Voice:** *The home run <u>was hit</u> by Tanya.*

In two cases, however, it is appropriate to use the passive voice:

- When you want to emphasize the receiver of the action rather than the doer

    The rescue workers <u>were praised</u> for their efforts. (emphasizes the receivers)

- When the doer is not important or easily identified

    Twenty votes are required to pass the bill. (the doer is not easily identified)

Conditional and Subjunctive Moods

Use the **conditional mood** when you need to express uncertainty about whether an action will occur:

> **Indicative Mood:** *I <u>am going</u> to play tennis.* (certain)
>
> **Conditional Mood:** *If it stops raining, I <u>might play</u>.* (uncertain)

You can use the **subjunctive mood** to express a state contrary to fact:

> **Indicative Mood:** *He <u>is</u> not an orthodontist.* (according to fact)
>
> **Subjunctive Mood:** *If he <u>were</u> an orthodontist, he could give me braces.* (contrary to fact)

Name _____ Date _____ Assignment _____

Apply the Standard

A. All of the sentences below are written in the passive voice. Seven would be stronger in the **active voice**. Rewrite them on the lines. If the passive voice is correct, write CORRECT.

1. Twenty officers are assigned to the mounted police.

....

2. Horses are ridden by the officers on the beat.

....

3. The new horses are trained by specialists.

....

4. Sometimes a riot is erupted on the street.

....

5. Excited mobs are nudged back by the horses.

....

6. Signs of crime are carefully watched for by Officer Sanchez.

....

7. Ringo, a stallion, is exercised on the beach.

....

8. Sadie, the oldest horse, is ridden by the newest officer.

....

9. The horses are taken care of by Officer McMurtry.

....

10. Special permission is required to visit the horses.

....

B. Write a sentence for each phrase or clause below. Use the conditional or subjunctive mood to express the attitude given in parentheses.

1. would be happy (express uncertainty) ....

2. if I were rich (express a state contrary to fact) ....

For use with Language 3a

Language 4a

> **4a. Determine or clarify the meaning of unknown and multiple-meaning words and phrases based on** *grade 8 reading and content,* **choosing flexibility from a range of strategies.**
>
> • **Use context (e.g., the overall meaning of a sentence or paragraph; a word's position or function in a sentence) as a clue to the meaning of a word or phrase.**

Explanation

When you come to an unfamiliar word in your reading, you can often use **context clues**—other words, phrases, and sentences—to figure out its meaning. Most context clues are found in nearby words. You might also find clues in the general meaning of the entire sentence. Finally, you might find clues in the unknown word's position or function in the sentence.

Examples

Clues in nearby words: Look for a word or phrase that may have a similar meaning to the unknown word or that might explain its meaning in another way.

> **Similar meaning:** *The song had an uneven* <u>tempo</u> *and we couldn't dance to a* **beat** *like that.*
>
> (The clue suggests that *tempo* means "the beat or rhythm of music.")
>
> **Opposite meaning:** *The rainy weather made her feel* <u>melancholy</u> *but her* **spirits rose** *when the sun came out.*
>
> (The clues suggest that *melancholy* means "sad.")
>
> **Explanation of meaning:** *No one wants to live in the* <u>squalid</u> *conditions of the* **slum.**
>
> (The clues suggest that *squalid* means "shabby" or "run-down.")

Clues in the meaning of the sentence: Look for the main idea of the sentence. Often you can use it to figure out the meaning of an unknown word.

> *Of course,* **children** *were the* <u>predominant</u> **age group** *of those attending the* **cartoon feature.**
>
> (The general meaning of the sentence suggests that *predominant* means "main.")

Clues in the word's function in the sentence: Look at where the word falls in the sentence. Think about its job, or function. Does it follow an article (*the, a*) or an adjective? If so, it is a noun. Does it express action? If so, it is a verb. Use that information, plus any of the first two types of clues, to figure out the unknown word's meaning.

> *The teacher* <u>deliberated</u> **whether to send students home** *early because of the* **bad weather.**
>
> (*Deliberated* expresses a mental action. Therefore, it's a verb. The general sense of the sentence suggests that *deliberated* means "thought seriously about.")

Name _____ Date _____ Assignment _____

Apply the Standard

A. Use context clues in the other words in the sentence to find the meaning of the underlined word. Write its definition on the line provided.

1. Knowing that exercise keeps you healthy, Rob does <u>calisthenics</u> daily. ....

2. Normally talkative, the student became <u>inarticulate</u> in the principal's office.
....

3. Su Lin likes to shop in small specialty shops, such as <u>boutiques</u>. ....

4. The scientist's <u>perseverance</u>, refusing to give up no matter what, paid off with a new discovery.

....

5. Dave thought that the detail was <u>irrelevant</u>, but I thought it was very important.

....

6. Her library card is <u>invalid</u> because she forgot to renew it. ....

7. A jeweler uses a special eyepiece to see if a gem is <u>genuine</u> or fake. ....

8. Keeping our rivers clean is not just a national issue; it's also a <u>global</u> one. ....

9. Coming in second was little <u>consolation</u> to the runner who had counted on winning the race.

....

10. Other firefighters were brave, but none showed as much <u>fortitude</u> as the captain.

....

B. Think about the underlined word's function and position in the sentence. Use that information, plus any other context clues, to define the underlined word. Write its meaning on the line.

1. <u>Felines</u> include lions, tigers, and leopards. ....

2. When the two sides could not agree, the talks ended in a <u>stalemate</u>. ....

3. The play will <u>commence</u> soon, so please take your seats. ....

4. It took twenty years for the fisherman to <u>accumulate</u> enough money to buy a new boat.

....

5. The student's half-hearted swipes were <u>ineffectual</u> in cleaning the white board.

....

For use with Language 4a

Language 4b

> **4b. Determine or clarify the meaning of unknown and multiple-meaning words and phrases based on *grade 8 reading and content,* choosing flexibly from a range of strategies.**
>
> • **Use common, grade-appropriate Greek or Latin affixes and roots as clues to the meaning of a word (e.g., *precede, recede, secede*).**

Explanation

When you come to an unfamiliar word in your reading, try breaking the word down into its parts. Look for affixes and roots. If you know the meanings of those word parts, you will have a good clue about the meaning of the unfamiliar word.

An **affix** is a word part that is attached to a base word in order to change the meaning of the base word. There are two kinds of affixes—**prefixes,** which are attached *before* the base word, and **suffixes,** which are attached *after* the base word. A **root** is the core of a word. Often the root is an old word that has come into the English language from an ancient language such as Latin or Greek.

Examples

This chart shows the meanings of some common Greek and Latin roots and affixes.

Word Part	Type	Origin	Meaning	Example
-phon-	root	Greek	"sound"	*telephone* (instrument for transmitting sounds)
-therm-	root	Greek	"heat"	*thermometer* (instrument for measuring heat)
-mob-, -mot-	root	Latin	"move"	*demote* (move down in rank)
-miss-, -mis-	root	Latin	"send"	*dismiss* (send away)
-ques-, -quer-	root	Latin	"ask"	*query* (ask about something)
-vid-, -vis-	root	Latin	"see"	*visible* (able to be seen)
post-	prefix	Latin	"after or later"	*postpone* (put off to a later time)
equi-	prefix	Latin	"equal"	*equator* (imaginary line across the center of Earth, equally distant from the poles)
super-	prefix	Latin	"more than"	*superhuman* (beyond normal human power)
-ance, -ence	suffix	Latin	"state or act of"	*appearance* (act of appearing)
-fy	suffix	Latin	"cause to be"	*beautify* (to make beautiful)
-ize	suffix	Latin	"to make"	*finalize* (to make complete or final)

Name _____ Date _____ Assignment _____

Apply the Standard

A. On the line, write the definition of the underlined word. Use the meaning of its highlighted root or affix, as well as any context clues, to help you uncover the meaning.

1. Snow fell so thickly that <u>**vis**ibility</u> on the highway was very low. ....

2. The room was chilly, so we turned up the <u>**therm**ostat</u>. ....

3. It was hard to hear the performer when her <u>micro**phone**</u> went dead. ....

4. A culture <u>trans**mits**</u> its values and traditions to its young people. ....

5. The <u>in**quis**itive</u> child wanted to know the names of all the toys on the shelf.

....

B. Use the meanings of the highlighted affixes to answer the questions. Write your answers on the lines.

1. For what reason might someone need to be hospital**ized**?

....

2. Would you complain about or praise a **super**lative perform**ance**?

....

3. What might a robber do to show repent**ance**?

....

4. If you fals**ify** a report, do you make it true or untrue?

....

5. Do **post**war events happen before, during, or after a war?

....

C. Use the affixes and roots in these words to figure out their meanings. Then write them on the lines.

1. missile ....

2. annoyance ....

3. standardize ....

4. symphony ....

5. superior ....

Language 4c

4c. **Determine or clarify the meaning of unknown and multiple-meaning words and phrases based** *on grade 8 reading and content,* **choosing flexibly from a range of strategies.**

• **Consult general and specialized reference materials (e.g., dictionaries, glossaries, thesauruses), both print and digital, to find the pronunciation of a word or determine or clarify its precise meaning or its part of speech.**

Explanation

A **dictionary** provides the meaning, pronunciation, and part of speech of words in a language. A **thesaurus** provides synonyms (words with similar meanings) for many words in a language. You can find dictionaries and thesauruses in print and online. Use them to help you clarify the meanings of unknown or multiple-meaning words.

Examples

Notice what this **dictionary entry** reveals about the word *annual*.

an•nual (an´ yoo- əl) *adj* **1** covering the period of a year **2** happening once a year; yearly: *annual rainfall* **3** for a year's time: *an annual wage* **4** completing the life cycle in one season: *annual* [L *annus*, year]

• Following the entry word are symbols that show the word's **pronunciation.** Note the stress mark that indicates which syllable is stressed (AN nual).

• The *adj.* tells the part of speech. *Annual* is an adjective. Other abbreviations include *v.* (verb), *n.* (noun), and *adv.* (adverb).

• The word's definition follows. If there is more than one definition for the word, each one is numbered.

• The word's **etymology,** or origins, appears in brackets. *Annual* comes from the Latin word *annus*.

Now notice what this **thesaurus entry** for the word *happy* offers.

happy (adjective) blissful, delighted, exuberant, joyful, pleased, tickled, thrilled

Antonyms: disgruntled, disheartened, displeased, downcast, joyless, sad, unhappy

• The part of speech follows the entry word.

• Synonyms are listed, followed by antonyms.

Name _____ Date _____ Assignment _____

Apply the Standard

Use the information in these dictionary and thesaurus entries to answer the questions.

Dictionary entry:

> **ad•vance** (əd van(t)s´) *v.* **1** to move forward: *advance a few feet* **2** to help the progress of: *advance a cause* **3** to raise to a higher rank; promote: *advance from teller to supervisor* **4** to give and expect to be paid back: *advance a loan* **5** to bring forward in time: *advance the time of the class* [Latin *abante* in front]

Thesaurus entry:

> **advance** (verb)
>
> 1. forge, go off, proceed, progress. *Antonyms:* halt, remain, stand, stay, stop
>
> 2. cultivate, encourage, forward, further, nurture. *Antonyms:* frustrate, hinder, inhibit

1. Which syllable in *advance* is the stressed syllable? ....

2. What part of speech is *advance*? ....

3. What language provided its origins? ....

4. What did the original word mean? ....

5. Which dictionary definition (1, 2, 3, or 4) relates to the use of *advance* in this sentence? *The bus advanced slowly down the avenue.* ....

6. Which dictionary definition (1, 2, 3, or 4) relates to the use of *advance* in this sentence? *The assistant hoped to be advanced to head chef.* ....

7. Rewrite this sentence, using a **synonym** for *advance* found in the thesaurus.

   Did the science experiment advance knowledge in that field?

   ....

8. Write two synonyms and two antonyms for the **first** meaning of *advance* shown in the thesaurus.

   ....

9. Write a sentence using an **antonym** for the second thesaurus meaning of *advance*.

   ....

10. Write a sentence using a **synonym** for the first thesaurus meaning of *advance*.

   ....

Language 4d

4d. **Determine or clarify the meaning of unknown and multiple-meaning words and phrases based on** *grade 8 reading and content,* **choosing flexibility from a range of strategies.**

 • **Verify the preliminary determination of the meaning of a word or phrase (e.g., by checking the inferred meaning in context or in a dictionary).**

Explanation

When you come to an unfamiliar word or phrase in your reading, look for **context clues** to help you figure out its meaning. Some clues might appear in nearby words or phrases. Others might be found in the general meaning of the sentence. If the meaning of the unknown word or phrase is still hard to understand, reread the sentence or passage for clues. Then read ahead. You may find clues in the sentences that follow the unknown word or phrase. You can also check your inferred meaning in a dictionary.

Examples

Nearby words: Look for words or phrases that give clues.

> *Usually Katie's decisions are* <u>*prudent*</u>*, but her choice to quit the team was not* ***sensible.***
> (The clue provides a synonym. It suggests that *prudent* means "sensible.")
> *Tony remained* ***hopeful*** *about reaching the goal, but Jose became* <u>*pessimistic*</u>*.*
> (The clue provides an antonym. It suggests that *pessimistic* means "lacking hope or trust.")
> *The* ***child*** *was delighted to receive the* ***dollhouse*** *and all of its* <u>*diminutive*</u> ***furniture.***
> (Together, the clues that suggest that *diminutive* means "very small.")

Meaning of the sentence: Often, the main idea of the sentence will suggest the meaning of an unknown word or phrase.

> *The comedian, telling one funny joke after another, had the audience* <u>*rolling in the aisles*</u>*.*
> (The general meaning of the sentence suggests that *rolling in the aisles* means "laughing hard.")

Sentences that follow: Read ahead. Often you can find clues in the words and phrases that appear in sentences that follow the unknown word or phrase.

> *Maria* <u>*contemplated*</u> *the decision. Minutes ticked by. Finally, her brother said, "You've thought long enough. What's your answer?"*
> (The third and fourth sentences suggest that *contemplated* means "thought about.")

Dictionary: If you have studied context clues, reread, and looked ahead in the text, but are still unsure of the meaning of an unfamiliar word or phrase, use a dictionary to verify its meaning.

Name _____ Date _____ Assignment _____

Apply the Standard

A. Use context clues to find the meaning of the underlined word or phrase. Write its definition on the line.

1. The club had to <u>recruit</u> members since not enough students signed up on their own. ....

2. It was nice to get <u>pristine</u> new textbooks instead of using the worn old books. ....

3. Making the honor roll was the deserved <u>culmination</u> of all his hard work and study. ....

4. The cat's eyes were <u>luminescent</u> at night, but everything else was dark. ....

5. Without hesitation, the <u>intrepid</u> fire fighters marched into the burning building. ....

6. To walk more than a couple of feet, the <u>feeble</u> man needed a cane. ....

7. Flu germs are <u>infectious</u>, but you can't catch an allergy from someone else. ....

8. The hot and thirsty soccer team <u>made a beeline</u> for the cool lemonade. ....

9. Mrs. Rodriguez's appearance is so tidy that there's <u>never a hair out of place</u>. ....

10. Do you <u>comprehend</u> the homework, or are you as confused as I am? ....

B. Read each group of sentences. Use context clues to find the meaning of each underlined word or phrase. Write its definition on the line. Then verify the meaning in a dictionary.

1. The results of the flood were <u>calamitous</u>. Not only were several people left homeless, but many of

   their business places were also destroyed. ....

2. Ellie is <u>unpretentious</u>. She never pretends to be something she isn't. I wish we all could be so sincere.

   ....

3. The youngest skater on the team was a <u>burgeoning</u> talent. Already she could do triple spins, and

   everybody expected her to do even better in the future. ....

4. The highlight of the hike was seeing the <u>gargantuan</u> waterfall. It was so huge that the hikers could

   hardly see the top, even if they strained their necks. ....

5. My father is a <u>backseat driver</u>. No matter who is driving, he gives directions on everything.

   ....

Language 5a

> **5a.** Demonstrate understanding of figurative language, word relationships, and
> nuances in word meanings.
>
> • Interpret figures of speech (e.g. verbal irony, puns) in context.

Explanation

Figurative language is imaginative writing. It is not meant to be taken literally, or word-for-word, as in this example: *The train's engine groans and whines as it labors up the hill.* Engines cannot literally groan or whine. The phrase is used figuratively to show that the engine is straining to pull the train. Figurative language is used to set a mood, convey a tone, and create imagery. It includes several figures of speech, such as *similes, metaphors, personification, puns,* and *irony.*

Examples

Figures of Speech		
Type	**Description**	**Example**
Simile	A comparison of two apparently unlike things that uses the words *like* or *as*.	The child was as quiet as a mouse.
Metaphor	Describing one thing as if it were something else. It implies comparison words such as *like* or *as*, but it doesn't use them.	The captain of the track team is a gazelle.
Personification	A comparison in which a nonhuman subject is made to seem human	The merry tumbleweed danced in the wind.
Pun	A humorous play on words that has more than one possible meaning.	If you want to be seen by a doctor, be patient.
Irony	The use of words to suggest the opposite of what is meant.	"What a lovely morning," moaned the tourist, looking at the pouring rain.

Context clues in the words and sentences that surround a figure of speech can help you understand its meaning. When you find a word or expression you do not understand, reread and read ahead for context clues. Once you have figured out a possible meaning, verify the meaning by inserting it in place of the unfamiliar word or expression. Reread the sentence. If it makes sense, the meaning you chose is probably correct. If the sentence does not make sense, read ahead to look for additional context clues.

Name _____ Date _____ Assignment _____

Apply the Standard

A. On the shorter line, identify the type of figurative language used in each sentences below: **simile, metaphor, personification,** or **irony.** Then use context clues to determine what the sentences mean. Using your own words, write the meaning on the longer line.

1. .... Fog was spread over the valley like a woolen blanket.

....

2. .... High on the hill, the grim old fort glared angrily at newcomers.

....

3. .... The breezes blew softly through the trees, murmuring their sleepy goodnights.

....

4. .... Excited about the project, the class was a fountain of ideas.

....

5. .... Her will to win was as tough as leather. "Nothing can beat me now," she told herself.

....

6. .... "Aren't we lucky to have such a feast," said Mr. Ray, staring gloomily at the plate of cold peas.

....

7. .... Whenever the stern principal was near, Rachel turned into a lamb.

....

B. Each item below contains a pun. On the lines, write the two different meanings that the word could have.

1. The baseball outfielder didn't catch the fly ball. "Let's just say I didn't have a ball," he said.

   Meaning 1: ....   **Meaning 2:** ....

2. The reporters pushed harder and harder to get more information. They don't call it the press for nothing.

   Meaning 1: ....   **Meaning 2:** ....

3. Bill asked Sue for a date, but when she gave him a fig, he was quite disappointed.

   Meaning 1: ....   **Meaning 2:** ....

Language 5b

5b. Demonstrate understanding of figurative language, word relationships, and nuances in word meanings.

• Use the relationship between particular words to better understand each of the words.

Explanation

An **analogy** compares two things that are similar in a certain way, but unlike in other ways. In other words, it shows a relationship between a set of words. Many tests include analogy problems as a way to test your knowledge of word meanings. An analogy item on a test contains two pairs of words. The relationship between the first pair of words is the same as the relationship between the second pair of words.

Examples

Each analogy features a specific type of relationship between the words, as in these examples:

- **Synonyms:**

  small is to *tiny* as *big* is to *large*

- **Antonyms:**

  happy is to *sad* as *neat* is to *messy*

- **Cause/Effect:**

  downpour is to *flooding* as *blizzard* is to *snowdrifts*

- **Part/Whole:**

  toe is to *foot* as *finger* is to *hand*

- **Item/Category:**

  student is to *class* as *singer* is to *choir*

- **Item/Use:**

  book is to *read* as *car* is to *drive*

- **Item/Place:**

  bee is to *hive* as *bird* is to *nest*

To figure out an analogy problem, ask yourself how the words in the first pair are related. For example, if the words in the first pair are antonyms, then the words in the second pair should also be antonyms. Thinking about these relationships helps readers and writers to understand the meanings of words.

Name _____ Date _____ Assignment _____

Apply the Standard

A. Study the relationship between the first pair of words. Then write a word to complete the second pair of words. Make sure that the second pair of words has the same relationship as the first pair of words. Then tell what type of analogy it is (synonyms, antonyms, cause/effect, part/whole, item/category, item/use, or item/place).

1. *brave* is to *courageous* as *intelligent* is to .... **Type:** ....

2. *left* is to *right* as *north* is to .... **Type:** ....

3. *laugh* is to *cry* as *take* is to .... **Type:** ....

4. *yellow* is to *color* as *seven* is to .... **Type:** ....

5. *eraser* is to *pencil* as *page* is to .... **Type:** ....

6. *sunrise* is to *dawn* as *sunset* is to .... **Type:** ....

7. *stripes* are to *zebra* as *spots* are to .... **Type:** ....

8. *shy* is to *timid* as *honest* is to .... **Type:** ....

9. *string* is to *violin* as *key* is to .... **Type:** ....

10. *couch* is to *living* room as *stove* is to .... **Type:** ....

B. Complete the analogies by adding a second pair of words to show the relationship indicated.

1. synonyms

   Incorrect is to *wrong* as .... is to ....

2. antonyms

   Above is to *below* as .... is to ....

3. cause/effect

   Gas pedal is to *go* as .... is to ....

4. part/whole

   Petal is to *flower* as .... is to ....

5. item/category

   Milk is to *dairy* as .... is to ....

Language 5c

> **5c.** Demonstrate understanding of figurative language, word relationships, and nuances in word meanings.
>
> - Distinguish among the connotations (associations) of words with similar denotations (definitions) (e.g., *bullheaded, willful, firm, persistent, resolute*).

Explanation

A word's **denotation** is its definition. Denotations are found in a dictionary. A word's **connotations** are the feeling or associations that it suggests. Connotations can be negative, positive, or neutral.

Examples

This chart shows four words that share the **same denotation** but have **different connotations**.

Word	Denotation	Connotation	Example Sentence
1. *slow*	moving without speed	moving without speed (neutral)	*The movements of a turtle are slow.*
2. *leisurely*		relaxed and easy (positive)	*They strolled through the park at a leisurely pace.*
3. *poky*		annoyingly slow (negative)	*"Hurry up!" he complained to his poky brother.*
4. *sluggish*		barely moving (negative)	*After a sluggish start, the game finally picked up.*

The denotation is the exact, literal meaning. The connotation contains more of the emotional content and expresses a feeling. For example, to say someone is *sluggish* is not a compliment. To say that someone is *poky* is almost a joking way of saying "hurry up." Finally, to describe someone as moving *leisurely* suggests that they are moving only as fast as they want because they can take all the time they want.

Connotations are frequently described as positive, negative, or neutral. Think of the connotations of words as you read and ask yourself why the author chose that particular word with that connotation.

Name _____ Date _____ Assignment _____

Apply the Standard

A. Use context clues and what you know about the meanings of words to tell whether the underlined word has a neutral, positive, or negative connotation. Circle your answer.

neutral positive negative **1.** "I got an A," the student <u>boasted</u>.

neutral positive negative **2.** "I'll be starting a new job," she <u>admitted</u>.

neutral positive negative **3.** The <u>lean</u> runners raced for the finish line.

neutral positive negative **4.** The <u>scrawny</u> cat meowed for food.

neutral positive negative **5.** After a week of sickness, he looked <u>gaunt</u>.

B. Use each word in a sentence. Then tell whether the word has a *neutral, positive,* or *negative* connotation. Circle your answer.

1. proud: ....

....

neutral   positive   negative

2. haughty: ....

....

neutral   positive   negative

3. strong-willed: ....

....

neutral   positive   negative

4. curious: ....

....

neutral   positive   negative

5. nosy: ....

....

neutral   positive   negative

For use with Language 5c

Language 6

> **6. Acquire and use accurately grade-appropriate general academic and domain-specific words and phrases; gather vocabulary knowledge when considering a word or phrase important to comprehension or expression.**

Explanation

In your schoolwork, you will come across many **academic** and **domain-specific** vocabulary words and phrases.

- **Academic words** include words that you use every day at school to solve problems, analyze a piece of literature, express your ideas, and so on.
  Examples include *analyze, contrast, predict,* and *confirm.*

- **Domain-specific words** are words that are specific to a course of study. In a science course, examples include *cell, gene,* and *gravity.* In a social studies course, examples include *alliance, legislature,* and *commerce.*

Learning the meanings of academic and domain-specific words and using them frequently will help you to complete assignments effectively and express yourself clearly.

Examples

In many of your courses, you are asked to complete tasks based on specific academic words and phrases. On many tests, you are asked to write essays that fulfill directions containing academic words and phrases. Here are examples:

Compare the **themes** of . . .	**Summarize** the **main idea** of . . .
Describe the author's **purpose** . . .	**Choose** the most likely **reason** for . . .
Explain the **causes** of . . .	**Determine** the meaning of . . .

In a literature course, you learn and use many domain-specific words and phrases, as in these examples:

drama	*plot*	*speaker*	*characterization*
metaphor	*biography*	*meter*	*table of contents*

Name _____ Date _____ Assignment _____

Apply the Standard

A. Write the letter of the matching definition on the line beside each word or phrase.

.... **1.** connotation

.... **2.** allusion

.... **3.** stage directions

.... **4.** foreshadowing

.... **5.** motive

.... **6.** drama

.... **7.** mood

.... **8.** statistics

.... **9.** viewpoint

.... **10.** persuade

a. *a reason for a character's action*

b. *convince someone to act or think a certain way*

c. *feeling or idea associated with a word*

d. *set of numbers that quantify information*

e. *the feeling created in readers by a literary work*

f. *words that tell actors how to move and speak*

g. *a reference to something well-known*

h. *a person's way of looking at something*

i. *a story written to be performed by actors*

j. *clues to what may happen later in a story*

B. Circle the letter of the answer that correctly completes each sentence.

1. The *resolution* of a plot...
- **a.** describes the setting
- **b.** tells the outcome
- **c.** introduces the main characters
- **d.** sets up the conflict

2. An example of an *external conflict* is a ....
- **a.** struggle with guilt
- **b.** need for friendship
- **c.** struggle against nature
- **d.** doubt about one's abilities

3. An example of a *genre* is ....
- **a.** poetry
- **b.** meter
- **c.** characterization
- **d.** author's style

4. The purpose of *persuasive writing* is to ....
- **a.** entertain readers
- **b.** provide information
- **c.** teach a moral
- **d.** convince readers to think a certain way

5. When you *analyze* an essay, you ....
- **a.** examine it in detail
- **b.** ask questions about it
- **c.** give your opinion on it
- **d.** guess what will happen next

Performance Tasks

Name _____ Date _____ Assignment _____

Performance Task 1

> **Literature 1**   Cite the textual evidence that most strongly supports an analysis of what the text says explicitly as well as inferences drawn from the text.*

Task: Support Analysis of a Story or Poem

Write a response to literature in which you cite textual evidence that most strongly supports your analysis of a story or poem. Explain both what the text says explicitly, as well as any inferences you have drawn from it.

Tips for Success

Present a response to a story or poem you have read. In your response, include these elements:

✓ a thesis statement that describes your response to the text

✓ evidence from the text that most strongly supports your analysis

✓ evidence from the text that strongly supports your inferences and conclusions

✓ evidence from the poem that explicitly supports the ideas you present

✓ language that is formal, precise, and follows the rules of standard English

Rubric for Self-Assessment

Criteria for Success	not very					very
How clear and effective is your thesis statement?	1	2	3	4	5	6
How clearly have you presented and supported your analysis of the text?	1	2	3	4	5	6
How well have you supported your analysis with explicit evidence from the text?	1	2	3	4	5	6
How well have you explained inferences and conclusions you drew from the text?	1	2	3	4	5	6
To what extent have you supported those inferences and conclusions with evidence from the text?	1	2	3	4	5	6
How successful is your use of standard English?	1	2	3	4	5	6
How well have you succeeded in using a formal style and appropriate tone for your audience?	1	2	3	4	5	6

* Other standards covered include Writing 4, 9; Speaking 4; Language 3.

For use with Literature 1

Name _____ Date _____ Assignment _____

Performance Task 1

> **Speaking and Listening 6** Adapt speech to a variety of contexts and tasks, demonstrating command of formal English when indicated or appropriate.

Task: Adapt Speech When Performing and Analyzing a Poem

Give a presentation in which you read a story passage or poem aloud. Then, present an analysis of the text to classmates and invite questions. Your analysis may focus on the author's word choice, the text's structure, or the overall theme of the work.

Tips for Success

Adapt the way you speak when performing and analyzing a story passage or poem. To prepare for your presentation, follow these tips for success:

- ✓ prepare a reading copy of the text in which you mark words to emphasize and places to pause
- ✓ read aloud the author's exact words, giving special emphasis to key ideas
- ✓ adopt a formal tone to present your analysis of the text
- ✓ invite questions and comments from your audience
- ✓ use a more informal tone when responding to audience questions and comments

Rubric for Self-Assessment

Criteria for Discussion	not very					very
How effectively did you mark up your reading copy of the poem?	1	2	3	4	5	6
How clearly and effectively did you perform the story passage or poem?	1	2	3	4	5	6
How thorough was your analysis of the text?	1	2	3	4	5	6
How well did you adapt your speech and tone for the analysis portion of your presentation?	1	2	3	4	5	6
How clearly did you explain your conclusions about the text?	1	2	3	4	5	6
How well did you adapt your speech and tone when answering audience questions?	1	2	3	4	5	6
How useful and accurate were your answers to questions?	1	2	3	4	5	6

Name _____ Date _____ Assignment _____

Performance Task 2

> **Literature 2** Determine a theme or central idea of a text and analyze its development over the course of the text, including its relationship to the characters, setting, and plot; provide an objective summary of the text.*

Task: Determine the Theme of a Story or Drama

First, write an objective summary of a story or drama. Then, using key details from your summary, write a response to literature in which you determine the theme or themes of the text and trace the theme's development over the course of the story or play, as reflected in characters, setting, and plot.

Tips for Success

Present a response to a story or play you have read. In your response, include these elements:

✓ an objective summary of the text's key details

✓ a statement of the text's theme (central idea)

✓ an awareness that a given text can have more than one theme

✓ a judgment of whether the theme is universal or specific to one time and place

✓ an explanation of how the key details convey the theme

✓ an analysis of the theme's development over the course of the story or play

✓ an analysis of how the characters, setting, and plot help to reveal the theme

✓ language that is formal, precise, and follows the rules of standard English

Rubric for Self-Assessment

Criteria for Success	not very					very
How clearly and objectively have you summarized the text?	1	2	3	4	5	6
How clearly and fully have you described the theme?	1	2	3	4	5	6
How thoroughly have your supported your analysis with text evidence?	1	2	3	4	5	6
How clearly have you explained the ways in which character, setting, and plot revealed theme?	1	2	3	4	5	6
How convincing is your analysis of the theme's development over the course of the play?	1	2	3	4	5	6
How successful is your use of standard English?	1	2	3	4	5	6
How well have you succeeded in using a formal style and appropriate tone for your audience?	1	2	3	4	5	6

* Other standards covered include Writing 2, 4; Language 1, 3, 5.

For use with Literature 2

Name _____ Date _____ Assignment _____

Performance Task 2

> **Speaking and Listening 4** Present claims and findings, emphasizing salient points in a focused, coherent manner with relevant evidence, sound valid reasoning, and well-chosen details; use appropriate eye contact, adequate volume, and clear pronunciation.

Task: Present Claims about a Story or Drama Effectively

Give a presentation in which you describe the theme of a story or drama and explain how its plot, characters, and setting led to your interpretation. Invite questions from listeners at the conclusion of your presentation.

Tips for Success

Give a presentation that explains the theme of a story or drama. As part of your presentation, include these elements:

✓ a clear statement of the theme or themes

✓ an analysis of the theme's development over the course of the text

✓ an analysis of how the characters, setting, and plot reveal theme

✓ relevant evidence and well-chosen details that support your reasoning

✓ appropriate eye contact; adequate volume and clear pronunciation

✓ thoughtful, focused replies to comments

Rubric for Self-Assessment

Criteria for Discussion	not very					very
How clearly did you present your claims and findings about the theme of the story or drama?	1	2	3	4	5	6
How logically did you present the theme's development throughout the text?	1	2	3	4	5	6
How compelling was your analysis of the way the characters, setting, and plot reveal theme?	1	2	3	4	5	6
How convincing were the evidence and details on which you based your determination of the theme?	1	2	3	4	5	6
How effectively did you make eye contact with the audience?	1	2	3	4	5	6
How well did you succeed in speaking clearly and loudly enough for your listeners to hear and understand you?	1	2	3	4	5	6

Name _____ Date _____ Assignment _____

Performance Task 3

Literature 3 Analyze how particular lines of dialogue or incidents in a story or drama propel the action, reveal aspects of a character, or provoke a decision.*

Task: Analyze How Dialogue Reveals Character

Write a response to literature in which you analyze how the dialogue in a story or drama reveals aspects of a character and reasons for his or her actions and decisions.

Tips for Success

Write a response to a story or drama you have read. In your response, include these elements:

- ✓ a brief description of the character you will be discussing, including his or her traits and motives

- ✓ revealing quotations of dialogue by that character or by others discussing that character

- ✓ an analysis of what the quoted dialogue tells the audience about the character and his or her actions or decisions

- ✓ language that is formal, precise, and follows the rules of standard English

Rubric for Self-Assessment

Criteria for Success	not very					very
How fully have you described the character and his or her traits and motives?	1	2	3	4	5	6
How well does the dialogue you chose reveal character?	1	2	3	4	5	6
How clear is your analysis of the way dialogue reveals the character's traits, actions, and decisions?	1	2	3	4	5	6
How successful is your use of standard English?	1	2	3	4	5	6
How well have you succeeded in using a formal style and appropriate tone for your audience?	1	2	3	4	5	6

* Other standards covered include Writing 2, 4; Speaking 4, 6; Language 1, 2, 3.

Name _____ Date _____ Assignment _____

Performance Task 3

Speaking and Listening 1 **Engage effectively in a range of collaborative discussions with diverse partners on grade 8 topics, texts, and issues, building on others' ideas and expressing your own clearly.**

Task: Discuss Responses to a Story or Drama

Participate in a group discussion in which you and several classmates discuss how particular incidents in a story or drama provoke a character's decision.

Tips for Success

Participate in a discussion about a story or play. Follow these tips for success:

- ✓ prepare by reading the story or drama and identifying at least two incidents that provoke characters to make decisions

- ✓ agree with all members of the group on guidelines and individual roles

- ✓ share your opinions regarding how the incidents provoke decisions

- ✓ provide evidence from the text to support your analysis

- ✓ pose questions that encourage group members to elaborate on their ideas

- ✓ respond to others' questions and comments with relevant observations and ideas

- ✓ summarize different speakers' responses to the passage

Rubric for Self-Assessment

Criteria for Discussion	not very					very
How successful were you at identifying incidents that provoked characters to make decisions?	1	2	3	4	5	6
How effective were the group's guidelines for the discussion?	1	2	3	4	5	6
How clearly did you present your analysis of the way incidents provoked decisions?	1	2	3	4	5	6
How convincing was the evidence for your analysis?	1	2	3	4	5	6
How effective were your questions in helping the group explore the relationship between incidents and decisions?	1	2	3	4	5	6
How relevant were your responses to others' questions and comments?	1	2	3	4	5	6
How clearly did you summarize others' responses?	1	2	3	4	5	6
How fully and equally did each member participate?	1	2	3	4	5	6

For use with Speaking and Listening 1

Name _____ Date _____ Assignment _____

Performance Task 4

> **Literature 4** Determine the meaning of words and phrases as they are used in
> a text, including figurative and connotative meanings; analyze the impact of
> specific word choices on meaning and tone, including analogies or allusions to
> other texts.*

Task: Analyze the Impact of Analogies and Allusions

Choose a text, such as a story or poem, that contains analogy or allusion. Then, write an essay in
which you explain the effect of analogies and/or allusions on the meaning and tone of the text.

Tips for Success

Present a response to a text you have read, such as a story or poem. In your response, include these
elements:

✓ definitions of the terms *analogy* and/or *allusion*

✓ an explanation of at least two analogies or allusions in the text: what they
  mean and what emotional associations they carry

✓ an analysis, using evidence from the text, of the effect the analogies or
  allusions have on the text's meaning and tone

✓ language that is formal, precise, and follows the rules of standard English

Rubric for Self-Assessment

Criteria for Success	not very					very
How clearly have you defined the terms *analogy* and/or *allusion*?	1	2	3	4	5	6
How well do the analogies or allusions you chose lend themselves to analysis?	1	2	3	4	5	6
How clearly have you explained the meaning of the analogies or allusions in the text?	1	2	3	4	5	6
How vividly have you explained the emotional associations of the analogies or allusions?	1	2	3	4	5	6
How well have you supported your analysis with evidence from the text?	1	2	3	4	5	6
How successful is your use of standard English?	1	2	3	4	5	6
How well have you succeeded in using a formal style and appropriate tone for your audience?	1	2	3	4	5	6

* Other standards covered include Writing 2, 4, 6, 9a; Speaking 4, 6; Language 1, 2, 3, 5.

For use with Literature 4

Name _____ Date _____ Assignment _____

Performance Task 4

> **Speaking and Listening 5** Integrate multimedia and visual displays into presentations to clarify information, strengthen claims and evidence, and add interest.

Task: Use Multimedia Components in a Presentation

Use multimedia components in a presentation in which you read a text aloud and then explain how its analogies and/or allusions affect its meaning and tone.

Tips for Success

Make a multimedia presentation about a text that contains analogy or allusion. As part of your presentation, include these elements:

✓ a poster-size copy of the text or a powerpoint version of the text in which you highlight the analogies and/or allusions in larger type or a different color ink

✓ images (either illustrations or photos) that convey the meaning of one or more of the analogies or allusions

✓ video or audio of you reading the text aloud, emphasizing passages that contain analogy or allusion

✓ music or sound effects to enhance the reading of the text

Rubric for Self-Assessment

Criteria for Discussion	not very					very
How effectively did the copy of the text clarify the location of the analogies and allustion?	1	2	3	4	5	6
How convincingly did the images help illustrate the meaning of the analogies and allusions?	1	2	3	4	5	6
How well did you convey the overall mood of the poem when you read it aloud?	1	2	3	4	5	6
How clearly did you explain the way the analogies and allusions enhanced the meaning of the text?	1	2	3	4	5	6
How effectively did the music or sound effects enhance the reading of the text?	1	2	3	4	5	6

Name _____ Date _____ Assignment _____

Performance Task 5

> **Literature 5** Compare and contrast the structure of two or more texts and analyze how the differing structure of each text contributes to its meaning and style.*

Task: Analyze the Different Structures of Two Short Stories

Write an essay in which you compare and contrast the structures of two texts, such as two different stories, a story and a poem, or a story and a drama. Then, explain how each text's structure contributes to its meaning and style.

Tips for Success

Write a comparison-and-contrast essay analyzing the structures of two short texts you have read. In your response, include these elements:

✓ diagrams of both texts' structures, with any special structural elements highlighted

✓ a point by point analysis comparing and contrasting how the structures contribute to the meanings and styles of the two texts

✓ evidence from the texts that supports your analysis

✓ language that is formal, precise, and follows the rules of standard English

Rubric for Self-Assessment

Criteria for Success	not very				very	
How clear and complete is your diagrams of the texts' structures?	1	2	3	4	5	6
How well does your analysis explain the similarities and differences between the two texts' structures?	1	2	3	4	5	6
How well does your analysis explain the way the texts' structures contribute to their meanings?	1	2	3	4	5	6
How well does your analysis explain the way the texts' structures contribute to their styles?	1	2	3	4	5	6
How effectively have you supported your analysis with evidence from the texts?	1	2	3	4	5	6
How successful is your use of standard English?	1	2	3	4	5	6
How well have you succeeded in using a formal style and appropriate tone for your audience?	1	2	3	4	5	6

* Other standards covered include Writing 1b, 2e, 4, 9; Speaking 4; Language 3.

Name _____ Date _____ Assignment _____

Performance Task 5

> **Speaking and Listening 1** Engage effectively in a range of discussions on grade 8 topics, texts, and issues, building on your others' ideas and expressing your own clearly.

Task: Discuss the Structures of Two Stories

Participate in a one-on-one discussion with a partner in which you explain how two texts' structures enhance their meanings and styles.

Tips for Success

Participate in a discussion comparing and contrasting how two short texts' structures contribute to their meanings and styles. Follow these tips for success.

- ✓ prepare by reading both texts and taking notes about their structures
- ✓ with your partner, develop on guidelines for participation
- ✓ give your analysis of how the texts' structures enhance their meanings and styles
- ✓ provide evidence from both texts to support your analysis
- ✓ listen carefully to and respectfully respond to your partner's analysis
- ✓ ask questions that will encourage further discussion

Rubric for Self-Assessment

Criteria for Discussion	not very					very
How thoroughly had you thought through your analysis before the discussion started?	1	2	3	4	5	6
How effective were the guidelines you established for the discussion?	1	2	3	4	5	6
How clear and accurate were your description of the texts' structures?	1	2	3	4	5	6
How convincing was your analysis of the way the structures enhanced the texts' meanings and styles?	1	2	3	4	5	6
How well did the evidence from the texts support your analysis?	1	2	3	4	5	6
How closely did you listen to your partner's analysis?	1	2	3	4	5	6
How effective were you at building on the ideas of your partner?	1	2	3	4	5	6
How respectful of your partner's opinions were your comments?	1	2	3	4	5	6

Name _____ Date _____ Assignment _____

Performance Task 6

Literature 6 Analyze how differences in the points of view of the characters and the audience or reader (e.g., created through the use of dramatic irony) create such effects as suspense or humor.*

Task: Analyze the Effects of Point of View

Write an essay in which you analyze how the differences between a character's point of view and the reader's point of view create dramatic irony or humor. Cite evidence in the story to support your analysis.

Tips for Success

Present an analysis of point of view in a short story you have read. In your response, include these elements:

✓ a brief, objective summary of the story

✓ a description of how the limited point of view of the character contrasts with the reader's more full point of view

✓ an analysis of the effect (such as suspense or humor) the use of dramatic irony achieves

✓ evidence from the story that supports the ideas you present

✓ language that is formal, precise, and follows the rules of standard English

Rubric for Self-Assessment

Criteria for Success	not very very
How clear and objective is your summary of the story?	1 2 3 4 5 6
How fully have you described the difference between the character's point of view and that of the reader?	1 2 3 4 5 6
How effectively have you described the effect of the use of dramatic irony?	1 2 3 4 5 6
How thoroughly have you supported your ideas with text evidence?	1 2 3 4 5 6
How well have you succeeded in using a formal style and appropriate tone for your audience?	1 2 3 4 5 6

*Other standards covered include: Writing 4, 9a; Language 1, 2, 3.

Name _____ Date _____ Assignment _____

Performance Task 6

> **Speaking and Listening 4** Present claims and findings, emphasizing salient points in a focused, coherent manner with relevant evidence, sound valid reasoning, and well-chosen details; use appropriate eye contact, adequate volume, and clear pronunciation.

Task: Present Claims Effectively

Give an oral presentation in which you explain how the use of irony in a story resulted in humor or suspense. Present your ideas in a logical and coherent manner, and support those ideas with evidence, reasoning, and well-chosen details.

Tips for Success

Give an oral presentation describing the use of dramatic irony in a short story you have read. Follow these tips for success:

✓ introduce the text story you will talk about, and provide a brief, objective summary of it

✓ explain the point of view of the character and how it differs from the point of view of the reader, creating dramatic irony

✓ describe ways in which the author's use of dramatic irony creates suspense or humor

✓ provide relevant evidence and details from the story that support your conclusions

✓ make appropriate eye contact with your audience

✓ maintain adequate volume and clear pronunciation

Rubric for Self-Assessment

Criteria for Discussion	not very				very	
How clearly and objectively did you summarize the story?	1	2	3	4	5	6
How compelling was your analysis of how the author creates dramatic irony?	1	2	3	4	5	6
How thoroughly did you analyze the effect the dramatic irony achieves?	1	2	3	4	5	6
How effectively did you present the evidence and details on which you based your analysis of the story?	1	2	3	4	5	6
How well did you succeed in speaking clearly and loudly enough for your listeners to understand you?	1	2	3	4	5	6

Name _____ Date _____ Assignment _____

Performance Task 7

> **Literature 7** Analyze the extent to which a filmed or live production of a story or drama stays faithful to or departs from the text or script, evaluating the choices made by the director or actors.*

Task: Analyze an Adaptation

Write an essay in which you analyze an adaptation of a short story and its film version. Evaluate the director's decisions on which story elements to keep and which to change as well as the actors' choices on how to bring the characters from the story to life.

Tips for Success

Develop an analysis of a short story and its film version. In your essay, include these elements:

✓ a thesis statement that sums up your conclusion

✓ a description of the similarities and differences between the plot of the story and the plot of the film

✓ an evaluation of how effectively the actors portrayed the story characters

✓ an analysis of how closely the settings in the film match those described in the text

✓ a judgment of why the changes were made from story to film and whether or not they were effective

✓ evidence from both versions that supports your opinions

✓ language that is formal, precise, and follows the rules of standard English

Rubric for Self-Assessment

Criteria for Success	not very					very
How clearly have you described the similarities and differences between the story and its film adaptation?	1	2	3	4	5	6
How fully have you analyzed and evaluated the actors' choices in portraying the story characters?	1	2	3	4	5	6
How clearly did you analyze the similarities and differences between the settings in the story and the film?	1	2	3	4	5	6
How thoroughly have you supported your conclusions with details from the text and film?	1	2	3	4	5	6
How well have you succeeded in using a formal style and appropriate tone for your audience?	1	2	3	4	5	6

* Other standards covered include: Writing 4, 9a; Speaking 4, 6; Language 1, 3, 6.

For use with Literature 7

Name _____ Date _____ Assignment _____

Performance Task 7

> **Speaking and Listening 5 Integrate multimedia and visual displays into presentations to clarify information, strengthen claims and evidence, and add interest.**

Task: Use Multimedia in a Presentation

Use multimedia components in a presentation in which you analyze the extent to which a film mirrors or departs from the short story on which it is based. Also provide an evaluation of the director's and actors' choices in bringing the story and its characters to life.

Tips for Success

Make a multimedia presentation about a film adaptation of a short story. As part of your presentation, you may wish to include these elements:

- ✓ a script to guide, organize, and focus your presentation

- ✓ a powerpoint or large poster in which you compare and contrast the plot, characters, dialogue, setting, overall mood, and theme of the two versions

- ✓ clips from the film, along with passages from original text, to highlight some of the changes

- ✓ sketches of how you imagined several story characters next to photos of the actors portraying those characters

- ✓ sketches or photos of how you imagined the settings next to photos of the settings in the film

Rubric for Self-Assessment

Criteria for Discussion	not very					very
How well organized and detailed was your script?	1	2	3	4	5	6
How effectively did the powerpoint or poster compare and contrast the two versions?	1	2	3	4	5	6
How effective was your analysis of the adaptation from page to screen?	1	2	3	4	5	6
How convincing was your evaluation of whether or not the adaptation of text to film was effective?	1	2	3	4	5	6
How useful was the display of your imagined settings versus those in the film?	1	2	3	4	5	6

Name _____ Date _____ Assignment _____

Performance Task 8

> **Literature 9** **Analyze how a modern work of fiction draws on themes, patterns of events, or character types from myths, traditional stories, or religious works such as the Bible, including describing how the material is rendered new.***

Task: Analyze How a Short Story Draws on Traditional Stories

Write an essay in which you analyze how a modern short story uses a theme, a pattern of events, or a character type from a myth or traditional or religious story and updates that material.

Tips for Success

Present an analysis of a story you have read. In your response, include these elements:

- ✓ a concise, clear thesis statement

- ✓ a description of what features or patterns (theme, events, characters) the story borrows from other literary works

- ✓ an analysis of how the author updated or freshened familiar themes, patterns, or character types

- ✓ an analysis of the effect that the reuse of familiar material has on your understanding and enjoyment of the story

- ✓ evidence from the text that supports your analysis

- ✓ language that is formal, precise, and follows the rules of standard English

Rubric for Self-Assessment

Criteria for Success	not very					very
How clear and concise is your thesis statement?	1	2	3	4	5	6
How accurately have you identified the elements in the modern story that have been borrowed from existing works?	1	2	3	4	5	6
How clear is your analysis of ways in which the modern author updated familiar material?	1	2	3	4	5	6
How compelling is your analysis of how the reuse of traditional material affects your understanding and enjoyment?	1	2	3	4	5	6
How well have you supported your analysis with details from the text?	1	2	3	4	5	6
How well have you succeeded in using a formal style and appropriate tone for your audience?	1	2	3	4	5	6

* Other standards covered include: Writing 4, 9a; Speaking 5, 6; Language 1, 2, 3.

For use with Literature 9

Name _____ Date _____ Assignment _____

Performance Task 8

> **Speaking and Listening 1 Engage effectively in a range of collaborative discussions with diverse partners on grade 8 topics, texts, and issues, building on others' ideas and expressing your own clearly.**

Task: Discuss How a Modern Story Draws on Traditional Sources

Participate in a teacher-led discussion in which you discuss how a modern story draws on themes, events, and character types from traditional stories and how authors update traditional material. Respond thoughtfully to and build on others' ideas.

Tips for Success

Participate in a discussion about the modern use of traditional story material. Follow these tips for success:

- ✓ prepare by reading the modern story and taking notes on elements of the story that echo patterns, plots, or characters of other stories

- ✓ with the group, develop guidelines for participation

- ✓ clearly express your ideas about ways in which this story draws on traditional materials

- ✓ provide evidence from the story that supports your analysis

- ✓ listen carefully to other participants' comments

- ✓ respond to others' comments with questions and comments that encourage further discussion

Rubric for Self-Assessment

Criteria for Discussion	not very					very
How well prepared were you for the group discussion?	1	2	3	4	5	6
How effective were the group's guidelines for participation?	1	2	3	4	5	6
How thought-provoking was your analysis of ways in which the modern story echoes traditional stories?	1	2	3	4	5	6
How convincing was the evidence from the stories in supporting your analysis?	1	2	3	4	5	6
How successful were you at building on the comments of others?	1	2	3	4	5	6

Name _____ Date _____ Assignment _____

Performance Task 9

> **Literature 10** By the end of the year, read and comprehend literature, including stories, dramas, and poems, at the high end of the grades 6–8 text complexity band independently and proficiently.*

Task: Read and Comprehend Literature

Read a collection of poetry of your choice (by a single author or several authors) and analyze what the poems you like best have in common.

Tips for Success

Read a collection of poetry of your choice and present a response to it. In your response, include these elements:

✓ a thesis statement that expresses your main conclusion

✓ an evaluation of the four or five poems from the collection you like best

✓ an analysis of what those poems have in common in terms of subject, theme, rhythm, rhyme, mood, setting, language, and/or author's style

✓ evidence from the poems that supports your analysis

✓ language that is formal, precise, and follows the rules of standard English

Rubric for Self-Assessment

Criteria for Success	not very					very
How clear and concise is your thesis statement?	1	2	3	4	5	6
How effective is your analysis of the similarities and differences in the poems' subjects and themes?	1	2	3	4	5	6
How effective is your analysis of the similarities and differences in the poems' rhythms and rhyme schemes?	1	2	3	4	5	6
How effective is your analysis of the similarities and differences in the poems' moods and settings?	1	2	3	4	5	6
How effective is your analysis of the similarities and differences in the poems' language and the poets' style?	1	2	3	4	5	6
How well have you supported your analysis with evidence from the text?	1	2	3	4	5	6
How successfully did you use standard English?	1	2	3	4	5	6

* Other standards covered include: Writing 4, 9a; Speaking 4; Language 1, 2, 3.

For use with Literature 10

Name _____ Date _____ Assignment _____

Performance Task 9

Speaking and Listening 6   Adapt speech to a variety of contexts and tasks, demonstrating command of formal English when indicated or appropriate.

Task: Adapt Speech Within a Presentation

Give a presentation in which you read two poems aloud and then explain what they have in common. Invite questions and comments from listeners at the conclusion of your presentation.

Tips for Success

Adapt the way you speak when analyzing poems and reading them aloud. Follow these tips for success:

- ✓ prepare reading copies of the poems in which you mark words you want to emphasize and places to pause

- ✓ rehearse reading aloud the poets' words exactly, adapting your voice to suit the subject matter and mood of each poem

- ✓ display or distribute copies of the poems to your audience so they can follow along as you read aloud

- ✓ switch to a more formal tone when you present your analysis of the poems and the details that support your analysis

- ✓ adapt your speech to a more informal tone when you respond to listener questions and comments

Rubric for Self-Assessment

Criteria for Discussion	not very					very
How effectively did you capture the mood of the poems as you read them aloud?	1	2	3	4	5	6
How well did you adapt your speech and tone during your analysis of the poems' similarities?	1	2	3	4	5	6
How convincing was the evidence from the poems in supporting your analysis?	1	2	3	4	5	6
How well did you adapt your speech and tone when answering audience questions?	1	2	3	4	5	6

For use with Speaking and Listening 6

Name _____ Date _____ Assignment _____

Performance Task 10

Informational Text 1   Cite the textual evidence that most strongly supports an analysis of what the text says explicitly as well as inferences drawn from the text.*

Task: Support Analysis of a Text

Write an essay in which you cite textual evidence to support your analysis of an informational text. Explain both what the text says explicitly and any inferences you have made.

Tips for Success

Present a response to an informational text. In your response, include these elements:

✓ a statement of the text's central idea

✓ an analysis of at least two supporting details that the text states explicitly

✓ an analysis of at least two inferences that you made while reading

✓ evidence from the text of the explicitly stated details

✓ evidence from the text that supports your inferences

✓ language that is formal, precise, and follows the rules of standard English

Rubric for Self-Assessment

Criteria for Success	not very					very
How clear is your statement of the text's central idea?	1	2	3	4	5	6
How well have you supported your analysis with explicit evidence from the text?	1	2	3	4	5	6
How clearly have you explained the inferences you drew from reading the text?	1	2	3	4	5	6
How well have you supported your inferences with evidence from the text?	1	2	3	4	5	6
How well have you succeeded in using a formal style and appropriate tone for your audience?	1	2	3	4	5	6

* Other standards covered include: Writing 4, 9a; Speaking 4; Language 1, 2, 3.

For use with Informational Text 1

Name _____ Date _____ Assignment _____

Performance Task 10

> **Speaking and Listening 5** Integrate multimedia and visual displays into presentations to clarify information, strengthen claims and evidence, and add interest.

Task: Use Multimedia Components in a Presentation

Use multimedia components in a presentation in which you expand on the subject matter or topic of an informational text. For example, you may want to explore the topic of the Civil War after having read a biography of Abraham Lincoln. Integrate the media into your presentation to add interest and to clarify the points you make. Allow time for a question-and-answer period at the end of your presentation.

Tips for Success

Develop a multimedia presentation that gives additional information on a topic in an informational text. As part of your presentation, you may wish to include these elements:

✓ a script that focuses your and guides your presentation

✓ a summary of the original informational text

✓ photographs or video footage that illustrate or clarify the topic of the text

✓ art or graphics that capture statistics or facts related to the topic

✓ as appropriate, music or artifacts that add interest to your presentation

Rubric for Self-Assessment

Criteria for Discussion	not very					very
How effective was the script you created?	1	2	3	4	5	6
How clear and concise was your summary of the original informational text?	1	2	3	4	5	6
How well did the photographs or video footage clarify or illustrate your chosen topic?	1	2	3	4	5	6
How effective was your use of art and/or graphics in adding interest to your presentation?	1	2	3	4	5	6
How fully were you able to respond to questions and comments of listeners?	1	2	3	4	5	6

Name _____ Date _____ Assignment _____

Performance Task 11

> **Informational Text 2** Determine a central idea of a text and analyze its development over the course of the text, including its relationship to supporting ideas; provide an objective summary of the text. *

Task: Analyze the Development of an Article's Central Idea

Write an essay on an article you have read, analyzing how the author develops its central idea. First, provide an objective summary of the article. Then, determine the article's central idea and analyze how the author develops it with supporting ideas.

Tips for Success

Include these elements in your analysis:

✓ an objective summary of the article

✓ a statement of the article's central idea

✓ an assessment of whether the central idea is first stated explicitly and then supported step by step or whether readers must infer the central idea

✓ an explanation of how the key details support, explain, or illustrate the central idea

✓ precise and formal language that follows the rules of standard English

Rubric for Self-Assessment

Criteria for Success	not very					very
How well did you summarize the article?	1	2	3	4	5	6
How accurately did you state the central idea?	1	2	3	4	5	6
How well did you assess how the central idea is revealed?	1	2	3	4	5	6
How convincing was your explanation of how the key details support the central idea?	1	2	3	4	5	6
How well did the examples you cited show the connection of the key details to the central idea?	1	2	3	4	5	6
How successfully did you use standard English?	1	2	3	4	5	6
How well did you succeed in using a formal style and a tone appropriate for your audience?	1	2	3	4	5	6

* Other standards covered include Writing 9b; Language 1, 3.

For use with Informational Text 2

Name _____ Date _____ Assignment _____

Performance Task 11

Speaking and Listening 1   Engage effectively in a range of collaborative group discussions (one-on-one, in groups, and teacher-led) with diverse partners on grade 8 topics, texts, and issues, building on others' ideas and expressing your own clearly.

Task: Discuss the Development of an Article's Central Idea

With several classmates, participate in a discussion analyzing the development of an article's central idea. Determine whether the central idea is stated explicitly or implied, and explore how key details support, explain, illustrate, or otherwise elaborate on it.

Tips for Success

As you participate in a discussion on the development of an article's central idea, follow these tips:

- ✓ Prepare by reading the article and identifying the central idea and at least four supporting details or ideas.

- ✓ With the group, establish goals for the discussion and assign individual roles, if necessary.

- ✓ Share your opinions on the development of the central idea.

- ✓ Pose questions that encourage other group members to expand on their opinions.

- ✓ Respond to others' questions and comments respectfully and with relevant points

Rubric for Self-Assessment

Criteria for Discussion	not very					very
How thoroughly did you prepare for the discussion?	1	2	3	4	5	6
How effective were you in helping to set the discussion guidelines?	1	2	3	4	5	6
How clear were your opinions on the development of the central idea?	1	2	3	4	5	6
How well did you support your opinions with evidence from the article?	1	2	3	4	5	6
How relevant were your responses to others' questions and opinions?	1	2	3	4	5	6
How polite and respectful of others' opinions were you?	1	2	3	4	5	6

For use with Speaking and Listening 1

Name _____ Date _____ Assignment _____

Performance Task 12

> **Informational Text 3** **Analyze how a text makes connections among and distinctions between individuals, ideas, or events (e.g., through comparisons, analogies, or categories).***

Task: Analyze an Essay

Write an analysis of an essay, noting how it uses various strategies to make connections among—and point out distinctions between—individuals, ideas, or events. Consider, for example, the author's use of strategies such as the following:

- comparison and contrast, to point out similarities and differences among items

- analogy, an extended comparison of a less familiar item with a more familiar one

- categorization, classifying an item with other similar items

Tips for Success

In your analysis of an essay, include these elements:

✓ the types of connections and distinctions the review makes

✓ an analysis of the author's use of strategies, such as comparison and contrast, analogy, and categorization

✓ an evaluation of the effectiveness of these ways of connecting ideas

✓ precise and formal language that follows the rules of standard English

Rubric for Self-Assessment

Criteria for Success	not very					very
How complete was your analysis of the essay?	1	2	3	4	5	6
How clear was your account of the connections and distinctions the essay makes?	1	2	3	4	5	6
How thorough was your analysis of the author's use of strategies such as comparison and contrast, analogy, and categorization?	1	2	3	4	5	6
How persuasive and well-supported was your evaluation of the connections and distinctions the essay makes?	1	2	3	4	5	6
How successfully did you use standard English?	1	2	3	4	5	6
How well did you succeed in using a formal style and a tone appropriate for your audience?	1	2	3	4	5	6

* Other standards covered include: Writing 4, 9b; Speaking 6; Language 1, 2, 3.

For use with Informational Text 3

Name _____ Date _____ Assignment _____

Performance Task 12

Speaking and Listening 4   Present claims and findings, emphasizing salient points in a focused, coherent manner with relevant evidence, sound valid reasoning, and well-chosen details; use appropriate eye contact, adequate volume, and clear pronunciation.

Task: Present Findings about a Movie Review

Give an oral presentation in which you analyze an essay. Focus on the author's use of comparison and contrast, analogy, and categorization to connect and differentiate ideas. Also, evaluate how well the author uses these strategies, supporting your assessments with well-chosen details and valid reasoning.

Tips for Success

As part of your presentation, do the following:

✓ Read the essay, or key passages from it, aloud to your audience.

✓ Analyze the author's use of comparison and contrast, analogy, and categorization.

✓ Support your analysis with well-chosen details and valid reasoning.

✓ Maintain eye contact with the audience and use appropriate gestures.

✓ Maintain an adequate volume, and make sure your pronunciation is clear.

✓ Invite the audience to ask questions, and answer these questions clearly and thoughtfully.

Rubric for Self-Assessment

Criteria for Discussion	not very					very
How clear and understandable was your reading of the essay?	1	2	3	4	5	6
How persuasive was your analysis of the essay's use of devices such as comparison and contrast, analogy, and categorization?	1	2	3	4	5	6
How effectively did you use evidence and sound reasoning?	1	2	3	4	5	6
How effectively did you maintain eye contact and use appropriate gestures?	1	2	3	4	5	6
How well did you succeed in speaking clearly and loudly enough for your listeners to follow you?	1	2	3	4	5	6
How clear and thoughtful were your replies to questions from the audience?	1	2	3	4	5	6

For use with Speaking and Listening 4

Name _____ Date _____ Assignment _____

Performance Task 13

Informational Text 4 Determine the meaning of words and phrases as they are used in a text, including figurative, connotative, and technical meanings; analyze the impact of specific word choices on meaning and tone, including analogies or allusions to other texts.*

Task: Analyze the Impact of Word Choices on Meaning and Tone

Write an essay in which you analyze the impact of word choices on the meaning and tone of a work of nonfiction. In your analysis, include analogies, allusions to other texts, and figurative, connotative, and technical meanings.

Tips for Success

In your essay, include these elements:

✓ definitions of the terms *analogy, allusion, figurative, connotative,* and *tone.*

✓ analysis of examples of figurative, connotative, and technical meanings

✓ explanation of how the word choices in the examples affect the overall meaning of the work

✓ explanation of how the word choices in the examples affect the tone of the work

✓ precise and formal language that follows the rules of standard English

Rubric for Self-Assessment

Criteria for Success	not very very
How clearly did you define the terms *analogy, allusion, figurative, connotative,* and *tone?*	1 2 3 4 5 6
How well did you interpret or define examples of figurative, connotative, and technical language?	1 2 3 4 5 6
How clearly did you explain how the word choices in the examples affect the overall meaning of the work?	1 2 3 4 5 6
How well did you explain how the word choices in the examples affect the tone of the work?	1 2 3 4 5 6
How successfully did you use standard English?	1 2 3 4 5 6
How well did you succeed in using a formal style and a tone appropriate for your audience?	1 2 3 4 5 6

* Other standards covered include: Writing 5, 9b; Speaking 4; Language 1, 2, 3.

Name _____ Date _____ Assignment _____

Performance Task 13

> **Speaking and Listening 6** Adapt speech to a variety of contexts and tasks, demonstrating command of formal English when indicated or appropriate.

Task: Adapt Your Speech to Different Contexts When Discussing Nonfiction

Give a presentation in which you interpret a work of nonfiction. First, read aloud passages from the work with examples of analogies, allusions, and figurative, connotative, and technical meanings. Then, have a partner interview you (as the author). Discuss how the word choices in these examples affect the essay's meaning and tone. Finally, still keeping in character, answer questions from the audience.

Tips for Success

Adapt your speaking style to a variety of contexts, as follows:

- ✓ Prepare a reading copy of the passages marking words to emphasize and places to pause.

- ✓ Rehearse your reading of the passages from the essay so you do not stumble over any words.

- ✓ Read the passages aloud using a formal style.

- ✓ As the author being interviewed, speak in a formal but friendly tone.

- ✓ Use a more informal tone when responding, as the author, to questions and comments from the audience.

Rubric for Self-Assessment

Criteria for Discussion	not very					very
How effectively did you mark up your reading copy of the work?	1	2	3	4	5	6
How well did your rehearsal prepare you for the public presentation of the passages?	1	2	3	4	5	6
Was your presentation of passages from the work free of errors and appropriately formal?	1	2	3	4	5	6
How well did you adopt a formal but friendly tone in the interview?	1	2	3	4	5	6
How insightful was your analysis of word choices on the essay's overall meaning and tone?	1	2	3	4	5	6
How well did you adopt an informal tone when responding to questions and comments from the audience?	1	2	3	4	5	6

Name _____ Date _____ Assignment _____

Performance Task 14

> **Informational Text 5** Analyze in detail the structure of a specific paragraph in a text, including the role of particular sentences in developing and refining a key concept.*

Task: Analyze a Paragraph in a Science Article

Write an essay analyzing the structure of a specific paragraph in a science article. Indicate the role individual sentences play in developing the key concept expressed by the paragraph.

Tips for Success

In your essay, include these elements:

✓ the topic sentence of the paragraph you chose

✓ an analysis of the function of each sentence in the paragraph, determining whether it develops the main idea of the paragraph, connects the paragraph's main idea to other ideas in the article, or engages readers' interest in the main idea

✓ an analysis of how sentences develop the paragraph's main idea—whether by explaining, illustrating, supporting, or qualifying it

✓ evidence from the text that supports your analysis

✓ precise, formal language that follows the rules of standard English

Rubric for Self-Assessment

Criteria for Success	not very					very
How suitable was the paragraph you chose to analyze?	1	2	3	4	5	6
How accurately did you identify the topic sentence?	1	2	3	4	5	6
How thoroughly did you analyze the function of each sentence?	1	2	3	4	5	6
How well did you analyze the ways individual sentences develop and refine the main idea?	1	2	3	4	5	6
How effectively did you support your analysis with textual evidence?	1	2	3	4	5	6
How well did you succeed in using a formal style, a tone appropriate for your audience, and standard English?	1	2	3	4	5	6

* Other standards covered include: Writing 4, 9b; Language 3.

Name _____ Date _____ Assignment _____

Performance Task 14

> **Speaking and Listening 1** Engage effectively in a range of collaborative discussions (one-on-one, in groups, and teacher-led) with diverse partners on *grade 8 topics, texts, and issues,* building on others' ideas and expressing their own clearly.

Task: Discuss a Paragraph in a Science Article

Participate in a teacher-led group discussion in which you analyze the structure of a specific paragraph in a science article and respond thoughtfully to others' ideas.

Tips for Success

To enhance your participation in the discussion, take the following steps:

✓ Prepare by reading the article and thinking through your analysis.

✓ Agree with other group members on guidelines for the discussion.

✓ Share your analysis of the paragraph's structure and the role of each sentence.

✓ Provide evidence from the article to support your analysis.

✓ Pose questions that encourage others to elaborate on their opinions.

✓ Build on others' ideas, making relevant observations and offering insights.

Rubric for Self-Assessment

Criteria for Discussion	not very					very
How thoroughly did you think through your analysis in preparing for the discussion?	1	2	3	4	5	6
How effective were you in helping to establish the discussion guidelines?	1	2	3	4	5	6
How coherent and was your analysis of the paragraph's structure and the role of each sentence?	1	2	3	4	5	6
How effectively did you present your analysis?	1	2	3	4	5	6
How useful were your questions in helping the group analyze the paragraph?	1	2	3	4	5	6
How well did you build on others' ideas?	1	2	3	4	5	6

Name _____ Date _____ Assignment _____

Performance Task 15

> **Informational Text 6**   **Determine an author's point of view or purpose in a text and analyze how the author acknowledges and responds to conflicting evidence or viewpoints.***

Task: Analyze Conflicting Viewpoints

Write an essay in which you identify the author's purpose in a persuasive speech and analyze how the author acknowledges and responds to conflicting evidence or viewpoints. Cite evidence in the essay to support your analysis.

Tips for Success

Write an essay explaining the author's purpose in a persuasive speech you have read or heard, analyzing how the author acknowledges and responds to conflicting evidence or viewpoints. In your essay, include these elements:

- ✓ an identification of the author's purpose(s) in the speech

- ✓ an explanation of why authors acknowledge and respond to conflicting evidence or viewpoints

- ✓ an analysis of how the author of this speech responds to conflicting evidence or viewpoints

- ✓ evidence from the speech that supports your opinions

- ✓ language that is formal, precise, and follows the rules of standard English

Rubric for Self-Assessment

Criteria for Success	not very					very
How accurately did you identify the author's purpose?	1	2	3	4	5	6
How clear was your explanation of why authors acknowledge and respond to conflicting evidence or viewpoints?	1	2	3	4	5	6
How useful was your analysis of how the author responds to conflicting evidence or viewpoints?	1	2	3	4	5	6
How well did you support your analysis with text evidence?	1	2	3	4	5	6
How well did you succeed in using a formal style, appropriate tone for your audience, and standard English?	1	2	3	4	5	6

* Other standards covered include Writing 4, 9b; Language 1, 2.

Name _____ Date _____ Assignment _____

Performance Task 15

Task: Present Claims about Conflicting Evidence

Give a presentation in which you deliver a persuasive speech and analyze how its author acknowledges and responds to conflicting evidence or viewpoints.

Tips for Success

Give a presentation analyzing how the author responds to conflicting viewpoints in a persuasive speech you have read or heard. As part of your presentation, include these elements:

✓ read the speech aloud in a persuasive manner

✓ analyze how the author acknowledges and responds to conflicting viewpoints

✓ provide relevant evidence and well-chosen details from the speech that support your analysis

✓ make appropriate eye contact and use appropriate body language

✓ maintain adequate volume and clear pronunciation

Rubric for Self-Assessment

Criteria for Discussion	not very					very
How persuasively did you deliver the speech?	1	2	3	4	5	6
How compelling was your analysis of how the author acknowledges and responds to conflicting viewpoints?	1	2	3	4	5	6
How convincing was the evidence from the speech to support your analysis?	1	2	3	4	5	6
How effectively did you present the conflicting viewpoints in your analysis?	1	2	3	4	5	6
How effectively did you use eye contact and body language in both the speech and your analysis?	1	2	3	4	5	6
How well did you succeed in speaking clearly and loudly enough for your listeners to follow you?	1	2	3	4	5	6

Name _____ Date _____ Assignment _____

Performance Task 16

> **Informational Text 7** Evaluate the advantages and disadvantages of using different mediums (e.g., print or digital text, video, multimedia) to present a particular topic or idea.*

Task: Evaluate a Radio Speech versus a Print Editorial

Write an essay in which you evaluate the advantages and disadvantages of a radio speech versus a print editorial on the same issue.

Tips for Success

Write an essay in which you evaluate the advantages and disadvantages of a radio speech you have heard versus a print editorial you have read on the same issue. In your essay, include these elements:

✓ an analysis of specific words and passages that are effective in a radio speech and in the print editorial

✓ an analysis of the advantages and disadvantages of the spoken word over the written word

✓ an evaluation of which version of the argument (in which medium) is more persuasive and why

✓ language that is formal, precise, and follows the rules of standard English

Rubric for Self-Assessment

Criteria for Success	not very					very
How well did you analyze which words and passages were effective in the radio speech?	1	2	3	4	5	6
How well did you analyze which words and passages were effective in the print editorial?	1	2	3	4	5	6
To what extent did you analyze the advantages of the spoken word over the written word?	1	2	3	4	5	6
How clearly did you evaluate which version of the argument is more persuasive and why?	1	2	3	4	5	6
How well did you succeed in using a formal style, appropriate tone for your audience, and standard English?	1	2	3	4	5	6

* Other standards covered include Writing 4, 9b; Speaking 1, 4, 5; Language 1, 3.

Name _____ Date _____ Assignment _____

Performance Task 16

Task: Discuss Television Commercials and Their Motives

With your class, view several television commercials and take notes on each. Then discuss in small groups the commercials and their motives.

Tips for Success

View several television commercials and discuss them in small groups. As part of your participation in the discussion, include these elements:

✓ refer to your notes on each commercial

✓ analyze the key words and images and their purposes

✓ analyze whether the information conveyed is credible or not

✓ analyze the techniques used (for example, celebrity spokespeople) to convey the messages

✓ analyze the motives behind the presentations

✓ respond to others' questions and comments with relevant points

Rubric for Self-Assessment

Criteria for Discussion	not very					very
How useful were your notes on the commercials?	1	2	3	4	5	6
How insightful was the group's analysis of the commercials key words and images?	1	2	3	4	5	6
How effective was the group's analysis of whether the commercials are credible or not?	1	2	3	4	5	6
How insightful was the group's analysis of the persuasive techniques used in the commercials?	1	2	3	4	5	6
How revealing was the group's analysis of the commercials' motives?	1	2	3	4	5	6
How relevant were your responses to others' questions?	1	2	3	4	5	6

Name _____ Date _____ Assignment _____

Performance Task 17

> **Informational Text 8** Delineate and evaluate the argument and specific claims in a
> text, assessing whether the reasoning is sound and the evidence is relevant and
> sufficient; recognize when irrelevant evidence is introduced.*

Task: Evaluate Claims in a Magazine Advertisement

Write an essay in which you evaluate the claims and identify irrelevant evidence in a magazine
advertisement.

Tips for Success

Write an essay in which you evaluate the claims and identify irrelevant evidence in a magazine
advertisement you have seen and read. In your essay, include these elements:

✓ a description of the advertisement's argument and claims

✓ an assessment of whether the reasoning is sound

✓ an analysis of whether the evidence to support claims is relevant and
sufficient

✓ identification of any evidence that is irrelevant

✓ identification of errors in logic, like false analogies

✓ language that is formal, precise, and follows the rules of standard English

Rubric for Self-Assessment

Criteria for Success	not very					very
How clearly did you describe the advertisement's argument and claims?	1	2	3	4	5	6
How accurately did you assess whether the reasoning is sound?	1	2	3	4	5	6
How effectively did you analyze whether the evidence to support claims is relevant and sufficient?	1	2	3	4	5	6
How accurately did you identify irrelevant evidence?	1	2	3	4	5	6
How accurately did you identify errors in logic?	1	2	3	4	5	6
How well did you succeed in using a formal style, appropriate tone for your audience, and standard English?	1	2	3	4	5	6

* Other standards covered include Writing 4, 9b; Speaking 1, 4, 5; Language 1, 3, 6.

Name _____ Date _____ Assignment _____

Performance Task 17

> **Speaking and Listening 3** Delineate a speaker's argument and specific claims, evaluating the soundness of the reasoning and relevance and sufficiency of the evidence and identifying when irrelevant evidence is introduced.

Task: Evaluate Claims in a Debate

In a small group, watch a debate (either on video or between students) and take notes on each speaker's argument, claims, and evidence. Then discuss the debaters' performances.

Tips for Success

Watch a debate and discuss it with a group. As part of your participation in the discussion, include these elements:

- ✓ refer to your notes on each debater's performance
- ✓ describe the argument and claims of each debater
- ✓ assess whether the reasoning is sound
- ✓ analyze whether the evidence to support claims is relevant and sufficient
- ✓ identify errors in logic, such as false analogies or bandwagon techniques
- ✓ respond to others' questions and comments with relevant points

Rubric for Self-Assessment

Criteria for Discussion	not very					very
How useful were your notes on the debaters?	1	2	3	4	5	6
How clearly did you describe each debater's argument and claims?	1	2	3	4	5	6
How accurately did you assess whether each debater's reasoning was sound?	1	2	3	4	5	6
How well did you analyze whether the evidence to support claims was relevant and sufficient?	1	2	3	4	5	6
How accurately did you identify any errors in logic?	1	2	3	4	5	6
How relevant were your responses to others' questions?	1	2	3	4	5	6

Name _____ Date _____ Assignment _____

Performance Task 18

Informational Text 9 Analyze a case in which two or more texts provide conflicting information on the same topic and identify where the texts disagree on matters of facts or interpretation.*

Task: Analyze History Articles That Disagree

Write an essay in which you compare and contrast two history articles that provide conflicting information on the same topic and identify where they disagree.

Tips for Success

Write an essay comparing two history articles you have read that provide conflicting information on the same topic. In your essay, include these elements:

✓ statements contrasting both articles' propositions and supporting details

✓ an analysis of where the articles differ on the facts

✓ research (where possible) to determine which facts are correct

✓ an analysis of where the articles agree on the facts but differ in their interpretations

✓ evidence from both texts that supports your analysis

✓ language that is formal, precise, and follows the rules of standard English

Rubric for Self-Assessment

Criteria for Success	not very					very
How clearly did you state the two articles' propositions and supporting details?	1	2	3	4	5	6
How insightful was your analysis of where the articles differ on the facts?	1	2	3	4	5	6
How successful was your research into which facts are true?	1	2	3	4	5	6
How comprehensive was your analysis of where the articles differ in their interpretations?	1	2	3	4	5	6
How well did you support your analysis with details from both articles?	1	2	3	4	5	6
How successfully did you use standard English?	1	2	3	4	5	6
How well did you succeed in using a formal style and appropriate tone for your audience?	1	2	3	4	5	6

* Other standards covered include Writing 4, 9b; Speaking 4; Language 1, 2, 3.

For use with Informational Text 9

Name _____ Date _____ Assignment _____

Performance Task 18

> **Speaking and Listening 6** Adapt speech to a variety of contexts and tasks, demonstrating command of formal English when indicated or appropriate.

Task: Adapt Speech When Contrasting Two History Articles

Choose a passage in each history article that reveals a conflict of either facts or interpretations with the other article. Read both passages aloud. Then analyze the differences, and share any research you have done to determine which article is more correct.

Tips for Success

Adapt the way you speak when contrasting the two history articles. As part of your performance, include these elements:

✓ prepare reading copies of both passages in which you mark words to emphasize and places to pause

✓ read aloud the authors' exact words, including any quotations

✓ speak in a formal tone when you analyze the differences between the passages and share your research

✓ avoid using incomplete sentences and filler words and phrases like "you know" and "I mean"

✓ switch to an informal tone when you respond to questions and comments from your audience

Rubric for Self-Assessment

Criteria for Discussion	not very					very
How usefully did you mark up your reading copy of the passages?	1	2	3	4	5	6
How accurately did you speak the authors' words?	1	2	3	4	5	6
How well did you adapt a formal speech and tone to share your analysis and research?	1	2	3	4	5	6
How successfully did you avoid using incomplete sentences and filler words?	1	2	3	4	5	6
How well did you adapt your speech and tone when responding to questions and comments?	1	2	3	4	5	6

Name _____ Date _____ Assignment _____

Performance Task 19

> **Informational Text 10** By the end of the year, read and comprehend literary
> nonfiction at the high end of the grades 6-8 text complexity band independently
> and proficiently.*

Task: Read and Comprehend a Science Book

Read a science book of your choice, meeting with a partner weekly to discuss your progress. Write an essay in which you identify two central ideas in the book and analyze their development over the course of a chapter or the entire book. In your meetings, you and your partner may want to discuss other central ideas as well.

Tips for Success

Read a science book of your choice and write an essay analyzing two central ideas in it. In your essay, include these elements:

✓ a statement of two central ideas in the book

✓ an analysis of how those central ideas are developed

✓ an identification of at least two key details that support each central idea you have identified

✓ evidence from the book that supports your analysis

✓ language that is formal, precise, and follows the rules of standard English

Rubric for Self-Assessment

Criteria for Success	not very				very	
How accurately did you identify two central ideas in the book?	1	2	3	4	5	6
How effectively did you analyze how those central ideas are developed?	1	2	3	4	5	6
How accurately did you identify details that support each central idea?	1	2	3	4	5	6
How well did you support your analysis with evidence from the book?	1	2	3	4	5	6
How successfully did you use standard English?	1	2	3	4	5	6
How well did you succeed in using a formal style and appropriate tone for your audience?	1	2	3	4	5	6

* Other standards covered include Writing 4, 9b; Speaking 4; Language 1, 2, 3.

Name _____ Date _____ Assignment _____

Performance Task 19

> **Speaking and Listening 1** Engage effectively in a range of collaborative discussions with a partner on *grade 8 topics, texts, and issues,* building on your partner's ideas and expressing your own clearly.

Task: Meet with a Partner Weekly to Discuss a Science Book

Participate in weekly discussions in which you talk about the ideas in a science book that interest you the most and respond thoughtfully to your partner's ideas and opinions.

Tips for Success

Participate in weekly discussions about reading and analyzing a science book of your choice. As part of your participation in the discussion, include these elements:

- ✓ prepare by reading several chapters of the book and thinking through your response to them

- ✓ agree with your partner on guidelines for equal and full participation

- ✓ summarize the main ideas of the chapters you have read this week

- ✓ analyze how well documented the book's information is

- ✓ evaluate how well the book is written

- ✓ use evidence from the book that supports your analysis

- ✓ listen to your partner's ideas and opinions about the book

Rubric for Self-Assessment

Criteria for Discussion	not very					very
How well did you know the portions of the book you had read so far?	1	2	3	4	5	6
How completely had you thought about the book before the discussion started?	1	2	3	4	5	6
How effectively did you and your partner establish guidelines for the discussion?	1	2	3	4	5	6
How helpful was your summary?	1	2	3	4	5	6
How useful was your analysis of the book's documentation?	1	2	3	4	5	6
How convincing was your evaluation of the quality of writing?	1	2	3	4	5	6
How effectively did you use evidence from the book?	1	2	3	4	5	6
How polite and respectful of your partner's opinions were you?	1	2	3	4	5	6